50% OFF Online Praxis Co... ...ep Course!

Dear Customer,

We consider it an honor and a privilege that you chose our Praxis Core Study Guide. As a way of showing our appreciation and to help us better serve you, we have partnered with Mometrix Test Preparation to offer you **50% off their online Praxis Core Online Course**. Many Praxis courses are needlessly expensive and don't deliver enough value. With their course, you get access to the best Praxis Core prep material, and you only pay half price.

Mometrix has structured their online course to perfectly complement your printed study guide. The Praxis Core Online Course contains **in-depth lessons** that cover all the most important topics, **150+ video reviews** that explain difficult concepts, over **700 practice questions** to ensure you feel prepared, and more than **650 digital flashcards**, so you can study while you're on the go.

Online Praxis Core Prep Course

Topics Covered:
- Reading
  - Literary Analysis
  - Theme and Plot
  - Elements of a Text
- Writing
  - Foundations of Grammar
  - Parts of an Essay
  - Style and Form
- Mathematics
  - Numbers and Operations
  - Proportions and Ratios
  - Systems of Equations

Course Features:
- Praxis Core Study Guide
  - Get content that complements our best-selling study guide.
- Full-Length Practice Tests
  - With over 700 practice questions, you can test yourself again and again.
- Mobile Friendly
  - If you need to study on the go, the course is easily accessible from your mobile device.
- Praxis Core Flashcards
  - Their course includes a flashcards mode with over 650 content cards for you to study.

To receive this discount, visit their website:
https://www.mometrix.com/university/praxis-core/ or simply scan this QR code with your smartphone. At the checkout page, enter the discount code: **APEXCORE50**

If you have any questions or concerns, please contact them at universityhelp@mometrix.com.

FREE

Free Study Tips DVD

In addition to the tips and content in this guide, we have created a FREE DVD with helpful study tips to further assist your exam preparation. **This FREE Study Tips DVD provides you with top-notch tips to conquer your exam and reach your goals.**

Our simple request in exchange for the strategy-packed DVD packed is that you email us your feedback about our study guide. We would love to hear what you thought about the guide, and we welcome any and all feedback—positive, negative, or neutral. It is our #1 goal to provide you with top quality products and customer service.

To receive your **FREE Study Tips DVD**, email freedvd@apexprep.com. Please put "FREE DVD" in the subject line and put the following in the email:

a. The name of the study guide you purchased.

b. Your rating of the study guide on a scale of 1-5, with 5 being the highest score.

c. Any thoughts or feedback about your study guide.

d. Your first and last name and your mailing address, so we know where to send your free DVD!

Thank you!

Praxis Core Study Guide Covering Math (5733), Reading (5713), and Writing (5723)

Academic Skills for Educators Exam Prep with Practice Test Questions [Updated for New Outlines]

Matthew Lanni

Written and edited by APEX Publishing.

ISBN 13: 9781637751756
ISBN 10: 1637751753

APEX Publishing is not connected with or endorsed by any official testing organization. APEX Publishing creates and publishes unofficial educational products. All test and organization names are trademarks of their respective owners.

The material in this publication is included for utilitarian purposes only and does not constitute an endorsement by APEX Publishing of any particular point of view.

For additional information or for bulk orders, contact info@apexprep.com.

Table of Contents

Test Taking Strategies

1. Reading the Whole Question

A popular assumption in Western culture is the idea that we don't have enough time for anything. We speed while driving to work, we want to read an assignment for class as quickly as possible, or we want the line in the supermarket to dwindle faster. However, speeding through such events robs us from being able to thoroughly appreciate and understand what's happening around us. While taking a timed test, the feeling one might have while reading a question is to find the correct answer as quickly as possible. Although pace is important, don't let it deter you from reading the whole question. Test writers know how to subtly change a test question toward the end in various ways, such as adding a negative or changing focus. If the question has a passage, carefully read the whole passage as well before moving on to the questions. This will help you process the information in the passage rather than worrying about the questions you've just read and where to find them. A thorough understanding of the passage or question is an important way for test takers to be able to succeed on an exam.

2. Examining Every Answer Choice

Let's say we're at the market buying apples. The first apple we see on top of the heap may *look* like the best apple, but if we turn it over we can see bruising on the skin. We must examine several apples before deciding which apple is the best. Finding the correct answer choice is like finding the best apple. Although it's tempting to choose an answer that seems correct at first without reading the others, it's important to read each answer choice thoroughly before making a final decision on the answer. The aim of a test writer might be to get as close as possible to the correct answer, so watch out for subtle words that may indicate an answer is incorrect. Once the correct answer choice is selected, read the question again and the answer in response to make sure all your bases are covered.

3. Eliminating Wrong Answer Choices

Sometimes we become paralyzed when we are confronted with too many choices. Which frozen yogurt flavor is the tastiest? Which pair of shoes look the best with this outfit? What type of car will fill my needs as a consumer? If you are unsure of which answer would be the best to choose, it may help to use process of elimination. We use "filtering" all the time on sites such as eBay® or Craigslist® to eliminate the ads that are not right for us. We can do the same thing on an exam. Process of elimination is crossing out the answer choices we know for sure are wrong and leaving the ones that might be correct. It may help to cover up the incorrect answer choice. Covering incorrect choices is a psychological act that alleviates stress due to the brain being exposed to a smaller amount of information. Choosing between two answer choices is much easier than choosing between all of them, and you have a better chance of selecting the correct answer if you have less to focus on.

4. Sticking to the World of the Question

When we are attempting to answer questions, our minds will often wander away from the question and what it is asking. We begin to see answer choices that are true in the real world instead of true in the world of the question. It may be helpful to think of each test question as its own little world. This world may be different from ours. This world may know as a truth that the chicken came before the egg or may assert that two plus two equals five. Remember that, no matter what hypothetical nonsense may be in the question, assume it to be true. If the question states that the chicken came before the egg, then choose your answer based on that truth. Sticking to the world of the question means placing all of our biases and assumptions aside and relying on the question to guide us to the correct answer. If we are simply looking for answers that are correct based on our own judgment, then we may choose incorrectly. Remember an answer that is true does not necessarily answer the question.

5. Key Words

If you come across a complex test question that you have to read over and over again, try pulling out some key words from the question in order to understand what exactly it is asking. Key words may be words that surround the question, such as *main idea, analogous, parallel, resembles, structured,* or *defines.* The question may be asking for the main idea, or it may be asking you to define something. Deconstructing the sentence may also be helpful in making the question simpler before trying to answer it. This means taking the sentence apart and obtaining meaning in pieces, or separating the question from the foundation of the question. For example, let's look at this question:

> Given the author's description of the content of paleontology in the first paragraph, which of the following is most parallel to what it taught?

The question asks which one of the answers most *parallels* the following information: The *description* of paleontology in the first paragraph. The first step would be to see *how* paleontology is described in the first paragraph. Then, we would find an answer choice that parallels that description. The question seems complex at first, but after we deconstruct it, the answer becomes much more attainable.

6. Subtle Negatives

Negative words in question stems will be words such as *not, but, neither,* or *except.* Test writers often use these words in order to trick unsuspecting test takers into selecting the wrong answer—or, at least, to test their reading comprehension of the question. Many exams will feature the negative words in all caps (*which of the following is NOT an example*), but some questions will add the negative word seamlessly into the sentence. The following is an example of a subtle negative used in a question stem:

> According to the passage, which of the following is *not* considered to be an example of paleontology?

If we rush through the exam, we might skip that tiny word, *not,* inside the question, and choose an answer that is opposite of the correct choice. Again, it's important to read the question fully, and double check for any words that may negate the statement in any way.

7. Spotting the Hedges

The word "hedging" refers to language that remains vague or avoids absolute terminology. Absolute terminology consists of words like *always, never, all, every, just, only, none,* and *must.* Hedging refers to words like *seem, tend, might, most, some, sometimes, perhaps, possibly, probability,* and *often.* In some cases, we want to choose answer choices that use hedging and avoid answer choices that use absolute terminology. It's important to pay attention to what subject you are on and adjust your response accordingly.

8. Restating to Understand

Every now and then we come across questions that we don't understand. The language may be too complex, or the question is structured in a way that is meant to confuse the test taker. When you come across a question like this, it may be worth your time to rewrite or restate the question in your own words in order to understand it better. For example, let's look at the following complicated question:

> Which of the following words, if substituted for the word *parochial* in the first paragraph, would LEAST change the meaning of the sentence?

Let's restate the question in order to understand it better. We know that they want the word *parochial* replaced. We also know that this new word would "least" or "not" change the meaning of the sentence. Now let's try the sentence again:

> Which word could we replace with *parochial*, and it would not change the meaning?

Restating it this way, we see that the question is asking for a synonym. Now, let's restate the question so we can answer it better:

> Which word is a synonym for the word *parochial*?

Before we even look at the answer choices, we have a simpler, restated version of a complicated question.

9. Predicting the Answer

After you read the question, try predicting the answer *before* reading the answer choices. By formulating an answer in your mind, you will be less likely to be distracted by any wrong answer choices. Using predictions will also help you feel more confident in the answer choice you select. Once you've chosen your answer, go back and reread the question-and-answer choices to make sure you have the best fit. If you have no idea what the answer may be for a particular question, forego using this strategy.

10. Avoiding Patterns

One popular myth in grade school relating to standardized testing is that test writers will often put multiple-choice answers in patterns. A runoff example of this kind of thinking is that the most common answer choice is "C," with "B" following close behind. Or, some will advocate certain made-up word patterns that simply do not exist. Test writers do not arrange their correct answer choices in any kind of pattern; their choices are randomized. There may even be times where the correct answer choice will be the same letter for two or three questions in a row, but we have no way of knowing when or if this might happen. Instead of trying to figure out what choice the test writer probably set as being correct, focus on what the *best answer choice* would be out of the answers you are presented with. Use the tips above, general knowledge, and reading comprehension skills in order to best answer the question, rather than looking for patterns that do not exist.

FREE DVD OFFER

Achieving a high score on your exam depends not only on understanding the content, but also on understanding how to apply your knowledge and your command of test taking strategies. **Because your success is our primary goal, we offer a FREE Study Tips DVD, which provides top-notch test taking strategies to help you optimize your testing experience.**

Our simple request in exchange for the strategy-packed DVD packed is that you email us your feedback about our study guide.

To receive your **FREE Study Tips DVD**, email freedvd@apexprep.com. Please put "FREE DVD" in the subject line and put the following in the email:

a. The name of the study guide you purchased.

b. Your rating of the study guide on a scale of 1-5, with 5 being the highest score.

c. Any thoughts or feedback about your study guide.

d. Your first and last name and your mailing address, so we know where to send your free DVD!

Introduction

Function of the Tests

Educational Testing Service (ETS) offers three Praxis Core Academic Skills for Educators exams: Mathematics, Reading, and Writing. These exams are intended to measure knowledge and skills required of candidates seeking careers as educators. The material tested on each of the three exams aligns with the Common Core State Standards for that subject and has been identified to be needed for college (especially teacher preparation programs) and career readiness for those on the path to careers as educators.

The Praxis Core exams are offered worldwide. However, they are primarily used in the United States, where certain states require them as part of the certification and licensing procedure. Certain professional associations and organizations also require them as part of their licensing process.

Administration of the Tests

Praxis Core Academic Skills for Educators exams are administered by computer at Prometric testing centers, universities, and other locations around the world throughout the year. All three tests may be taken in one administration or each can be taken separately. Whether taken as a combined test or separately, test takers receive an individual score for each component (Mathematics, Reading, and Writing).

When the Praxis Core tests are taken separately, each testing session takes two hours. When combined, the entire testing session takes five hours. These quoted timeframes include time for tutorials and entry of demographic information.

The tests are only available in English, but non-native English speakers may be eligible for extended testing time. Test takers with disabilities can request accommodations as per the Americans with Disabilities Act.

Format of the Tests

The tests are administered via computer. The Mathematics test consists of selected-response questions with one answer or multiple answers, and numeric-entry questions, where test takers generate their own responses. The Reading test contains only selected-response questions, and the Writing test contains selected-response questions and two essays. Test takers may answer the questions in any order and mark questions to return to later.

The content of the three exams is as follows:

Test	Allotted Time (min)	Number of Questions
Mathematics	85	56
Reading	85	56
Writing	40 60	40 selected-response 2 essays

The Math test addresses four content areas: Number and Quantity, Algebra and Functions, Geometry, and Statistics and Probability. The Reading test includes three content areas: Key Ideas and Details; Craft, Structure, and Language Skills; and Integration of Knowledge and Ideas. Lastly, the Writing test has two major domains: Text Types, Purposes, and Production; and Language and Research Skills for Writing.

Scoring

Raw scores are calculated from the number of correct responses; there is no penalty for incorrect answers Raw scores are converted to scaled scores from 100 to 200, which enables scores to be compared, regardless of the test version. The passing score varies because each state can set their own minimum scores. Test takers should review the requirements of the state in which they want to work.

Study Prep Plan for the Praxis Core Academic Skills for Educators

1 Breathe

Reducing stress is key when preparing for your test.

2 Build

Create a study plan to help you stay on track.

3 Begin

Stick with your study plan. You've got this!

1 Week Study Plan

Day 1	Day 2	Day 3	Day 4	Day 5	Day 6	Day 7
Mathematics	Algebra and Functions	Geometry	Statistics and Probability	Reading	Writing	Take Your Exam!

2 Week Study Plan

Day 1	Day 2	Day 3	Day 4	Day 5	Day 6	Day 7
Number and Quantity	Performing Operations on Rational Numbers	Algebra and Functions	Functions	Geometric Measurement and Dimension	Statistics and Probability	Practice Questions

Day 8	Day 9	Day 10	Day 11	Day 12	Day 13	Day 14
Key Ideas and Details	Integration of Knowledge and Ideas	Practice Questions	Text Production: Writing Arguments	Language Skills	Practice Questions	Take Your Exam!

30 Day Study Plan

Day 1	Day 2	Day 3	Day 4	Day 5	Day 6	Day 7
Number and Quantity	The Real Number System	Performing Operations on Rational Numbers	Rational and Irrational Numbers	Algebra and Functions	Systems of Equations and Inequalities	Geometry

Day 8	Day 9	Day 10	Day 11	Day 12	Day 13	Day 14
Geometric Measurement and Dimension	Statistics and Probability	Chance Processes and Probability Models	Linear Regression Models	Practice Questions	Answer Explanations	Key Ideas and Details

Day 15	Day 16	Day 17	Day 18	Day 19	Day 20	Day 21
Craft, Structure, and Language Skills	Evaluating the Author's Point of View in a Given Text	Integration of Knowledge and Ideas	Owners' Manuals	Evaluating Arguments and Claims	Practice Questions	Answer Explanations

Day 22	Day 23	Day 24	Day 25	Day 26	Day 27	Day 28
Text Production: Writing Arguments	Text Production: Writing Informative/ Explanatory Texts	Language Skills	Word Choice	Research Skills	Practice Questions	Answer Explanations

Day 29	Day 30
Essays 1 & 2	Take Your Exam!

Mathematics

Number and Quantity

Ratios and Proportional Relationships

<u>Ratio Concepts and Reasoning</u>

Recall that a **ratio** is the comparison of two different quantities. Comparing 2 apples to 3 oranges results in the ratio 2:3, which can be expressed as the fraction $\frac{2}{5}$. Note that order is important when discussing ratios. The number mentioned first is the **antecedent**, and the number mentioned second is the **consequent**. Note that the consequent of the ratio and the denominator of the fraction are *not* the same. When there are 2 apples to 3 oranges, there are five fruit total; two fifths of the fruit are apples, while three fifths are oranges. The ratio 2:3 represents a different relationship than the ratio 3:2. Also, it is important to make sure that when discussing ratios that have units attached to them, the two quantities use the same units. For example, to think of 8 feet to 4 yards, it would make sense to convert 4 yards to feet by multiplying by 3. Therefore, the ratio would be 8 feet to 12 feet, which can be expressed as the fraction $\frac{8}{20}$. Also, note that it is proper to refer to ratios in lowest terms. Therefore, the ratio of 8 feet to 4 yards is equivalent to the fraction $\frac{2}{5}$.

Many real-world problems involve ratios. Often, problems with ratios involve proportions, as when two ratios are set equal to find the missing amount. However, some problems involve deciphering single ratios. For example, consider an amusement park that sold 345 tickets last Saturday. If 145 tickets were sold to adults and the rest of the tickets were sold to children, what would the ratio of the number of adult tickets to children's tickets be? A common mistake would be to say the ratio is 145:345. However, 345 is the total number of tickets sold, not the number of children's tickets. There were $345 - 145 = 200$ tickets sold to children. The correct ratio of adult to children's tickets is 145:200. As a fraction, this expression is written as $\frac{145}{345}$, which can be reduced to $\frac{29}{69}$.

While a ratio compares two measurements using the same units, **rates** compare two measurements with different units. Examples of rates would be \$200 for 8 hours of work, or 500 miles traveled per 20 gallons. Because the units are different, it is important to always include the units when discussing rates. Key words in rate problems include for, per, on, from, and in. Just as with ratios, it is important to write rates in lowest terms. A common rate in real-life situations is cost per unit, which describes how much one item/unit costs. When evaluating the cost of an item that comes in several sizes, the cost per unit rate can help buyers determine the best deal. For example, if 2 quarts of soup was sold for \$3.50 and 3 quarts was sold for \$4.60, to determine the best buy, the cost per quart should be found. $\frac{\$3.50}{2\ \text{qt}} = \$1.75$ per quart, and $\frac{\$4.60}{3\ \text{qt}} = \$1.53$ per quart. Therefore, the better deal would be the 3-quart option.

Rate of change problems involve calculating a quantity per some unit of measurement. Usually, the unit of measurement is time. For example, meters per second is a common rate of change. To calculate this measurement, find the distance traveled in meters and divide by total time traveled. The result is the average speed over the entire time interval. Another common rate of change used in the real world is miles per hour.

Consider the following problem that involves calculating an average rate of change in temperature. Last Saturday, the temperature at 1:00 a.m. was 34 degrees Fahrenheit, and at noon, the temperature had increased to 75 degrees Fahrenheit. What was the average rate of change over that time interval? The average rate of change is calculated by finding the change in temperature and dividing it by the total hours elapsed. Therefore, the rate of change was equal to:

$$\frac{75 - 34}{12 - 1} = \frac{41}{11}$$

degrees per hour. This quantity rounded to two decimal places is equal to 3.73 degrees per hour.

A common rate of change that appears in algebra is the slope calculation. Given a linear equation in one variable, $y = mx + b$, the **slope**, m, is equal to:

$$\frac{rise}{run} \text{ or } \frac{change \text{ } in \text{ } y}{change \text{ } in \text{ } x}$$

In other words, slope is equivalent to the ratio of the vertical and horizontal changes between any two points on a line. The vertical change is known as the **rise**, and the horizontal change is known as the **run**. Given any two points on a line (x_1, y_1) and (x_2, y_2), slope can be calculated with the formula:

$$m = \frac{y_2 - y_1}{x_2 - x_1} = \frac{\Delta y}{\Delta x}$$

Common real-world applications of slope include determining how steep a staircase should be, calculating how steep a road is, and determining how to build a wheelchair ramp.

Many times, problems involving rates and ratios involve proportions. A proportion states that two ratios (or rates) are equal. The property of cross products can be used to determine if a proportion is true, meaning both ratios are equivalent. If $\frac{a}{b} = \frac{c}{d}$, then to clear the fractions, multiply both sides by the least common denominator, bd. This results in $ad = bc$, which is equal to the result of multiplying along both diagonals. For example, $\frac{4}{40} = \frac{1}{10}$ grants the cross product $4 \times 10 = 40 \times 1$, which is equivalent to $40 = 40$ and shows that this proportion is true. Cross products are used when proportions are involved in real-world problems. Consider the following: If 3 pounds of fertilizer will cover 75 square feet of grass, how many pounds are needed for 375 square feet? To solve this problem, set up a proportion using two ratios. Let x equal the unknown quantity, pounds needed for 375 feet. Setting the two ratios equal to one another yields the equation:

$$\frac{3}{75} = \frac{x}{375}$$

Cross-multiplication gives:

$$3 \times 375 = 75x$$

Therefore, $1,125 = 75x$. Divide both sides by 75 to get $x = 15$. Therefore, 15 pounds of fertilizer are needed to cover 375 square feet of grass.

Another application of proportions involves similar triangles. If two triangles have corresponding angles with the same measurements and corresponding sides with proportional measurements, the triangles are said to be similar. If two angles are the same, the third pair of angles are equal as well because the sum of all angles in a triangle is equal to 180 degrees. Each pair of equivalent angles are known as

corresponding angles. Corresponding sides face the corresponding angles, and it is true that corresponding sides are in proportion. For example, consider the following set of similar triangles:

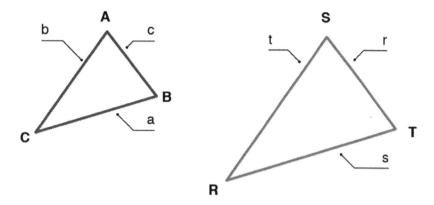

Angles A and S have the same measurement, angles C and R have the same measurement, and angles B and T have the same measurement. Therefore, the following proportion can be set up from the sides:

$$\frac{c}{r} = \frac{a}{s} = \frac{b}{t}$$

This proportion can be helpful in finding missing lengths in pairs of similar triangles. For example, if the following triangles are similar, a proportion can be used to find the missing side lengths, a and b.

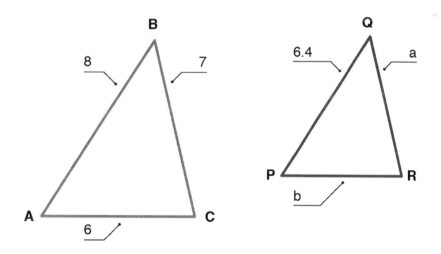

The proportions $\frac{8}{6.4} = \frac{6}{b}$ and $\frac{8}{6.4} = \frac{7}{a}$ can both be cross-multiplied and solved to obtain $a = 5.6$ and $b = 4.8$.

A real-life situation that uses similar triangles involves measuring shadows to find heights of unknown objects. Consider the following problem: A building casts a shadow that is 120 feet long, and at the same time, another building that is 80 feet high casts a shadow that is 60 feet long. How tall is the first building? Each building, together with the sun rays and shadows casted on the ground, forms a triangle. They are similar because each building forms a right angle with the ground, and the sun rays form equivalent angles. Therefore, these two pairs of angles are both equal. Because all angles in a triangle add up to 180 degrees, the third angles are equal as well. Both shadows form corresponding sides of the triangle, the buildings form corresponding sides, and the sun rays form corresponding sides. Therefore, the triangles are similar, and the following proportion can be used to find the missing building length:

$$\frac{120}{x} = \frac{60}{80}$$

Cross multiply to obtain the equation $9600 = 60x$. Then, divide both sides by 60 to obtain $x = 160$. This means that the first building is 160 feet high.

Analyzing Proportional Relationships and Using Them to Solve Real-World Problems

Fractions appear in everyday situations, and in many scenarios, they appear in the real-world as ratios and in proportions. A **ratio** is formed when two different quantities are compared. For example, in a group of 50 people, if there are 33 females and 17 males, the ratio of females to males is 33 to 17. This expression can be written in the fraction form as $\frac{33}{50}$, where the denominator is the sum of females and males, or by using the ratio symbol, 33:17. The order of the number matters when forming ratios. In the same setting, the ratio of males to females is 17 to 33, which is equivalent to $\frac{17}{50}$ or 17:33. A **proportion** is an equation involving two ratios. The equation $\frac{a}{b} = \frac{c}{d}$, or $a:b = c:d$ is a proportion, for real numbers a, b, c, and d. Usually, in one ratio, one of the quantities is unknown, and cross-multiplication is used to solve for the unknown. Consider,

$$\frac{1}{4} = \frac{x}{5}$$

To solve for x, cross-multiply to obtain $5 = 4x$. Divide each side by 4 to obtain the solution $x = \frac{5}{4}$. It is also true that percentages are ratios in which the second term is 100 minus the first term. For example, 65% is 65:35 or $\frac{65}{100}$. Therefore, when working with percentages, one is also working with ratios.

Real-world problems frequently involve proportions. For example, consider the following problem: If 2 out of 50 pizzas are usually delivered late from a local Italian restaurant, how many would be late out of 235 orders? The following proportion would be solved with x as the unknown quantity of late pizzas:

$$\frac{2}{50} = \frac{x}{235}$$

Cross multiplying results in $470 = 50x$. Divide both sides by 50 to obtain $x = \frac{470}{50}$, which in lowest terms is equal to $\frac{47}{5}$. In decimal form, this improper fraction is equal to 9.4. Because it does not make sense to answer this question with decimals (portions of pizzas do not get delivered) the answer must be rounded. Traditional rounding rules would say that 9 pizzas would be expected to be delivered late. However, to be safe, rounding up to 10 pizzas out of 235 would probably make more sense.

Percentages

Percentages are defined as parts per one hundred. To convert a decimal to a percentage, move the decimal point two units to the right and place the percent sign after the number. Percentages appear in many scenarios in the real world. It is important to make sure the statement containing the percentage is translated to a correct mathematical expression. Be aware that it is extremely common to make a mistake when working with percentages within word problems.

An example of a word problem containing a percentage is the following: 35% of people speed when driving to work. In a group of 5,600 commuters, how many would be expected to speed on the way to their place of employment? The answer to this problem is found by finding 35% of 5,600. First, change the percentage to the decimal 0.35. Then compute the product:

$$0.35 \times 5,600 = 1,960$$

Therefore, it would be expected that 1,960 of those commuters would speed on their way to work based on the data given. In this situation, the word "of" signals to use multiplication to find the answer.

Another way percentages are used is in the following problem: Teachers work 8 months out of the year. What percent of the year do they work? To answer this problem, find what percent of 12 the number 8 is, because there are 12 months in a year. Therefore, divide 8 by 12, and convert that number to a percentage:

$$\frac{8}{12} = \frac{2}{3} = 0.66\overline{6}$$

The percentage rounded to the nearest tenth place tells us that teachers work 66.7% of the year. Percentage problems can also find missing quantities like in the following question: 60% of what number is 75? To find the missing quantity, turn the question into an equation. Let x be equal to the missing quantity. Therefore, $0.60x = 75$. Divide each side by 0.60 to obtain 125. Therefore, 60% of 125 is equal to 75.

Sales tax is an important application relating to percentages because tax rates are usually given as percentages. For example, a city might have an 8% sales tax rate. Therefore, when an item is purchased with that tax rate, the real cost to the customer is 1.08 times the price in the store. For example, a $25 pair of jeans costs the customer:

$$\$25 \times 1.08 = \$27$$

If the sales tax rate is unknown, it can be determined after an item is purchased. If a customer visits a store and purchases an item for $21.44, but the price in the store was $19, they can find the tax rate by first subtracting:

$$\$21.44 - \$19$$

to obtain $2.44, the sales tax amount. The sales tax is a percentage of the in-store price. Therefore, the tax rate is:

$$\frac{2.44}{19} = 0.128$$

which has been rounded to the nearest thousandths place. In this scenario, the actual sales tax rate given as a percentage is 12.8%.

Solving Unit Rate Problems
A **unit rate** is a rate with a denominator of one. It is a comparison of two values with different units where one value is equal to one. Examples of unit rates include 60 miles per hour and 200 words per minute. Problems involving unit rates may require some work to find the unit rate. For example, if Mary travels 360 miles in 5 hours, what is her speed, expressed as a unit rate? The rate can be expressed as the following fraction: $\frac{360\ miles}{5\ hours}$. The denominator can be changed to one by dividing by five. The numerator will also need to be divided by five to follow the rules of equality. This division turns the fraction into $\frac{72\ miles}{1\ hour}$,

13

which can now be labeled as a unit rate because one unit has a value of one. Another type question involves the use of unit rates to solve problems. For example, if Trey needs to read 300 pages and his average speed is 75 pages per hour, will he be able to finish the reading in 5 hours? The unit rate is 75 pages per hour, so the total of 300 pages can be divided by 75 to find the time. After the division, the time it takes to read is four hours. The answer to the question is yes, Trey will finish the reading within 5 hours.

The Real Number System

Operations with Fractions

Once the rules for integers are understood, operations with fractions and decimals can be mastered. Recall that a **rational number** can be written as a fraction and can be converted to a decimal through division. If a rational number is negative, the rules for adding, subtracting, multiplying, and dividing integers must be used. If a rational number is in fraction form, performing addition, subtraction, multiplication, and division is more complicated than when working with integers. First, consider addition. To add two fractions having the same denominator, add the numerators and then reduce the fraction. When an answer is a fraction, it should always be in lowest terms. **Lowest terms** means that every common factor, other than 1, between the numerator and denominator is divided out. For example:

$$\frac{2}{8} + \frac{4}{8} = \frac{6}{8} = \frac{6 \div 2}{8 \div 2} = \frac{3}{4}$$

Both the numerator and denominator of $\frac{6}{8}$ have a common factor of 2, so 2 is divided out of each number to put the fraction in lowest terms. If denominators are different in an addition problem, the fractions must be converted to have common denominators. The **least common denominator (LCD)** of all the given denominators must be found, and this value is equal to the **least common multiple (LCM)** of the denominators. This non-zero value is the smallest number that is a multiple of both denominators. Then, each original fraction can be written as an equivalent fraction using the new denominator. Once in this form, process of adding with like denominators is completed. For example, consider $\frac{1}{3} + \frac{4}{9}$. The LCD is 9 because 9 is the smallest multiple of both 3 and 9. The fraction $\frac{1}{3}$ must be rewritten with 9 as its denominator. Therefore, multiply both the numerator and denominator by 3. Multiplying by $\frac{3}{3}$ is the same as multiplying times 1, which does not change the value of the fraction. Therefore, an equivalent fraction is $\frac{3}{9}$, and:

$$\frac{1}{3} + \frac{4}{9} = \frac{3}{9} + \frac{4}{9} = \frac{7}{9}$$

which is in lowest terms. Subtraction is performed in a similar manner; once the denominators are equal, the numerators are then subtracted. The following is an example of addition of a positive and a negative fraction:

$$-\frac{5}{12} + \frac{5}{9} = -\frac{5 \times 3}{12 \times 3} + \frac{5 \times 4}{9 \times 4} = -\frac{15}{36} + \frac{20}{36} = \frac{5}{36}$$

Common denominators are not used in multiplication and division. To multiply two fractions, multiply the numerators together and the denominators together. Then, write the result in lowest terms.

For example:

$$\frac{2}{3} \times \frac{9}{4} = \frac{18}{12} = \frac{3}{2}$$

14

Alternatively, the fractions could be factored first to cancel out any common factors before performing the multiplication. For example:

$$\frac{2}{3} \times \frac{9}{4} = \frac{2}{3} \times \frac{3 \times 3}{2 \times 2} = \frac{3}{2}$$

This second approach is helpful when working with larger numbers, as common factors might not be obvious. Multiplication and division of fractions are related because the division of two fractions is changed into a multiplication problem. This means that dividing a fraction by another fraction is the same as multiplying the first fraction by the reciprocal of the second fraction, so that second fraction must be inverted, or "flipped," to be in reciprocal form. For example:

$$\frac{11}{15} \div \frac{3}{5} = \frac{11}{15} \times \frac{5}{3} = \frac{55}{45} = \frac{11}{9}$$

The fraction $\frac{5}{3}$ is the reciprocal of $\frac{3}{5}$. It is possible to multiply and divide numbers containing a mix of integers and fractions. In this case, convert the integer to a fraction by placing it over a denominator of 1. For example, a division problem involving an integer and a fraction is:

$$3 \div \frac{1}{2} = \frac{3}{1} \times \frac{2}{1} = \frac{6}{1} = 6$$

Finally, when performing operations with rational numbers that are negative, the same rules apply as when performing operations with integers. For example, a negative fraction times a negative fraction results in a positive value, and a negative fraction subtracted from a negative fraction results in a negative value.

Converting Non-Negative Fractions, Decimals, and Percentages
Within the number system, different forms of numbers can be used. It is important to be able to recognize each type, as well as work with, and convert between, the given forms. The **real number system** comprises natural numbers, whole numbers, integers, rational numbers, and irrational numbers. Natural numbers, whole numbers, integers, and irrational numbers typically are not represented as fractions, decimals, or percentages.

Rational numbers, however, can be represented as any of these three forms. A **rational number** is a number that can be written in the form $\frac{a}{b}$, where a and b are integers, and b is not equal to zero. In other words, rational numbers can be written in a fraction form.

The value a is the **numerator,** and b is the **denominator.** If the numerator is equal to zero, the entire fraction is equal to zero. Non-negative fractions can be less than 1, equal to 1, or greater than 1. Fractions are less than 1 if the numerator is smaller (less than) than the denominator.

For example, $\frac{3}{4}$ is less than 1. A fraction is equal to 1 if the numerator is equal to the denominator. For instance, $\frac{4}{4}$ is equal to 1. Finally, a fraction is greater than 1 if the numerator is greater than the denominator: the fraction $\frac{11}{4}$ is greater than 1. When the numerator is greater than the denominator, the fraction is called an **improper fraction**.

An improper fraction can be converted to a **mixed number**, a combination of both a whole number and a fraction. To convert an improper fraction to a mixed number, divide the numerator by the denominator.

Write down the whole number portion, and then write any remainder over the original denominator. For example, $\frac{11}{4}$ is equivalent to $2\frac{3}{4}$. Conversely, a mixed number can be converted to an improper fraction by multiplying the denominator by the whole number and adding that result to the numerator.

Fractions can be converted to decimals. With a calculator, a fraction is converted to a decimal by dividing the numerator by the denominator. For example:

$$\frac{2}{5} = 2 \div 5 = 0.4$$

Sometimes, rounding might be necessary. Consider:

$$\frac{2}{7} = 2 \div 7 = 0.28571429$$

This decimal could be rounded for ease of use, and if it needed to be rounded to the nearest thousandth, the result would be 0.286. If a calculator is not available, a fraction can be converted to a decimal manually. First, find a number that, when multiplied by the denominator, has a value equal to 10, 100, 1,000, etc. Then, multiply both the numerator and denominator times that number. The decimal form of the fraction is equal to the new numerator with a decimal point placed as many place values to the left as there are zeros in the denominator.

For example, to convert $\frac{3}{5}$ to a decimal, multiply both the numerator and denominator by 2, which results in $\frac{6}{10}$. The decimal is equal to 0.6 because there is one zero in the denominator, and so the decimal place in the numerator is moved one unit to the left. In the case where rounding would be necessary while working without a calculator, an approximation must be found. A number close to 10, 100, 1,000, etc. can be used. For example, to convert $\frac{1}{3}$ to a decimal, the numerator and denominator can be multiplied by 33 to turn the denominator into approximately 100, which makes for an easier conversion to the equivalent decimal. This process results in $\frac{33}{99}$ and an approximate decimal of 0.33. Once in decimal form, the number can be converted to a percentage. Multiply the decimal by 100 and then place a percent sign after the number. For example, 0.614 is equal to 61.4%. In other words, move the decimal place two units to the right and add the percentage symbol.

Solving Multi-Digit Problems, Common Factors, and Multiples

Solving Real-World One- or Multi-Step Problems with Rational Numbers

One-step problems take only one mathematical step to solve. For example, solving the equation $5x = 45$ is a one-step problem because the one step of dividing both sides of the equation by 5 is the only step necessary to obtain the solution $x = 9$. The **multiplication principle of equality** is the one step used to isolate the variable. The equation is of the form $ax = b$, where a and b are rational numbers. Similarly, the **addition principle of equality** could be the one step needed to solve a problem. In this case, the equation would be of the form $x + a = b$ or $x - a = b$, for real numbers a and b.

A multi-step problem involves more than one step to find the solution, or it could consist of solving more than one equation. An equation that involves both the addition principle and the multiplication principle is a two-step problem, and an example of such an equation is:

$$2x - 4 = 5$$

To solve, add 4 to both sides and then divide both sides by 2. An example of a two-step problem involving two separate equations is $y = 3x, 2x + y = 4$. The two equations form a system that must be solved together in two variables. The system can be solved by the substitution method. Since y is already solved for in terms of x, replace y with $3x$ in the equation $2x + y = 4$, resulting in:

$$2x + 3x = 4$$

Therefore, $5x = 4$ and $x = \frac{4}{5}$. Because there are two variables, the solution consists of a value for both x and for y. Substitute $x = \frac{4}{5}$ into either original equation to find y. The easiest choice is $y = 3x$. Therefore:

$$y = 3 \times \frac{4}{5} = \frac{12}{5}$$

The solution can be written as the ordered pair $\left(\frac{4}{5}, \frac{12}{5}\right)$.

Real-world problems can be translated into both one-step and multi-step problems. In either case, the word problem must be translated from the verbal form into mathematical expressions and equations that can be solved using algebra. An example of a one-step real-world problem is the following: A cat weighs half as much as a dog living in the same house. If the dog weighs 14.5 pounds, how much does the cat weigh? To solve this problem, an equation can be used. In any word problem, the first step must be defining variables that represent the unknown quantities. For this problem, let x be equal to the unknown weight of the cat. Because two times the weight of the cat equals 14.5 pounds, the equation to be solved is: $2x = 14.5$. Use the multiplication principle to divide both sides by 2. Therefore, $x = 7.25$, and the cat weighs 7.25 pounds.

Most of the time, real-world problems are more difficult than this one and are multi-step problems. The following is an example of a multi-step problem: The sum of two consecutive page numbers is equal to 437. What are those page numbers? First, define the unknown quantities. If x is equal to the first page number, then $x + 1$ is equal to the next page number because they are consecutive integers. Their sum is equal to 437. Putting this information together results in the equation:

$$x + x + 1 = 437$$

To solve, first collect like terms to obtain:

$$2x + 1 = 437$$

Then, subtract 1 from both sides and then divide by 2. The solution to the equation is $x = 218$. Therefore, the two consecutive page numbers that satisfy the problem are 218 and 219. It is always important to make sure that answers to real-world problems make sense. For instance, it should be a red flag if the solution to this same problem resulted in decimals, which would indicate the need to check the work. Page numbers are whole numbers; therefore, if decimals are found to be answers, the solution process should be double-checked for mistakes.

Factorization
Factorization is the process of breaking up a mathematical quantity, such as a number or polynomial, into a product of two or more factors. For example, a factorization of the number 16 is:

$$16 = 8 \times 2$$

If multiplied out, the factorization results in the original number. A **prime factorization** is a specific factorization when the number is factored completely using prime numbers only. For example, the prime factorization of 16 is:

$$16 = 2 \times 2 \times 2 \times 2$$

A factor tree can be used to find the prime factorization of any number. Within a factor tree, pairs of factors are found until no other factors can be used, as in the following factor tree of the number 84:

A factor tree

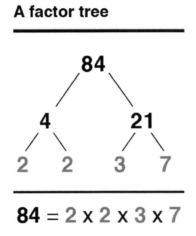

$$84 = 2 \times 2 \times 3 \times 7$$

It first breaks 84 into 21 × 4, which is not a prime factorization. Then, both 21 and 4 are factored into their primes. The final numbers on each branch consist of the numbers within the prime factorization. Therefore,

$$84 = 2 \times 2 \times 3 \times 7$$

Factorization can be helpful in finding greatest common divisors and least common denominators.

Also, a factorization of an algebraic expression can be found. Throughout the process, a more complicated expression can be decomposed into products of simpler expressions. To factor a polynomial, first determine if there is a greatest common factor. If there is, factor it out. For example, $2x^2 + 8x$ has a greatest common factor of $2x$ and can be written as:

$$2x(x + 4)$$

Once the greatest common monomial factor is factored out, if applicable, count the number of terms in the polynomial. If there are two terms, is it a difference of squares, a sum of cubes, or a difference of cubes?

If so, the following rules can be used:

$$a^2 - b^2 = (a + b)(a - b)$$

$$a^3 + b^3 = (a + b)(a^2 - ab + b^2)$$

$$a^3 - b^3 = (a - b)(a^2 + ab + b^2)$$

18

If there are three terms, and if the trinomial is a perfect square trinomial, it can be factored into the following:

$$a^2 + 2ab + b^2 = (a + b)^2$$

$$a^2 - 2ab + b^2 = (a - b)^2$$

If not, try factoring into a product of two binomials in the form of $(x + p)(x + q)$. For example, to factor $x^2 + 6x + 8$, determine what two numbers have a product of 8 and a sum of 6. Those numbers are 4 and 2, so the trinomial factors into $(x + 2)(x + 4)$.

Finally, if there are four terms, try factoring by grouping. First, group terms together that have a common monomial factor. Then, factor out the common monomial factor from the first two terms. Next, look to see if a common factor can be factored out of the second set of two terms that results in a common binomial factor. Finally, factor out the common binomial factor of each expression, for example:

$$xy - x + 5y - 5 = x(y - 1) + 5(y - 1) = (y - 1)(x + 5)$$

After the expression is completely factored, check the factorization by multiplying it out; if this results in the original expression, then the factoring is correct. Factorizations are helpful in solving equations that consist of a polynomial set equal to 0. If the product of two algebraic expressions equals zero, then at least one of the factors is equal to zero. Therefore, factor the polynomial within the equation, set each factor equal to zero, and solve. For example:

$$x^2 + 7x - 18 = 0$$

This can be solved by factoring into:

$$(x + 9)(x - 2) = 0$$

Set each factor equal to zero, and solve to obtain $x = -9$ and $x = 2$.

Performing Operations on Rational Numbers

The four basic operations include addition, subtraction, multiplication, and division. The result of addition is a **sum**, the result of subtraction is a **difference**, the result of multiplication is a **product**, and the result of division is a **quotient**. Each type of operation can be used when working with rational numbers; however, the basic operations need to be understood first while using simpler numbers before working with fractions and decimals.

These operations should first be learned using whole numbers. Addition needs to be done column by column. To add two whole numbers, add the ones column first, then the tens columns, then the hundreds, etc. If the sum of any column is greater than 9, a one must be carried over to the next column.

For example, the following is the result of 482 + 924:

$$
\begin{array}{r}
1 \\
482 \\
+924 \\
\hline
1406
\end{array}
$$

Notice that the sum of the tens column was 10, so a one was carried over to the hundreds column. Subtraction is also performed column by column. Subtraction is performed in the ones column first, then the tens, etc. If the number on top is less than the number below, a one must be borrowed from the column to the left. For example, the following is the result of 5,424 − 756:

$$
\begin{array}{r}
4\ 13\ 11\ 14 \\
5\,4\,2\,4 \\
-\ 7\ 5\ 6 \\
\hline
4\ 6\ 6\ 8
\end{array}
$$

Notice that a one is borrowed from the tens, hundreds, and thousands place. After subtraction, the answer can be checked through addition. A check of this problem would be to show that:

$$756 + 4{,}668 = 5{,}424$$

In multiplication, the number on top is known as the multiplicand, and the number below is the multiplier. Complete the problem by multiplying the multiplicand by each digit of the multiplier. Make sure to place the ones value of each result under the multiplying digit in the multiplier. The final product is found by adding each partial product. The following example shows the process of multiplying 46 times 37:

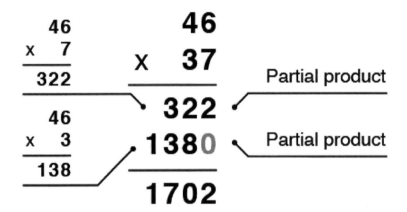

Finally, division can be performed using long division. When dividing, the first number is known as the **dividend,** and the second is the **divisor.** For example, with $a \div b = c$, a is the dividend, b is the divisor, and c is the quotient. For long division, place the dividend within the division bar and the divisor on the outside. For example, with $8{,}764 \div 4$, refer to the first problem in the diagram below. The first digit, 8, is divisible by 4 two times. Therefore, 2 goes above the division bar over the 8. Then, multiply 4 times 2 to get 8, and that product goes below the 8. Subtract to get 0, and then carry down the second digit, 7. Continue the same steps. $7 \div 4 = 1$ R3, so 1 is written above the 7. Multiply 4 times 1 to get 4, and write it below the 7. Subtract to get 3, and carry the 6 down next to the 3. Continuing this process for the next two digits results in a 9 and a 1. The final subtraction results in a 0, which means that 8,764 is evenly divisible by 4 with no remaining numbers.

The second example shows that:

$$4{,}536 \div 216 = 21$$

The steps are a little different because 216 cannot be contained in 4 or 5, so the first step is placing a 2 above the 3 because there are 2 216's in 453. Finally, the third example shows that:

$$546 \div 31 = 17 \text{ R}19$$

The 19 is a remainder. Notice that the final subtraction does not result in a 0, which means that 546 is not divisible by 31. The remainder can also be written as a fraction over the divisor to say that:

$$546 \div 31 = 17\frac{19}{31}$$

```
      2 1 9 1
   4 | 8 7 6 4
     8 ↓
     0 7
       4 ↓
       3 6
       3 6 ↓
         0 4
           4
           0
```

```
           2 1
   2 1 6 | 4 5 3 6
         4 3 2 ↓
           2 1 6
           2 1 6
               0
```

```
         1 7  r  1 9
   3 1 | 5 4 6
       3 1 ↓
         2 3 6
         2 1 7
           1 9
```

A remainder can have meaning in a division problem with real-world application. For example, consider the third example,

$$546 \div 31 = 17 \text{ R}19$$

Let's say that we had $546 to spend on calculators that cost $31 each, and we wanted to know how many we could buy. The division problem would answer this question. The result states that 17 calculators could be purchased, with $19 left over. Notice that the remainder will never be greater than or equal to the divisor.

Once the operations are understood with whole numbers, they can be used with negative numbers. There are many rules surrounding operations with negative numbers. First, consider addition with integers. The sum of two numbers can first be shown using a number line. For example, to add $-5 + (-6)$, plot the point -5 on the number line. Adding a negative number is the same as subtracting, so move 6 units to the left. This process results in landing on -11 on the number line, which is the sum of -5 and -6. If adding a positive number, move to the right. While visualizing this process using a number line is useful for understanding, it is more efficient to learn the rules of operations. When adding two numbers with the same sign, add the absolute values of both numbers, and use the common sign of both numbers as the sign of the sum. For example, to add $-5 + (-6)$, add their absolute values:

$$5 + 6 = 11$$

Then, introduce a negative symbol because both addends are negative. The result is -11. To add two integers with unlike signs, subtract the lesser absolute value from the greater absolute value, and apply the sign of the number with the greater absolute value to the result. For example, the sum $-7 + 4$ can be computed by finding the difference $7 - 4 = 3$ and then applying a negative because the value with the larger absolute value is negative. The result is -3. Similarly, the sum $-4 + 7$ can be found by computing the same difference but leaving it as a positive result because the addend with the larger absolute value is positive. Also, recall that any number plus 0 equals that number. This is known as the **Addition Property of 0**.

Subtracting two integers with opposite signs can be computed by changing to addition to avoid confusion. The rule is to add the first number to the opposite of the second number. The opposite of a number is the number with the same value on the other side of 0 on the number line. For example, -2 and 2 are opposites. Consider $4 - 8$. Change this to adding the opposite as follows: $4 + (-8)$. Then, follow the rules of addition of integers to obtain -4. Secondly, consider $-8 - (-2)$. Change this problem to adding the opposite as $-8 + 2$, which equals -6. Notice that subtracting a negative number functions the same as adding a positive number.

Multiplication and division of integers are actually less confusing than addition and subtraction because the rules are simpler to understand. If two factors in a multiplication problem have the same sign, the result is positive. If one factor is positive and one factor is negative, the result, known as the **product**, is negative. For example:

$$(-9)(-3) = 27$$

and

$$9(-3) = -27$$

Also, any number times 0 always results in 0. If a problem consists of several multipliers, the result is negative if it contains an odd number of negative factors, and the result is positive if it contains an even number of negative factors. For example:

$$(-1)(-1)(-1)(-1) = 1$$

and

$$(-1)(-1)(-1)(-1)(-1) = -1$$

These two problems are also examples of repeated multiplication, which can be written in a more compact notation using exponents. The first example can be written as $(-1)^4 = 1$, and the second example can be written as $(-1)^5 = -1$. Both are exponential expressions; -1 is the base in both instances, and 4 and 5 are the respective exponents. Note that a negative number raised to an odd power is always negative, and a negative number raised to an even power is always positive. Also, $(-1)^4$ is not the same as -1^4. In the first expression, the negative is included in the parentheses, but it is not in the second expression. The second expression is found by evaluating 1^4 first to get 1 and then by applying the negative sign to obtain -1.

Similar rules apply within division. First, consider some vocabulary. When dividing 14 by 2, it can be written in the following ways:

$$14 \div 2 = 7 \text{ or } \frac{14}{2} = 7$$

14 is the **dividend,** 2 is the **divisor,** and 7 is the **quotient**. If two numbers in a division problem have the same sign, the quotient is positive. If two numbers in a division problem have different signs, the quotient is negative. For example:

$$14 \div (-2) = -7$$

and

$$-14 \div (-2) = 7$$

To check division, multiply the quotient times the divisor to obtain the dividend. Also, remember that 0 divided by any number is equal to 0. However, any number divided by 0 is undefined. It just does not make sense to divide a number by 0 parts.

If more than one operation is to be completed in a problem, follow the **Order of Operations**. The mnemonic device, PEMDAS, states the order in which addition, subtraction, multiplication, and division need to be done. It also includes when to evaluate operations within grouping symbols and when to incorporate exponents. PEMDAS, which some remember by thinking "please excuse my dear Aunt Sally," refers to parentheses, exponents, multiplication, division, addition, and subtraction. First, complete any operation within parentheses or any other grouping symbol like brackets, braces, or absolute value symbols. Note that this does not refer to when parentheses are used to represent multiplication like $(2)(5)$. An operation is not within parentheses like it is in (2×5). Then, any exponents must be computed. Next, multiplication and division are performed from left to right.

Finally, addition and subtraction are performed from left to right. The following is an example in which the operations within the parentheses need to be performed first, so the order of operations must be applied to the exponent, subtraction, addition, and multiplication within the grouping symbol:

$$9 - 3(3^2 - 3 + 4 \cdot 3)$$

$$9 - 3(3^2 - 3 + 4 \cdot 3) \quad \text{Work within the parentheses first}$$

$$= 9 - 3(9 - 3 + 12)$$

$$= 9 - 3(18)$$

$$= 9 - 54$$

$$= -45$$

Operations can be performed on rational numbers in decimal form. Recall that to write a fraction as an equivalent decimal expression, divide the numerator by the denominator. For example:

$$\frac{1}{8} = 1 \div 8 = 0.125$$

With the case of decimals, it is important to keep track of place value. To add decimals, make sure the decimal places are in alignment and add vertically. If the numbers do not line up because there are extra or missing place values in one of the numbers, then zeros may be used as placeholders.

For example, $0.123 + 0.23$ becomes:

$$
\begin{array}{r}
0.123 \\
+\ 0.230 \\
\hline
0.353
\end{array}
$$

Subtraction is done the same way. Multiplication and division are more complicated. To multiply two decimals, place one on top of the other as in a regular multiplication process and do not worry about lining up the decimal points. Then, multiply as with whole numbers, ignoring the decimals. Finally, in the solution, insert the decimal point as many places to the left as there are total decimal values in the original problem. Here is an example of a decimal multiplication problem:

$$
\begin{array}{r}
0.52 \quad \textit{2 decimal places} \\
\times \quad 0.2 \quad \textit{1 decimal place} \\
\hline
0.104 \quad \textit{3 decimal places}
\end{array}
$$

The answer to 52 times 2 is 104, and because there are three decimal values in the problem, the decimal point is positioned three units to the left in the answer.

The decimal point plays an integral role throughout the whole problem when dividing with decimals. First, set up the problem in a long division format. If the divisor is not an integer, move the decimal to the right as many units as needed to make it an integer. The decimal in the dividend must be moved to the right the same number of places to maintain equality. Then, complete division normally. Below is an example of long division with decimals. The problem is $12.72 \div 0.06$:

**Long division
with decimals**

$$
\begin{array}{r}
212 \\
6\,\overline{)\,1272} \\
\underline{12}\downarrow \\
07 \\
\underline{6}\downarrow \\
12
\end{array}
$$

The decimal point in 0.06 needed to move two units to the right to turn it into an integer (6), so it also needed to move two units to the right in 12.72 to make it 1,272. The quotient is 212. To check a division problem, multiply the answer by the divisor to see if the result is equal to the dividend.

Sometimes it is helpful to round answers that are in decimal form. First, find the place to which the rounding needs to be done. Then, look at the digit to the right of it. If that digit is 4 or less, the number in the place value to its left stays the same, and everything to its right becomes a 0. This process is known as **rounding down.** If that digit is 5 or higher, the number in the place value to its left increases by 1, and every number to its right becomes a 0. This is called rounding up. Excess 0s at the end of a decimal can be dropped. For example, 0.145 rounded to the nearest hundredth place would be rounded up to 0.15, and 0.145 rounded to the nearest tenth place would be rounded down to 0.1.

Another operation that can be performed on rational numbers is the square root. Dealing with real numbers only, the **positive square root** of a number is equal to one of the two repeated positive factors of that number. For example,

$$\sqrt{49} = \sqrt{7 \times 7} = 7$$

A **perfect square** is a number that has a whole number as its square root. Examples of perfect squares are 1, 4, 9, 16, 25, etc. If a number is not a perfect square, an approximation can be used with a calculator. For example, $\sqrt{67} = 8.185$, rounded to the nearest thousandth place. Taking the square root of a fraction that includes perfect squares involves breaking up the problem into the square root of the numerator separate from the square root of the denominator.

For example:

$$\sqrt{\frac{16}{25}} = \frac{\sqrt{16}}{\sqrt{25}} = \frac{4}{5}$$

If the fraction does not contain perfect squares, a calculator can be used. Therefore, $\sqrt{\frac{2}{5}} = 0.632$, rounded to the nearest thousandth place. A common application of square roots involves the **Pythagorean theorem**. Given a right triangle, the sum of the squares of the two legs equals the square of the hypotenuse.

For example, consider the following right triangle:

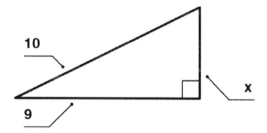

The missing side, x, can be found using the Pythagorean theorem:

$$9^2 + x^2 = 10^2$$

$$81 + x^2 = 100$$

$$x^2 = 19$$

To solve for x, take the square root of both sides. Therefore, $x = \sqrt{19} = 4.36$, which has been rounded to two decimal places.

In addition to the square root, the cube root is another operation. If a number is a **perfect cube**, the cube root of that number is equal to one of the three repeated factors. For example:

$$\sqrt[3]{27} = \sqrt[3]{3 \times 3 \times 3} = 3$$

A negative number has a cube root, which will also be a negative number. For example:

$$\sqrt[3]{-27} = \sqrt[3]{(-3)(-3)(-3)} = -3$$

Similar to square roots, if the number is not a perfect cube, a calculator can be used to find an approximation. Therefore, $\sqrt[3]{\frac{2}{3}} = 0.873$, rounded to the nearest thousandth place.

Higher-order roots also exist. The number relating to the root is known as the **index.** Given the following root, $\sqrt[3]{64}$, 3 is the index, and 64 is the **radicand.** The entire expression is known as the **radical.** Higher-order roots exist when the index is larger than 3. They can be broken up into two groups: even and odd roots. Even roots, when the index is an even number, follow the properties of square roots. They are found by finding the number that, when multiplied by itself the number of times indicated by the index, results in the radicand. For example, the fifth root of 32 is equal to 2 because:

$$\sqrt[5]{32} = \sqrt[5]{2 \times 2 \times 2 \times 2 \times 2} = 2$$

Odd roots, when the index is an odd number, follow the properties of cube roots. A negative number has an odd root. Similarly, an odd root is found by finding the single factor that is repeated that many times to obtain the radicand. For example, the 4th root of 81 is equal to 3 because $3^4 = 81$. This radical is written as $\sqrt[4]{81} = 3$.

When performing operations with rational numbers, it might be helpful to round the numbers in the original problem to get a rough idea of what the answer should be. For example, if you walked into a grocery store and had a $20 bill, you could round each item to the nearest dollar and add up all the items to make sure that you will have enough money when you check out. This process involves obtaining an estimation of what the exact total would be. In other situations, it might be helpful to round to the nearest $10 amount or $100 amount.

Front-end rounding might be helpful as well in many situations. In this type of rounding, the first digit of a number is rounded to the highest possible place value. Then, all digits following the first become 0. Consider a situation in which you are at the furniture store and want to estimate your total on three pieces of furniture that cost $434.99, $678.99, and $129.99. Front-end rounding would round these three amounts to $500, $700, and $200. Therefore, the estimate of your total would be $500 + $700 + $200 =

$1,400, compared to the exact total of $1,243.97. In this situation, the estimate is not that far off the exact answer.

Rounding is useful both for approximation when an exact answer is not needed and for comparison when an exact answer is needed. For instance, if you had a complicated set of operations to complete and your estimate was $1,000, but you obtained an exact answer of $100,000, then you know something is off. You might want to check your work to see if you made a mistake because an estimate should not be that different from an exact answer. Estimates can also be helpful with square roots. If the square root of a number is unknown, then you can use the closest perfect square to help you approximate. For example, $\sqrt{50}$ is not equal to a whole number, but 50 is close to 49, which is a perfect square, and $\sqrt{49} = 7$. Therefore, $\sqrt{50}$ is a little bit larger than 7. The actual approximation, rounded to the nearest thousandth, is 7.071.

Various Strategies and Algorithms Used to Perform Operations on Rational Numbers
As mentioned, **rational numbers** are any numbers that can be written as a fraction of integers. Operations to be performed on rational numbers include adding, subtracting, multiplying, and dividing. Essentially, this refers to performing these operations on fractions. For the denominators to become 35, the first fraction must be multiplied by 7 and the second by 5. For example, the problem $\frac{3}{5} + \frac{6}{7}$ requires that the common multiple be found between 5 and 7. The smallest number that divides evenly by 5 and 7 is 35. For the denominators to become 35, the first fraction must be multiplied by 7 and the second by 5. The fraction $\frac{3}{5}$ can be multiplied by 7 on the top and bottom to yield the fraction $\frac{21}{35}$. The fraction $\frac{6}{7}$ can be multiplied by 5 to yield the fraction $\frac{30}{35}$. Now that the fractions have the same denominator, the numerators can be added. The answer to the addition problem becomes:

$$\frac{3}{5} + \frac{6}{7} = \frac{21}{35} + \frac{30}{35} = \frac{51}{35}$$

The same technique can be used to subtract fractions. Multiplication and division may seem easier to perform because finding common denominators is unnecessary. If the problems reads $\frac{1}{3} \times \frac{4}{5}$, then the numerators and denominators are multiplied by each other and the answer is found to be $\frac{4}{15}$. For division, the problem must be changed to multiplication before performing operations. To complete a fraction division problem, you need to leave, change, and flip before multiplying. If the problems reads $\frac{3}{7} \div \frac{3}{4}$, then the first fraction is *left* alone, the operation is *changed* to multiplication, and then the last fraction is *flipped*. The problem becomes:

$$\frac{3}{7} \times \frac{4}{3} = \frac{12}{21}$$

Rational numbers can also be negative. When two negative numbers are added, the result is a negative number with an even greater magnitude. When a negative number is added to a positive number, the result depends on the value of each addend. For example, $-4 + 8 = 4$ because the positive number is larger than the negative number. For multiplying two negative numbers, the result is positive. For example, $-4 \times -3 = 12$, where the negatives cancel out and yield a positive answer.

Rational and Irrational Numbers
Rational numbers can be whole or negative numbers, fractions, or repeating decimals because these numbers can all be written as fractions. Examples of rational numbers include $\frac{1}{2}$, $\frac{5}{4}$, 2.75 and 8. The number

8 is rational because it can be expressed as a fraction: $\frac{8}{1} = 8$. **Rational exponents** are used to express the root of a number raised to a specific power. For example, $3^{\frac{1}{2}}$ has a base of 3 and rational exponent of $\frac{1}{2}$.

The square root of 3 raised to the first power can be written as $\sqrt[2]{3^1}$. Any number with a rational exponent can be written this way. The **numerator**, or number on top of the fraction, becomes the whole number exponent and the **denominator**, or bottom number of the fraction, becomes the root. Another example is $4^{\frac{3}{2}}$. It can be rewritten as the square root of four to the third power, or $\sqrt[2]{4^3}$. To simplify this, first solve for 4 to the third power:

$$4^3 = 4 \times 4 \times 4 = 64$$

Then take the square root of 64, written as $\sqrt[2]{64}$, which yields an answer of 8. Another way of stating the answer would be 4 to power of $\frac{3}{2}$ is eight, or that 4 to the power of $\frac{3}{2}$ is the square root of 4 cubed,

$$\sqrt[2]{4}^3 = 2^3 = 2 \times 2 \times 2 = 8$$

The *n*th root of a is given as $\sqrt[n]{a}$, which is called a **radical.** Typical values for *n* are 2 and 3, which represent the square and cube roots. In this form, *n* represents an integer greater than or equal to 2, and a is a real number. If *n* is even, a must be nonnegative, and if *n* is odd, a can be any real number. This radical can be written in exponential form as $a^{\frac{1}{n}}$. Therefore, $\sqrt[4]{15}$ is the same as $15^{\frac{1}{4}}$ and $\sqrt[3]{-5}$ is the same as $(-5)^{\frac{1}{3}}$.

In a similar fashion, the *n*th root of *a* can be raised to a power *m*, which is written as $\left(\sqrt[n]{a}\right)^m$. This expression is the same as $\sqrt[n]{a^m}$. For example:

$$\sqrt[2]{4^3} = \sqrt[2]{64} = 8 = \left(\sqrt[2]{4}\right)^3 = 2^3$$

Because $\sqrt[n]{a} = a^{\frac{1}{n}}$, both sides can be raised to an exponent of *m*, resulting in:

$$\left(\sqrt[n]{a}\right)^m = \sqrt[n]{a^m} = a^{\frac{m}{n}}$$

This rule allows:

$$\sqrt[2]{4^3} = \left(\sqrt[2]{4}\right)^3 = 4^{\frac{3}{2}}$$

$$(2^2)^{\frac{3}{2}} = 2^{\frac{6}{2}} = 2^3 = 8$$

Negative exponents can also be incorporated into these rules. Any time an exponent is negative, the base expression must be flipped to the other side of the fraction bar and rewritten with a positive exponent. For instance:

$$2^{-3} = \frac{1}{2^3} = \frac{1}{8}$$

Therefore, two more relationships between radical and exponential expressions are:

$$a^{-\frac{1}{n}} = \frac{1}{\sqrt[n]{a}} \text{ and } a^{-\frac{m}{n}} = \frac{1}{\sqrt[n]{a^m}} = \frac{1}{\left(\sqrt[n]{a}\right)^m}$$

Thus:

$$8^{-\frac{1}{3}} = \frac{1}{\sqrt[3]{8}} = \frac{1}{2}$$

All of these relationships are very useful when simplifying complicated radical and exponential expressions. If an expression contains both forms, use one of these rules to change the expression to contain either all radicals or all exponential expressions. This process makes the entire expression much easier to work with, especially if the expressions are contained within equations.

Consider the following example:

$$\sqrt{x} \times \sqrt[4]{x}$$

It is written in radical form; however, it can be simplified into one radical by using exponential expressions first. The expression can be written as $x^{\frac{1}{2}} \times x^{\frac{1}{4}}$. It can be combined into one base by adding the exponents as:

$$x^{\frac{1}{2}+\frac{1}{4}} = x^{\frac{3}{4}}$$

Writing this back in radical form, the result is $\sqrt[4]{x^3}$.

Quartiles

Solving Problems by Quantitative Reasoning
Ordering and Comparing Rational Numbers
Whole numbers are the numbers 0, 1, 2, 3, …. Examples of other whole numbers would be 413 and 8,431. Notice that numbers such as 4.13 and $\frac{1}{4}$ are not included in whole numbers. **Counting numbers**, also known as **natural numbers**, consist of all whole numbers except for the zero. In set notation, the natural numbers are the set $\{1, 2, 3, …\}$. The entire set of whole numbers and negative versions of those same numbers comprise the set of numbers known as **integers.** Therefore, in set notation, the integers are $\{…, -3, -2, -1, 0, 1, 2, 3, …\}$. Examples of other integers are $-4,981$ and $90,131$. A number line is a great way to visualize the integers. Integers are labeled on the following number line:

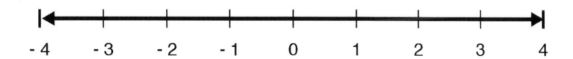

The arrows on the right- and left-hand sides of the number line show that the line continues indefinitely in both directions.

Fractions also exist on the number line as parts of a whole. For example, if an entire pie is cut into two pieces, each piece is half of the pie, or $\frac{1}{2}$. The top number in any fraction, known as the **numerator,** defines how many parts there are. The bottom number, known as the **denominator,** states how many pieces the whole is divided into. Fractions can also be negative or written in their corresponding decimal form.

A **decimal** is a number that uses a decimal point and numbers to the right of the decimal point representing the part of the number that is less than 1. For example, 3.5 is a decimal and is equivalent to the fraction $\frac{7}{2}$ or the mixed number $3\frac{1}{2}$. The decimal is found by dividing 2 into 7. Other examples of fractions are $\frac{2}{7}$, $\frac{-3}{14}$, and $\frac{14}{27}$.

Any number that can be expressed as a fraction is known as a **rational number.** Basically, if a and b are any integers and $b \neq 0$, then $\frac{a}{b}$ is a rational number. Any integer can be written as a fraction where the denominator is 1, so therefore the rational numbers consist of all fractions and all integers.

Any number that is not rational is known as an irrational number. Consider the number

$$\pi = 3.141592654 \ldots.$$

The decimal portion of that number extends indefinitely. In that situation, a number can never be written as a fraction. Another example of an irrational number is $\sqrt{2} = 1.414213662 \ldots.$ Again, this number cannot be written as a ratio of two integers.

Together, the set of all rational and irrational numbers makes up the **real numbers.** The number line contains all real numbers. To graph a number other than an integer on a number line, it needs to be plotted between two integers. For example, 3.5 would be plotted halfway between 3 and 4.

Even numbers are integers that are divisible by 2. For example, 6, 100, 0, and −200 are all even numbers. **Odd numbers** are integers that are not divisible by 2. If an odd number is divided by 2, the result is a fraction. For example, −5, 11, and −121 are odd numbers.

Prime numbers consist of natural numbers greater than 1 that are not divisible by any other natural numbers other than themselves and 1. For example, 3, 5, and 7 are prime numbers. If a natural number is not prime, it is known as a **composite number**. 8 is a composite number because it is divisible by both 2 and 4, which are natural numbers other than itself and 1.

The **absolute value** of any real number is the distance from that number to 0 on the number line. The absolute value of a number can never be negative. For example, the absolute value of both 8 and −8 is 8 because they are both 8 units away from 0 on the number line. This is written as $|8| = |-8| = 8$.

Ordering rational numbers is a way to compare two or more different numerical values. Determining whether two amounts are equal, less than, or greater than is the basis for comparing both positive and negative numbers. Also, a group of numbers can be compared by ordering them from the smallest amount to the largest amount. A few symbols are necessary to use when ordering rational numbers. The **equals sign**, $=$, shows that the two quantities on either side of the symbol have the same value. For example, $\frac{12}{3} = 4$ because both values are equivalent. Another symbol that is used to compare numbers is $<$, which represents "less than." With this symbol, the smaller number is placed on the left and the larger number is placed on the right. Always remember that the symbol's "mouth" opens up to the larger number. When comparing negative and positive numbers, it is important to remember that the number occurring to the left on the number line is always smaller and is placed to the left of the symbol. This idea might seem confusing because some values could appear at first glance to be larger, even though they are not. For example, $-5 < 4$ is read "negative 5 is less than 4." Here is an image of a number line for help:

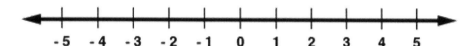

The symbol $\leq$ represents "less than or equal to," and it joins $<$ with equality. Therefore, both $-5 \leq 4$ and $-5 \leq -5$ are true statements and "-5 is less than or equal to both 4 and -5." Other symbols are $>$ and $\geq$, which represent "greater than" and "greater than or equal to." Both $4 \geq -1$ and $-1 \geq -1$ are correct ways to use these symbols.

Here is a chart of these four inequality symbols:

Symbol	Definition
$<$	less than
$\leq$	less than or equal to
$>$	greater than
$\geq$	greater than or equal to

Comparing integers is a straightforward process, especially when using the number line, but the comparison of decimals and fractions is not as obvious. When comparing two non-negative decimals, compare digit by digit, starting from the left. The larger value contains the first larger digit. For example, 0.1456 is larger than 0.1234 because the value 4 in the hundredths place in the first decimal is larger than the value 2 in the hundredths place in the second decimal. When comparing a fraction with a decimal, convert the fraction to a decimal and then compare in the same manner. Finally, there are a few options when comparing fractions. If two non-negative fractions have the same denominator, the fraction with the larger numerator is the larger value. If they have different denominators, they can be converted to equivalent fractions with a common denominator to be compared, or they can be converted to decimals to be compared.

When comparing two negative decimals or fractions, a different approach must be used. It is important to remember that the smaller number exists to the left on the number line. Therefore, when comparing two negative decimals by place value, the number with the larger first place value is smaller due to the negative sign. Whichever value is closer to 0 is larger. For instance, -0.456 is larger than -0.498 because of the values in the hundredth places. If two negative fractions have the same denominator, the fraction with the larger numerator is smaller because of the negative sign.

Converting Within and Between Standard and Metric Systems

When working with dimensions, sometimes the given units don't match the formula, and conversions must be made. When performing operations with rational numbers, it might be helpful to round the numbers in the original problem to get a rough idea of what the answer should be. This system expands to three places above the base unit and three places below. These places correspond to prefixes that each signify a specific base of 10.

The following table shows the conversions:

kilo-	hecto-	deka-	base	deci-	centi-	milli-
1,000 times the base	100 times the base	10 times the base		1/10 times the base	1/100 times the base	1/1000 times the base

To convert between units within the metric system, values with a base ten can be multiplied. The decimal can also be moved in the direction of the new unit by the same number of zeros on the number. For example, 3 meters is equivalent to 0.003 kilometers. The decimal moved three places (the same number of zeros for kilo-) to the left (the same direction from base to kilo-). Three meters is also equivalent to 3,000 millimeters. The decimal is moved three places to the right because the prefix milli- is three places to the right of the base unit.

The English Standard system, which is used in the United States, uses the base units of foot for length, pound for weight, and gallon for liquid volume. Conversions within the English Standard system are not as easy as those within the metric system because the former does not use a base ten model. The following table shows the conversions within this system.

Length	Weight	Capacity
1 foot (ft) = 12 inches (in) 1 yard (yd) = 3 feet 1 mile (mi) = 5280 feet 1 mile = 1760 yards	1 pound (lb) = 16 ounces (oz) 1 ton = 2000 pounds	1 tablespoon (tbsp) = 3 teaspoons (tsp) 1 cup (c) = 16 tablespoons 1 cup = 8 fluid ounces (oz) 1 pint (pt) = 2 cups 1 quart (qt) = 2 pints 1 gallon (gal) = 4 quarts

When converting within the English Standard system, most calculations include a conversion to the base unit and then another to the desired unit. For example, take the following problem: 3 qt = _____ c. There is no straight conversion from quarts to cups, so the first conversion is from quarts to pints. There are 2 pints in 1 quart, so there are 6 pints in 3 quarts. This conversion can be solved as a proportion:

$$\frac{3 \text{ qt}}{x} = \frac{1 \text{ qt}}{2 \text{ pt}}$$

It can also be observed as a ratio 2:1, expanded to 6:3. Then the 6 pints must be converted to cups. The ratio of pints to cups is 1:2, so the expanded ratio is 6:12. For 6 pints, the measurement is 12 cups. This problem can also be set up as one set of fractions to cancel out units. It begins with the given information and cancels out matching units on top and bottom to yield the answer. Consider the following expression:

$$\frac{3 \text{ qt}}{1} \times \frac{2 \text{ pt}}{1 \text{ qt}} \times \frac{2 \text{ c}}{1 \text{ pt}}$$

It's set up so that units on the top and bottom cancel each other out:

$$\frac{3 \text{ q̶t̶}}{1} \times \frac{2 \text{ p̶t̶}}{1 \text{ q̶t̶}} \times \frac{2 \text{ c}}{1 \text{ p̶t̶}}$$

The numbers can be calculated as $3 \times 2 \times 2$ on the top and 1 on the bottom. It still yields an answer of 12 cups.

This process of setting up fractions and canceling out matching units can be used to convert between standard and metric systems. A few common equivalent conversions are 2.54 cm = 1 in, 3.28 ft = 1 m, and 2.205 lb = 1 kg. Writing these as fractions allows them to be used in conversions. For the problem 5 meters = ___ ft, use the feet-to-meter conversion and start with the expression:

$$\frac{5 \text{ m}}{1} \times \frac{3.28 \text{ ft}}{1 \text{ m}}$$

The "meters" will cancel each other out, leaving "feet" as the final unit. Calculating the numbers yields 16.4 feet. This problem only required two fractions. Others may require longer expressions, but the underlying rule stays the same. When a unit in the numerator of a fraction matches a unit in the denominator, then they cancel each other out. Using this logic and the conversions given above, many units can be converted between and within the different systems.

The conversion between Fahrenheit and Celsius is found in a formula:

$$°C = (°F - 32) \times \frac{5}{9}$$

For example, to convert 78°F to Celsius, the given temperature would be entered into the formula:

$$°C = (78 - 32) \times \frac{5}{9}$$

Solving the equation, the temperature comes out to be 25.56°C. To convert in the other direction, the formula becomes:

$$°F = °C \times \frac{9}{5} + 32$$

Remember the order of operations when calculating these conversions.

Applying Estimation Strategies and Rounding Rules to Real-World Problems
Sometimes it is helpful to find an estimated answer to a problem rather than working out an exact answer. An estimation might be much quicker to find, and it might be all that is required given the scenario. For example, if Aria goes grocery shopping and has only a $100 bill to cover all of her purchases, it might be appropriate for her to estimate the total of the items she is purchasing to determine if she has enough

money to cover them. Also, an estimation can help determine if an answer makes sense. For instance, if you estimate that an answer should be in the 100s, but your result is a fraction less than 1, something is probably wrong in the calculation.

The first type of estimation involves rounding. As mentioned, **rounding** consists of expressing a number in terms of the nearest decimal place like the tenth, hundredth, or thousandth place, or in terms of the nearest whole number unit like tens, hundreds, or thousands place. When rounding to a specific place value, look at the digit to the right of the place. If it is 5 or higher, round the number to its left up to the next value, and if it is 4 or lower, keep that number at the same value.

For instance, 1,654.2674 rounded to the nearest thousand is 2,000, and the same number rounded to the nearest thousandth is 1,654.267. Rounding can make it easier to estimate totals at the store. Items can be rounded to the nearest dollar. For example, a can of corn that costs $0.79 can be rounded to $1.00, and then all other items can be rounded in a similar manner and added together. When working with larger numbers, it might make more sense to round to higher place values.

For example, when estimating the total value of a dealership's car inventory, it would make sense to round the car values to the nearest thousands place. The price of a car that is on sale for $15,654 can be estimated at $16,000. All other cars on the lot could be rounded in the same manner and then added together. Depending on the situation, it might make sense to calculate an over-estimate.

For example, to make sure Aria has enough money at the grocery store, rounding up for each item would ensure that she will have enough money when it comes time to pay. A $0.40 item rounded up to $1.00 would ensure that there is a dollar to cover that item. Traditional rounding rules would round $0.40 to $0, which does not make sense in this particular real-world setting. Aria might not have a dollar available at checkout to pay for that item if she uses traditional rounding. It is up to the customer to decide the best approach when estimating.

Estimating is also very helpful when working with measurements. Bryan is updating his kitchen and wants to retile the floor. Again, an over-measurement might be useful. Also, rounding to nearest half-unit might be helpful. For instance, one side of the kitchen might have an exact measurement of 14.32 feet, and the most useful measurement needed to buy tile could be estimating this quantity to be 14.5 feet. If the kitchen was rectangular and the other side measured 10.9 feet, Bryan might round the other side to 11 feet. Therefore, Bryan would find the total tile necessary according to the following area calculation: $14.5 \times 11 = 159.5$ square feet. To make sure he purchases enough tile, Bryan would probably want to purchase at least 160 square feet of tile. This is a scenario in which an estimation might be more useful than an exact calculation. Having more tile than necessary is better than having an exact amount, in case any tiles are broken or otherwise unusable.

Finally, estimation is helpful when exact answers are necessary. Consider a situation in which Sabina has many operations to perform on numbers with decimals, and she is allowed a calculator to find the result. Even though an exact result can be obtained with a calculator, there is always a possibility that Sabina could make an error while inputting the data. For example, she could miss a decimal place, or misuse a parenthesis, causing a problem with the actual order of operations. A quick estimation at the beginning could help ensure that her final answer is within the correct range. Sabina has to find the exact total of 10 cars listed for sale at the dealership. Each price has two decimal places included to account for both dollars and cents. If one car is listed at $21,234.43 but Sabina incorrectly inputs into the calculator the price of $2,123.443, this error would throw off the final sum by almost $20,000. A quick estimation at the beginning, by rounding each price to the nearest thousands place and finding the sum of the prices, would give Sabina an amount to compare the exact amount to. This comparison would let Sabina see if an error was made in her exact calculation.

Algebra and Functions

Seeing Structure in Expressions

Applying an Understanding of Arithmetic to Algebraic Expressions

Translating Phrases and Sentences into Expressions, Equations, and Inequalities

When presented with a real-world problem, the first step is to determine what unknown quantity must be solved for. Use a **variable**, such as x or t, to represent that unknown quantity. Sometimes there can be two or more unknown quantities. In this case, either choose an additional variable, or if a relationship exists between the unknown quantities, express the other quantities in terms of the original variable. After choosing the variables, form algebraic expressions and/or equations that represent the verbal statement in the problem. The following table shows examples of vocabulary used to represent the different operations:

Addition	Sum, plus, total, increase, more than, combined, in all
Subtraction	Difference, less than, subtract, reduce, decrease, fewer, remain
Multiplication	Product, multiply, times, part of, twice, triple
Division	Quotient, divide, split, each, equal parts, per, average, shared

The combination of operations and variables form both mathematical expression and equations. The differences between expressions and equations are that there is no equals sign in an expression, and that expressions are evaluated to find an unknown quantity, while equations are solved to find an unknown quantity. Also, inequalities can exist within verbal mathematical statements. Instead of a statement of equality, expressions state quantities are *less than, less than or equal to, greater than,* or *greater than or equal to.* Another type of inequality is when a quantity is said to be not equal to another quantity ($\neq$).

The steps for solving inequalities in one variable are the same steps for solving equations in one variable. The addition and multiplication principles are used. However, to maintain a true statement when using the $<, \leq, >,$ and $\geq$ symbols, if a negative number is either multiplied times both sides of an inequality or divided from both sides of an inequality, the sign must be flipped. For instance, consider the following inequality:

$$3 - 5x \leq 8$$

First, 3 is subtracted from each side to obtain $-5x \leq 5$. Then, both sides are divided by -5, while flipping the sign, to obtain $x \geq -1$. Therefore, any real number greater than or equal to -1 satisfies the original inequality.

Adding and Subtracting Linear Algebraic Expressions

To add and subtract linear algebraic expressions, you must combine like terms. Like terms are terms that have the same variable with the same exponent. In the following example, the x-terms can be added because the variable and exponent are the same. These terms add to be $9x$. Terms without a variable component are called constants. These terms will add to be nine.

Example: Add $(3x - 5) + (6x + 14)$

$3x - 5 + 6x + 14$ Rewrite without parentheses

$3x + 6x - 5 + 14$ Commutative property of addition

$9x + 9$ Combine like terms

When subtracting linear expressions, be careful to add the opposite when combining like terms. Do this by distributing -1, which is multiplying each term inside the second parenthesis by negative one. Remember that distributing -1 changes the sign of each term.

Example: Subtract $(17x + 3) - (27x - 8)$

$17x + 3 - 27x + 8$ Distributive Property

$17x - 27x + 3 + 8$ Commutative property of addition

$-10x + 11$ Combine like terms

Example: Simplify by adding or subtracting:

$(6m + 28z - 9) + (14m + 13) - (-4z + 8m + 12)$

$6m + 28z - 9 + 14m + 13 + 4z - 8m - 12$ Distributive Property

$6m + 14m - 8m + 28z + 4z - 9 + 13 - 12$ Commutative Property of

Addition

$12m + 32z - 8$ Combine like terms

Solving Problems Using Numerical and Algebraic Expressions

Translating sentences describing relationships between variables and constants to algebraic expressions and equations involves recognizing key words that represent mathematical operations. This process is known as **modeling.** For simplicity, let x be the variable, or the unknown quantity. Statements that include the four operations addition, subtraction, multiplication, and division exist in sentences that model linear relationships. For example, words and phrases that represent addition are "sum," "more than," and "increased by." Words and phrases that represent subtraction are "minus," "decreased by," "subtracted from," "difference," "less", "fewer than," and "less than." Words and phrases that represent multiplication are "times," "product of," "twice," "double," and "triple." Finally, words and phrases that represent division are "divided by," "quotient," and "reciprocal."

Most of the time, these words and phrases are combined to represent expressions that deal with one or more operation. For example, "ten subtracted from nine times a number" would be represented as $9x - 10$, and "the quotient of a number and 7 increased by 8" would be represented as $\frac{x}{7} + 8$. The word problems that typically use these expressions will have a statement of equality. For instance, the problem could say "ten subtracted from nine times a number equals 20; find that number." In this case, the algebraic expression shown previously would be set equal to 20 and then solved for x.

$$9x - 10 = 20$$

Add ten to both sides and then divide by 9 to get the solution $x = \frac{30}{9}$, which reduces to $x = \frac{10}{3}$.

Other types of expressions, besides linear expressions, can be the results of modeling. If the variable is raised to a power other than 1, the result is a **polynomial expression**. The path of an object thrown up into the air is a common example of this. The graph of an object represents an upside-down parabola, which is modeled by an equation of the type $y = -ax^2$. In this case, a represents the height of the object at its highest point before coming back down to the ground, and the negative sign shows that the parabola is upside down.

Here is the graph of a parabola:

Parabola

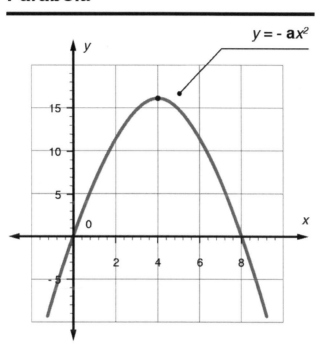

Rewriting Simple Rational Expressions

A **rational expression** is a fraction or a ratio in which both the numerator and denominator are polynomials that are not equal to zero. A polynomial is a mathematical expression containing addition, subtraction, or multiplication of one or more constants multiplied by variables raised to positive powers.

Here are some examples of rational expressions: $\frac{2x^2+6x}{x}$, $\frac{x-2}{x^2-6x+8}$, and $\frac{x^3-1}{x+2}$. Such expressions can be simplified using different forms of division. The first example can be simplified in two ways. Then, cancelling out an x in each numerator and the x in each denominator results in $2x + 6$. It also can be simplified using factoring and then crossing out common factors in the numerator and denominator. For instance, it can be written as:

$$\frac{2x(x + 3)}{x} = 2(x + 3) = 2x + 6$$

The second expression above can also be simplified using factoring. It can be written as:

$$\frac{x - 2}{(x - 2)(x - 4)} = \frac{1}{x - 4}$$

Finally, the third example can only be simplified using long division, as there are no common factors in the numerator and denominator. First, divide the first term of the numerator by the first term of the denominator, then write the result in the quotient. Then, multiply the divisor by that number and write it below the dividend. Subtract and continue the process until each term in the divisor is accounted for. Here is the actual long division:

Simplifying Expressions Using Long Division

$$
\begin{array}{r}
x^2 \quad - 2x \quad + 4 \\
x + 2 \overline{\smash{)}\; x^3 - 1} \\
\underline{x^3 \quad + 2x^2 } \\
- 2x^2 - 1 \\
\underline{- 2x^2 \quad - 4x } \\
4x \quad - 1 \\
\underline{4x \quad + 8} \\
- 9
\end{array}
$$

Interpreting Parts of Nonlinear Expressions in Terms of Their Context

If a quantity increases or decreases at a constant rate as another quantity increases, then this idea is represented as a **linear expression**, and the graph of such a relationship is a straight line. All other relationships are nonlinear, and nonlinear expressions must be used as mathematical representations of such instances.

Common nonlinear relationships that exist between two quantities are *inverse* **variation equations**, which are represented by equations such as $y = \frac{k}{x}$ and $y = \frac{k}{x^2}$ with constants k, **quadratic equations** of the form $y = ax^2 + bx + c$, and **exponential equations** of the form $y = a^x$.

Inverse variation situations arise when, as one quantity increases, the other quantity decreases in proportion. For instance, as a person increases the speed of a car she is driving, the time it takes to reach the destination decreases. This is a nonlinear relationship regarding inverse variation.

Recall that quadratic equations are used to model something shaped like a parabola. For instance, if a ball is thrown into the air, it travels higher and higher and eventually slows down to reach its highest point, then stops dropping at a faster and faster rate. A quadratic equation must be used to tell the position of the ball given the amount of time since the ball was thrown. This relationship is nonlinear.

Finally, an exponential equation is used to model something with exponential growth or decay. If something grows exponentially, such as compound interest, the amount is multiplied times a growth factor for every increase in x. If something decays exponentially, the amount is multiplied times a factor between 0 and 1 for every increase in x. When a population is declining, an exponential decay equation can be used to represent the situation.

Generating Equivalent Expressions

Creating Equivalent Expressions Involving Rational Exponents and Radicals

Re-writing complex radical expressions as equivalent forms with rational exponents can help to simplify them. The rule that helps this conversion is:

$$\sqrt[n]{x^m} = x^{\frac{m}{n}}$$

If $m = 1$, the rule is simply $\sqrt[n]{x} = x^{\frac{1}{n}}$. For instance, consider the following expression: $\sqrt[4]{x}\sqrt[2]{y}$. This can be written as one radical expression, but first it needs to be converted to an equivalent expression. The equivalent expression is $x^{\frac{1}{4}}y^{\frac{1}{2}}$. The goal is to have one radical, which means one index n, so a common denominator of the exponents must be found. The common denominator is 4, so an equivalent expression is $x^{\frac{1}{4}}y^{\frac{2}{4}}$. The exponential rule $a^m b^m = (ab)^m$ can be used to factor $\frac{1}{4}$ out of both variables.

This process results in the expression $(xy^2)^{\frac{1}{4}}$, and its equivalent radical form is $\sqrt[4]{xy^2}$. Converting to rational exponents has allowed the entire expression to be written as one radical.

Another type of problem could involve going in the opposite direction—starting with rational exponents and using an equivalent radical form to simplify the expression. For instance, $32^{\frac{1}{5}}$ might not seem obviously equal to 2. However, putting it in its equivalent radical form $\sqrt[5]{32}$ shows that it is equivalent to the fifth root of 32, which is 2.

Creating an Equivalent Form of an Algebraic Expression

Two algebraic expressions are equivalent if they represent the same value, even if they look different. To obtain an equivalent form of an algebraic expression, follow the laws of algebra. For instance, addition and multiplication are both commutative and associative. Therefore, terms in an algebraic expression can be added in any order and multiplied in any order.

For instance, $4x + 2y$ is equivalent to $2y + 4x$ and:

$$y \times 2 + x \times 4$$

Also, the distributive law allows a number to be distributed throughout parentheses, as in the following:

$$a(b + c) = ab + ac$$

The expressions on both sides of the equals sign are equivalent. Collecting like terms is also important when working with equivalent forms because the simplest version of an expression is always the easiest one to work with.

An expression is not an equation; therefore, expressions cannot undergo multiplication, division, addition, or subtraction and still have equivalent expressions. These processes can only happen in equations when the same step is performed on both sides of the equals sign.

Using the Distributive Property to Generate Equivalent Linear Algebraic Expressions
The Distributive Property:
$$a(b + c) = ab + ac$$

The **distributive property** is a way of taking a factor and multiplying it through a given expression in parentheses. Each term inside the parentheses is multiplied by the outside factor, eliminating the parentheses. The following example shows how to distribute the number 3 to all the terms inside the parentheses.

Example: Use the distributive property to write an equivalent algebraic expression:

$3(2x + 7y + 6)$

$3(2x) + 3(7y) + 3(6)$ Distributive property

$6x + 21y + 18$ Simplify

Because $a - b$ can be written $a + (-b)$, the distributive property can be applied in the example below:

Example: Use the distributive property to write an equivalent algebraic expression.

$7(5m - 8)$

$7[5m + (-8)]$ Rewrite subtraction as addition of -8

$7(5m) + 7(-8)$ Distributive property

$35m - 56$ Simplify

In the following example, note that the factor of 2 is written to the right of the parentheses but is still distributed as before.

Example: Use the distributive property to write an equivalent algebraic expression:

$(3m + 4x - 10)2$

$(3m)2 + (4x)2 + (-10)2$ Distributive property

$6m + 8x - 20$ Simplify

Example: $-(-2m + 6x)$

In this example, the negative sign in front of the parentheses can be interpreted as $-1(-2m + 6x)$

$-1(-2m + 6x)$

$-1(-2m) + (-1)(6x)$ Distributive property

$2m - 6x$ Simplify

Determining the Most Suitable Form of an Expression or Equation

When given a problem, it is necessary to determine the best form of an expression or equation to use, given the context. Usually this involves some algebraic manipulation. If an equation is given, the simplest form of the equation is best. Simplifying involves using the distributive property, collecting like terms, etc., If an equation is needed to be solved, properties involving performing the same operation on both sides of the equation must be used. For instance, if a number is added to one side of the equals sign, it must be added to the other side as well. This maintains a true equation.

If an expression is given, simplifying can only involve properties allowing to rewrite the expression as an equivalent form. If there is no equals sign, mathematical operations cannot be performed on the expression, unless it is a rational expression. A rational expression can be written in the form of a fraction, in which the numerator and denominator are both polynomials and the denominator is not equal to zero. Rational expressions can always be multiplied times a form of 1. For example, consider the following rational expression involving radicals: $\frac{2}{\sqrt{2}}$. It is incorrect to write a fraction with a root in the denominator, and therefore the expression must be rationalized. Multiply the fraction times $\frac{\sqrt{2}}{\sqrt{2}}$, a form of 1. This results in:

$$\frac{2}{\sqrt{2}} \times \frac{\sqrt{2}}{\sqrt{2}} = \frac{2\sqrt{2}}{\sqrt{4}} = \frac{2\sqrt{2}}{2} = \sqrt{2}$$

This is the most suitable form of the expression.

Reasoning with Equations and Inequalities

The Connection Between Proportional Relationships and Linear Equations

Linear growth involves a quantity, the **dependent variable**, increasing or decreasing at a constant rate as another quantity, the **independent variable**, increases as well. The graph of linear growth is a straight line. Linear growth is represented as the following equation: $y = mx + b$, where m is the **slope** of the line, also known as the **rate of change**, and b is the **y-intercept**. If the y-intercept is 0, then the linear growth is actually known as **direct variation**. If the slope is positive, the dependent variable increases as the independent variable increases, and if the slope is negative, the dependent variable decreases as the independent variable increases.

A linear function that models a linear relationship between two quantities is of the form $y = mx + b$, or in function form:

$$f(x) = mx + b$$

In a linear function, the value of y depends on the value of x, and y increases or decreases at a constant rate as x increases. Therefore, the independent variable is x, and the dependent variable is y. The graph of a linear function is a line, and the constant rate can be seen by looking at the steepness, or slope, of the line. If the line increases from left to right, the slope is positive. If the line slopes downward from left to right, the slope is negative. In the function, m represents slope. Each point on the line is an **ordered pair** (x, y), where x represents the x-coordinate of the point and y represents the y-coordinate of the point. The point where $x = 0$ is known as the y-intercept, and it is the place where the line crosses the y-axis. If $x = 0$ is plugged into $f(x) = mx + b$, the result is $f(0) = b$, so therefore, the point $(0, b)$ is the y-intercept of the line. The derivative of a linear function is its slope.

Consider the following situation. A taxicab driver charges a flat fee of $2 per ride and $3 a mile. This statement can be modeled by the function $f(x) = 3x + 2$ where x represents the number of miles and $f(x) = y$ represents the total cost of the ride. The total cost increases at a constant rate of $2 per mile, and that is why this situation is a linear relationship. The slope $m = 3$ is equivalent to this rate of change. The flat fee of $2 is the y-intercept. It is the place where the graph crosses the x-axis, and it represents the cost when $x = 0$, or when no miles have been traveled in the cab. The y-intercept in this situation represents the flat fee.

Solving Equations Using Reasoning

The reasonableness of an answer found in a math problem gives evidence to the accuracy of the work. If the answer is not reasonable, the work should be redone in order to find the error and correct the problem. Problems that involve fractions and decimals are good places to use reasonableness to check answers. For example, Karen has $63.75 to spend on sodas for her family gathering. If each soda costs $1.50, how many can she buy? The answer can be found by division, but because there are decimals, an estimate can be found by rounding the two numbers and doing easy division. The money can round to $64 and the sodas can round to $2. An estimate is 32 sodas. When the actual division is done, the answer should be close to 32. If not, it is a sign that there is an error in the math.

One-Variable Linear Equations and Inequalities

Solving Equations in One Variable

An **equation in one variable** is a mathematical statement where two algebraic expressions in one variable, usually x, are set equal. To solve the equation, the variable must be isolated on one side of the equals sign. The addition and multiplication principles of equality are used to isolate the variable. The **addition principle of equality** states that the same number can be added to or subtracted from both sides of an equation. Because the same value is being used on both sides of the equals sign, equality is maintained.

For example, the equation $2x - 3 = 5x$ is equivalent to both:

$$2x - 3 + 2 = 5x + 2$$

and

$$2x - 3 - 5 = 5x - 5$$

This principle can be used to solve the following equation:

$$x + 5 = 4$$

The variable x must be isolated, so to move the 5 from the left side, subtract 5 from both sides of the equals sign. Therefore:

$$x + 5 - 5 = 4 - 5$$

So, the solution is $x = -1$. This process illustrates the idea of an **additive inverse** because subtracting 5 is the same as adding -5. Basically, add the opposite of the number that must be removed to both sides of the equals sign. The multiplication principle of equality states that equality is maintained when both sides of an equation are multiplied or divided by the same number.

For example, $4x = 5$ is equivalent to both $16x = 20$ and $x = \frac{5}{4}$. Multiplying both sides times 4 and dividing both sides by 4 maintains equality. Solving the equation $6x - 18 = 5$ requires the use of both principles. First, apply the addition principle to add 18 to both sides of the equals sign, which results in $6x = 23$.

Then use the multiplication principle to divide both sides by 6, giving the solution $x = \frac{23}{6}$. Using the multiplication principle in the solving process is the same as involving a multiplicative inverse. A *multiplicative inverse* is a value that, when multiplied by a given number, results in 1. Dividing by 6 is the same as multiplying by $\frac{1}{6}$, which is both the reciprocal and multiplicative inverse of 6.

When solving linear equations, check the answer by plugging the solution back into the original equation. If the result is a false statement, something was done incorrectly during the solution procedure. Checking the example above gives the following:

$$6 \times \frac{23}{6} - 18 = 23 - 18 = 5$$

Therefore, the solution is correct.

Some equations in one variable involve fractions or the use of the distributive property. In either case, the goal is to obtain only one variable term and then use the addition and multiplication principles to isolate that variable.

Consider the equation $\frac{2}{3}x = 6$. To solve for x, multiply each side of the equation by the reciprocal of $\frac{2}{3}$, which is $\frac{3}{2}$. This step results in:

$$\frac{3}{2} \times \frac{2}{3}x = \frac{3}{2} \times 6$$

which simplifies into the solution $x = 9$. Now consider the equation:

$$3(x + 2) - 5x = 4x + 1$$

Use the distributive property to clear the parentheses. Therefore, multiply each term inside the parentheses by 3. This step results in:

$$3x + 6 - 5x = 4x + 1$$

Next, collect like terms on the left-hand side. **Like terms** are terms with the same variable or variables raised to the same exponent(s). Only like terms can be combined through addition or subtraction. After collecting like terms, the equation is:

$$-2x + 6 = 4x + 1$$

Finally, apply the addition and multiplication principles. Add $2x$ to both sides to obtain:

$$6 = 6x + 1$$

Then, subtract 1 from both sides to obtain $5 = 6x$. Finally, divide both sides by 6 to obtain the solution $\frac{5}{6} = x$.

Two other types of solutions can be obtained when solving an equation in one variable. There could be no solution, or the solution set could contain all real numbers.

Consider the equation:

$$4x = 6x + 5 - 2x$$

First, the like terms can be combined on the right to obtain:

$$4x = 4x + 5$$

Next, subtract $4x$ from both sides. This step results in the false statement $0 = 5$. There is no value that can be plugged into x that will ever make this equation true. Therefore, there is no solution. The solution procedure contained correct steps, but the result of a false statement means that no value satisfies the equation. The symbolic way to denote that no solution exists is $\emptyset$.

Next, consider the equation:

$$5x + 4 + 2x = 9 + 7x - 5$$

Combining the like terms on both sides results in:

$$7x + 4 = 7x + 4$$

The left-hand side is exactly the same as the right-hand side. Using the addition principle to move terms, the result is $0 = 0$, which is always true. Therefore, the original equation is true for any number, and the solution set is all real numbers. The symbolic way to denote such a solution set is $\mathbb{R}$, or in interval notation, $(-\infty, \infty)$.

Solving a Linear Inequality in One Variable
A **linear equation in x** can be written in the form $ax + b = 0$. A **linear inequality** is very similar, although the equals sign is replaced by an inequality symbol such as $<, >, \leq,$ or $\geq$. In any case, a can never be 0. Some examples of linear inequalities in one variable are $2x + 3 < 0$ and $4x - 2 \leq 0$. Solving an inequality involves finding the set of numbers that, when plugged into the variable, makes the inequality a true statement.

These numbers are known as the **solution set** of the inequality. To solve an inequality, use the same properties that are necessary in solving equations. First, add or subtract variable terms and/or constants to obtain all variable terms on one side of the equals sign and all constant terms on the other side. Then, either multiply or divide both sides by the same number to obtain an inequality that gives the solution

44

set. When multiplying or dividing by a negative number, change the direction of the inequality symbol. The solution set can be graphed on a number line. Consider the linear inequality:

$$y - 2x - 5 > x + 6$$

First, add 5 to both sides and subtract x from both sides to obtain $-3x > 11$. Then, divide both sides by -3, making sure to change the direction of the inequality symbol. These steps result in the solution $x < -\frac{11}{3}$. Therefore, any number less than $-\frac{11}{3}$ satisfies this inequality.

Systems of Equations and Inequalities

Systems of Linear Inequalities in Two Variables

A system of linear inequalities in two variables consists of two inequalities in two variables, x and y. For example, the following is a system of linear inequalities in two variables:

$$\begin{cases} 4x + 2y < 1 \\ 2x - y \leq 0 \end{cases}$$

The curly brace on the left side shows that the two inequalities are grouped together. A solution of a single inequality in two variables is an ordered pair that satisfies the inequality. For example, (1, 3) is a solution of the linear inequality $y \geq x + 1$ because when plugged in, it results in a true statement. The graph of an inequality in two variables consists of all ordered pairs that make the solution true. Therefore, the entire solution set of a single inequality contains many ordered pairs, and the set can be graphed by using a half plane. A **half plane** consists of the set of all points on one side of a line. If the inequality consists of $>$ or $<$, the line is dashed because no solutions actually exist on the line shown. If the inequality consists of $\geq$ or $\leq$, the line is solid and solutions are on the line shown. To graph a linear inequality, graph the corresponding equation found by replacing the inequality symbol with an equals sign. Then pick a test point that exists on either side of the line. If that point results in a true statement when plugged into the original inequality, shade in the side containing the test point. If it results in a false statement, shade in the opposite side.

Algebraically Solving Linear Equations or Inequalities in One Variable

A linear equation in one variable can be solved using the following steps:

1. Simplify both sides of the equation by removing all parentheses, using the distributive property, and collecting all like terms.

2. Collect all variable terms on one side of the equation and all constant terms on the other side by adding the same quantity to or subtracting the same quantity from both sides.

3. Isolate the variable by either multiplying or dividing both sides of the equation by the same number.

4. Check the answer.

The only difference between solving linear inequalities versus equations is that when multiplying by a negative number or dividing by a negative number, the direction of the inequality symbol must be reversed.

If an equation contains multiple fractions, it might make sense to clear the equation of fractions first by multiplying all terms by the least common denominator. Also, if an equation contains several decimals, it might make sense to clear the decimals as well by multiplying times a factor of 10. If the equation has decimals in the hundredths place, multiply every term in the equation by 100.

Algebraically Solving Systems of Two Linear Equations in Two Variables

There are two algebraic methods to finding solutions. The first is **substitution**. This process is better suited for systems when one of the equations is already solved for one variable, or when solving for one variable is easy to do. The equation that is already solved for is substituted into the other equation for that variable, and this process results in a linear equation in one variable. This equation can be solved for the given variable, and then that solution can be plugged into one of the original equations, which can then be solved for the other variable. This last step is known as **back-substitution**, and the end result is an ordered pair.

The following is an example of a system that is suited for substitution:

$$y = 4x + 2$$

$$2x + 3y = 9$$

The other method is known as **elimination,** or the **addition method**. This is better suited when the equations are in standard form:

$$Ax + By = C$$

The goal in this method is to multiply one or both equations times numbers that result in opposite coefficients. Then, add the equations together to obtain an equation in one variable. Solve for the given variable, then take that value and back-substitute to obtain the other part of the ordered pair solution.

The following is an example of a system that is suited for elimination:

$$2x + 3y = 8$$

$$4x - 2y = 10$$

Note that in order to check an answer when solving a system of equations, the solution must be checked in both original equations to show that it solves not only one of the equations, but both of them.

If either solution results in an untrue statement when inserted into the original equation, then there is no solution to the system. Finally, if throughout either solution procedure the process results in the variables dropping out, which gives a statement that is always true, there are infinitely many solutions.

Representing and Solving Equations and Inequalities Graphically

Solving a system of linear inequalities must be done graphically. Follow the process as described above for both given inequalities. The solution set to the entire system is the region that is in common to every graph in the system. For example, here is the solution to the following system:

$$\begin{cases} y \geq 3 - x \\ y \leq -3 - x \end{cases}$$

The solution to $\begin{cases} y \geq 3 - x \\ y \leq -3 - x \end{cases}$

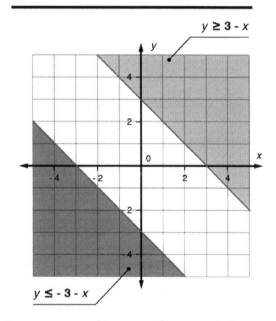

Note that there is no region in common, so this system has no solution.

Systems of Two Linear Equations in Two Variables

An example of a system of two linear equations in two variables is the following:

$$2x + 5y = 8$$

$$5x + 48y = 9$$

A solution to a system of two linear equations is an ordered pair that satisfies both the equations in the system. A system can have one solution, no solution, or infinitely many solutions. The solution can be found through a graphing technique. The solution to a system of equations is actually equal to the point where both lines intersects. If the lines intersect at one point, there is one solution and the system is said to be **consistent**. However, if the two lines are parallel, they will never intersect and there is no solution. In this case, the system is said to be **inconsistent.** Third, if the two lines are actually the same line, there are infinitely many solutions and the solution set is equal to the entire line. The lines are dependent. Here is a summary of the three cases:

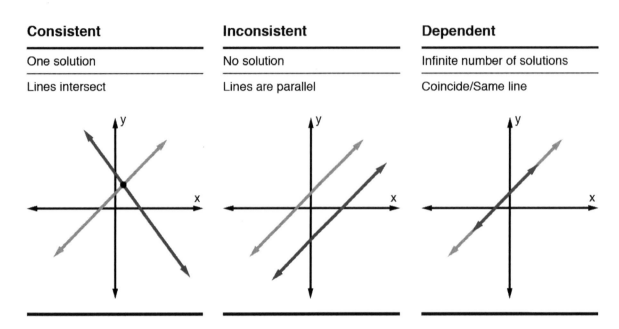

Consistent	Inconsistent	Dependent
One solution	No solution	Infinite number of solutions
Lines intersect	Lines are parallel	Coincide/Same line

Consider the following system of equations:

$$y + x = 3$$

$$y - x = 1$$

To find the solution graphically, graph both lines on the same xy-plane. Graph each line using either a table of ordered pairs, the x- and y-intercepts, or slope and the y-intercept. Then, locate the point of intersection.

The graph is shown here:

The System of Equations $\begin{cases} y + x = 3 \\ y - x = 1 \end{cases}$

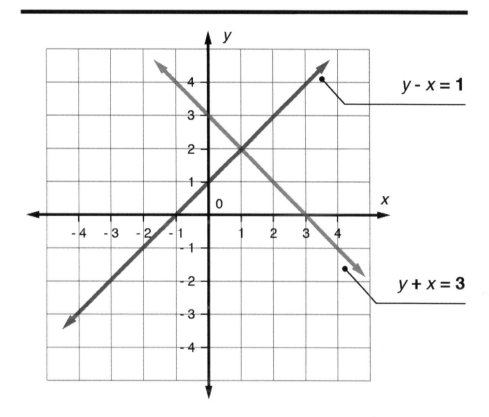

It can be seen that the point of intersection is the ordered pair (1, 2). This solution can be checked by plugging it back into both original equations to make sure it results in true statements. This process results in:

$$2 + 1 = 3$$

$$2 - 1 = 1$$

Both equations are true, so the solution is correct.

The following system has no solution:

$$y = 4x + 1$$

$$y = 4x - 1$$

Both lines have the same slope and different y-intercepts, so they are parallel, meaning that they run alongside each other and never intersect.

Finally, the following solution has infinitely many solutions:

$$2x - 7y = 12$$

$$4x - 14y = 24$$

Note that the second equation is equal to the first equation times 2. Therefore, they are the same line. The solution set can be written in set notation as $\{(x, y)|2x - 7y = 12\}$, which represents the entire line.

Functions

Interpreting Functions

A **relation** is any set of ordered pairs (x, y). The values listed first in the ordered pairs, known as the x-coordinates, make up the domain of the relation. The values listed second, known as the y-coordinates, make up the range. A relation in which every member of the domain corresponds to only one member of the range is known as a **function**. A function cannot have a member of the domain corresponding to two members of the range. Functions are most often given in terms of equations instead of ordered pairs. For instance, here is an equation of a line:

$$y = 2x + 4$$

In function notation, this can be written as:

$$f(x) = 2x + 4$$

The expression $f(x)$ is read "f of x" and it shows that the inputs, the x-values, get plugged into the function and the output is $y = f(x)$. The set of all inputs are in the domain, and the set of all outputs are in the range.

The x-values are known as the **independent variables** of the function and the y-values are known as the **dependent variables** of the function. The y-values depend on the x-values. For instance, if $x = 2$ is plugged into the function shown above, the y-value depends on that input.

$$f(2) = 2 \times 2 + 4 = 8.$$

Therefore, $f(2) = 8$, which is the same as writing the ordered pair (2, 8). To graph a function, graph it in equation form. Therefore, replace $f(x)$ with y and plot ordered pairs.

Due to the definition of a function, the graph of a function cannot have two of the same x-components paired to different y-component. For example, the ordered pairs (3, 4) and (3, -1) cannot be in a valid function. Therefore, all graphs of functions pass the **vertical line test**. If any vertical line intersects a graph in more than one place, the graph is not that of a function. For instance, the graph of a circle is not a function because one can draw a vertical line through a circle and intersect the circle twice. Common functions include lines and polynomials, which pass the vertical line test.

Interpreting the Variables and Constants in Expressions for Linear Functions within the Context Presented

A **linear function** of the form $f(x) = mx + b$ has two important quantities: m and b. The quantity m represents the slope of the line, and the quantity b represents the y-intercept of the line. When the function represents a real-life situation or a mathematical model, these two quantities are very meaningful. The slope, m, represents the rate of change, or the amount y increases or decreases given an increase in x. If m is positive, the rate of change is positive, and if m is negative, the rate of change is negative. The y-intercept, b, represents the amount of quantity y when x is 0. In many applications, if the x-variable is never a negative quantity, the y-intercept represents the initial amount of the quantity y. The x-variable often represents time, so it makes sense that it would not be negative.

Consider the following example. These two equations represent the cost, C, of t-shirts, x, at two different printing companies:

$$C(x) = 7x$$

$$C(x) = 5x + 25$$

The first equation represents a scenario in which each t-shirt costs $7. In this equation, x varies directly with y. There is no y-intercept, which means that there is no initial cost for using that printing company. The rate of change is 7, which is price per shirt. The second equation represents a scenario that has both an initial cost and a cost per t-shirt. The slope of 5 shows that each shirt is $5. The y-intercept of 25 shows that there is an initial cost of using that company. Therefore, it makes sense to use the first company at $7 per shirt when only purchasing a small number of t-shirts. However, any large orders would be cheaper from the second company because eventually that initial cost would become negligible.

Building Functions

When given data in ordered pairs, choosing an appropriate function or equation to model the data is important. Besides linear relationships, other common relationships that exist are quadratic and exponential. A helpful way to determine what type of function to use is to find the difference between consecutive dependent variables. Basically, find pairs of ordered pairs where the x-values increase by 1, and take the difference of the y-values. If the differences in the y-values are always the same value, then the function is **linear**. If the differences in the y-values when the x-values increase by 1 are not the same, the function could be quadratic or exponential. If the differences are not the same, find differences of those differences. If consecutive differences are the same, then the function is **quadratic.** If consecutive differences are not the same, try taking ratios of consecutive y-values. If the ratios are the same, the data have an exponential relationship and an **exponential** function should be used.

For example, the ordered pairs (1, 4), (2, 6), (3 ,8), and (4,10) have a linear relationship because the difference in y-values is 2 for every increase in x of 1. The ordered pairs (1, 0), (2, 3), (3, 10), and (4, 21) have a nonlinear relationship. The first differences in y-values are 3, 7, and 11, however, consecutive second differences are both 4. Third, the ordered pairs (1, 10), (2, 30), (3, 90), and (4, 270) have an exponential relationship. Taking ratios of consecutive y-values leads to a common ratio of 4.

The general form of a **quadratic equation** is $y = ax^2 + bx + c$, and its vertex form is $y = a(x - h)^2 + k$, with vertex (h, k). If the vertex and one other point are known, the vertex form should be used to solve for a. If three points, not the vertex, are known, the general form should be used. The three points create a system of three equations in three unknowns that can be solved for.

The general form of an exponential function is $y = b \times a^x$, where a is the base and b is the y-intercept.

Radical Functions

Recall that a **radical expression** is an expression involving a square root, a cube root, or a higher order root such as fourth root, fifth root, etc. The expression underneath the radical is known as the **radicand** and the **index** is the number corresponding to the root. An index of 2 corresponds to a square root. A radical function is a function that involves a radical expression. For instance, $\sqrt{x+1}$ is a radical expression, $x + 1$ is the radicand, and the corresponding function is:

$$y = \sqrt{x+1}$$

It can also be written in function notation as:

$$f(x) = \sqrt{x+1}$$

If the root is even, meaning a square root, fourth root, etc., the radicand must be positive. Therefore, in order to find the domain of a radical function with an even index, set the radicand greater than or equal to zero and find the set of numbers that satisfies that inequality. The domain of $f(x) = \sqrt{x+1}$ is all numbers greater than or equal to -1. The range of this function is all non-negative real numbers because the square root, or any even root, can never output a negative number. The domain of an odd root is all real numbers because the radicand can be negative in an odd root.

Piecewise Functions

A **piecewise function** is basically a function that is defined in pieces or sections. The graph of the function behaves differently over different intervals along the x-axis, or different intervals of its domain. Therefore, the function is defined using different mathematical expressions over these intervals. The function is not defined by only one equation. In a piecewise function, the function is actually defined by two or more equations, where each equation is used over a specific interval of the domain. Here is a graph of a piecewise function:

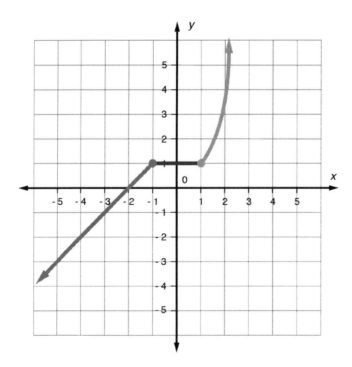

Notice that from $(-\infty, -1]$, the graph is a line with positive slope. From $[-1, 1]$ the graph is a horizontal line. Finally, from $[1, \infty)$ the graph is a nonlinear curve. Both the domain and range of this function are all real numbers, expressed as $(-\infty, \infty)$.

Piecewise functions can also have discontinuities, which are jumps in the graph. When drawing a graph, if the pencil must be picked up at any point to continue drawing, the graph has a discontinuity. Here is the graph of a piecewise function with discontinuities at $x = 1$ and $x = 2$:

A Piecewise Function

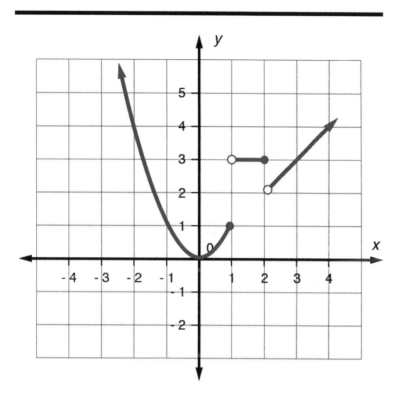

The open circle at a point indicates that the endpoint is not included in that part of the graph, and the closed circle indicates that the endpoint is included. The domain of this function is all real numbers; however, the range is all non-negative real numbers $[0, \infty)$.

Polynomial Functions

A **polynomial function** is a function containing a polynomial expression, which is an expression containing constants and variables combined using the four mathematical operations. The degree of a polynomial depends on the largest exponent in the expression. Typical polynomial functions are **quartic,** with a degree of 4, **cubic,** with a degree of 3, and **quadratic,** with a degree of 2. Note that the exponents on the variables can only be non-negative integers. The domain of any polynomial function is all real numbers because any number plugged into a polynomial expression grants a real number output. An example of a quartic polynomial equation is:

$$y = x^4 + 3x^3 - 2x + 1$$

The **zeros** of a polynomial function are the points where its graph crosses the y-axis. In order to find the number of real zeros of a polynomial function, use **Descartes' Rule of Signs**, which states that the number of possible positive real zeros is equal to the number of sign changes in the coefficients. If there is only one sign change, there is only one positive real zero. In the example above, the signs of the coefficients are positive, positive, negative, and positive. Therefore, the sign changes two times and thus, there are at most two positive real zeros. The number of possible negative real zeros is equal to the number of sign changes in the coefficients when plugging $-x$ into the equation. Again, if there is only one sign change, there is only one negative real zero. The polynomial result when plugging $-x$ into the equation is:

$$y^4 - 3x^3 + 2x + 1$$

The sign changes two times, so there are, at most, two negative real zeros. Another polynomial equation this rule can be applied to is:

$$y = x^3 + 2x - x - 5$$

There is only one sign change in the terms of the polynomial, so there is exactly one real zero. When plugging $-x$ into the equation, the polynomial result is:

$$-x^3 - 2x - x - 5$$

There are no sign changes in this polynomial, so there are no possible negative zeros.

Logarithmic Functions

For $x > 0, b > 0, b \neq 1$, the function $f(x) = \log_b x$ is known as the **logarithmic function** with base b. With $y = \log_b x$, its exponential equivalent is $b^y = x$. In either case, the **exponent** is y and the **base** is b. Therefore, $3 = \log_2 8$ is the same as $2^3 = 8$. So, in order to find the logarithm with base 2 of 8, find the exponent that when 2 is raised to that value results in 8. Similarly, $\log_3 243 = 5$. In order to do this mentally, ask the question, what exponent does 3 need to be raised to that results in 243? The answer is 5. Most logarithms do not have whole number results. In this case, a calculator can be used. A calculator typically has buttons with base 10 and base e (Euler's number, the base in the natural log), so the change of base formula can be used to calculate these logs. For instance:

$$\log_3 55 = \frac{\log 55}{\log 3} = 3.64$$

Similarly, the natural logarithm with base e could be used to obtain the same result:

$$\log_3 55 = \frac{\ln 55}{\ln 3} = 3.64$$

The domain of a logarithmic function $f(x) = \log_b x$ is all positive real numbers. This is because the exponent must be a positive number. The range of a logarithmic function $f(x) = \log_b x$ is all real numbers. The graphs of all logarithmic functions of the form $f(x) = \log_b x$ always pass through the point (1, 0) because anything raised to the power of 0 is 1.

Therefore, such a function always has an *x*-intercept at 1. If the base is greater than 1, the graph increases from the left to the right along the *x*-axis. If the base is between 0 and 1, the graph decreases from the left to the right along the *x*-axis. In both situations, the *y*-axis is a vertical asymptote. The graph will never touch the *y*-axis, but it does approach it closely. Here are the graphs of the two cases of logarithmic functions:

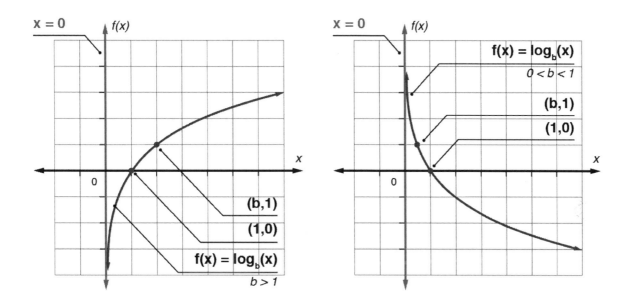

Geometry

Congruence and Similarity

Relationships Between Geometric Figures

Basic shapes are those polygons that are made up of straight lines and angles and can be described by their number of sides and concavity. Some examples of those shapes are rectangles, triangles, hexagons, and pentagons. These shapes have identifying characteristics on their own, but they can also be decomposed into other shapes. For example, the following can be described as one hexagon, as seen in the first figure. It can also be decomposed into six equilateral triangles. The last figure shows how the hexagon can be decomposed into three rhombuses.

Decomposing a Hexagon

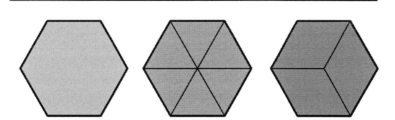

More complex shapes can be formed by combining basic shapes or lining them up side by side. Below is an example of a house. This house is one figure all together but can be decomposed into seven different shapes. The chimney is a parallelogram, and the roof is made up of two triangles. The bottom of the house is a square alongside three triangles. There are many other ways of decomposing this house. Different shapes can be used to line up together and form one larger shape. The area for the house can be calculated by finding the individual areas for each shape, then adding them all together. For this house, there would be the area of four triangles, one square, and one parallelogram. Adding these all together would result in the area of the house as a whole. Decomposing and composing shapes is commonly done with a set of tangrams. A **tangram** is a set of shapes that includes different size triangles, rectangles, and parallelograms.

A Tangram of a House

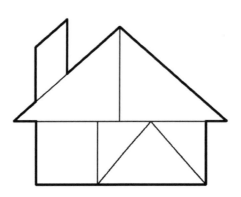

Defining and Applying Knowledge of Shapes and Solids

Shapes are defined by their angles and number of sides. A shape with one continuous side, where all points on that side are equidistant from a center point is called a **circle.** A shape made with three straight line segments is a **triangle.** A shape with four sides is called a **quadrilateral,** but more specifically a *square*, **rectangle, parallelogram,** or **trapezoid,** depending on the interior angles. These shapes are two-dimensional and only made of straight lines and angles.

Solids can be formed by combining these shapes and forming three-dimensional figures. While two-dimensional figures have only length and height, three-dimensional figures also have depth. Examples of solids may be prisms or spheres. The four figures below have different names based on their sides and dimensions. Figure 1 is a **cone**, a three-dimensional solid formed by a circle at its base and the sides combining to one point at the top. Figure 2 is a **triangle**, a shape with two dimensions and three line segments. Figure 3 is a cylinder made up of two base circles and a rectangle to connect them in three dimensions. Figure 4 is an **oval** formed by one continuous line in two dimensions; it differs from a circle because not all points are equidistant from the center.

Shapes and Solids

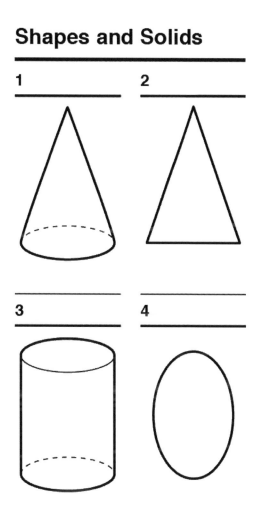

The **cube** in Figure 5 below is a three-dimensional solid made up of squares. Figure 6 is a **rectangle** because it has four sides that intersect at right angles. More specifically, it is a square because the four sides are equal in length. Figure 7 is a pyramid because the bottom shape is a square and the sides are all triangles. These triangles intersect at a point above the square. Figure 8 is a circle because it is made up of one continuous line where the points are all equidistant from one center point.

Shapes and Solids

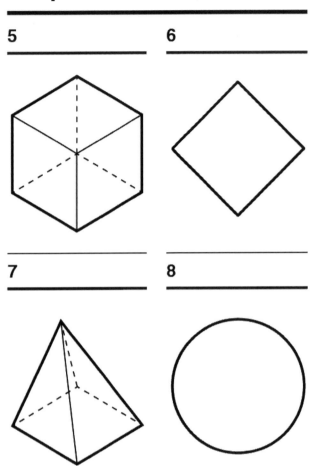

5

6

7

8

Transformations of a Plane

Two figures are **congruent** if they have the same shape and same size, meaning same angle measurements and equal side lengths. Two figures are similar if they have the same angle measurements but not side lengths. Basically, angles are congruent in similar triangles and their side lengths are constant multiples of each other. Proving two shapes are similar involves showing that all angles are the same; proving two shapes are congruent involves showing that all angles are the same *and* that all sides are the same. If two pairs of angles are congruent in two triangles, then those triangles are similar because their third angles have to be equal due to the fact that all three angles add up to 180 degrees.

There are five main theorems that are used to prove congruence in triangles. Each theorem involves showing that different combinations of sides and angles are the same in two triangles, which proves the triangles are congruent. The **side-side-side (SSS) theorem** states that if all sides are equal in two triangles, the triangles are congruent. The **side-angle-side (SAS) theorem** states that if two pairs of sides and the included angles are equal in two triangles then the triangles are congruent. Similarly, the **angle-side-angle (ASA) theorem** states that if two pairs of angles and the included side lengths are equal in two triangles, the triangles are similar. The **angle-angle-side (AAS) theorem** states that two triangles are congruent if they have two pairs of congruent angles and a pair of corresponding equal side lengths that are not included. Finally, the **hypotenuse-leg (HL) theorem** states that if two right triangles have equal

58

hypotenuses and an equal pair of shorter sides, the triangles are congruent. An important item to note is that angle-angle-angle (AAA) is not enough information to prove congruence because the three angles could be equal in two triangles, but their sides could be different lengths.

Right Triangles

The Pythagorean Theorem and Right Triangles

Within right triangles, trigonometric ratios can be defined for the acute angle within the triangle. Consider the following right triangle. The side across from the right angle is known as the **hypotenuse,** the acute angle being discussed is labeled θ, the side across from the acute angle is known as the **opposite** side, and the other side is known as the **adjacent** side.

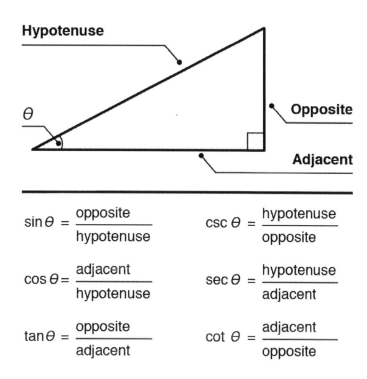

$$\sin\theta = \frac{\text{opposite}}{\text{hypotenuse}} \qquad \csc\theta = \frac{\text{hypotenuse}}{\text{opposite}}$$

$$\cos\theta = \frac{\text{adjacent}}{\text{hypotenuse}} \qquad \sec\theta = \frac{\text{hypotenuse}}{\text{adjacent}}$$

$$\tan\theta = \frac{\text{opposite}}{\text{adjacent}} \qquad \cot\theta = \frac{\text{adjacent}}{\text{opposite}}$$

The six trigonometric ratios are shown above as well. "Sin" is short for sine, "cos" is short for cosine, "tan" is short for tangent, "csc" is short for cosecant, "sec" is short for secant, and "cot" is short for cotangent. A mnemonic device exists that is helpful to remember the ratios. SOHCAHTOA stands for Sine = Opposite/Hypotenuse, Cosine = Adjacent/Hypotenuse, and Tangent = Opposite/Adjacent. The other three trigonometric ratios are reciprocals of sine, cosine, and tangent because $\csc\theta = \frac{1}{\sin\theta}$, $\sec\theta = \frac{1}{\cos\theta}$, and $\cot\theta = \frac{1}{\tan\theta}$.

The **Pythagorean Theorem** expresses an important relationship between the three sides of a right triangle. It states that the square of the hypotenuse is equal to the sum of the squares of the other two sides. When using the Pythagorean Theorem, the hypotenuse is labeled as side c, the opposite is labeled as side a, and the adjacent side is side b.

The theorem can be seen in the following diagram:

The Pythagorean Theorem

$a^2 + b^2 = c^2$

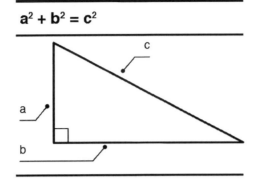

Both the trigonometric ratios and Pythagorean Theorem can be used in problems that involve finding either a missing side or missing angle of a right triangle. Look to see what sides and angles are given and select the correct relationship that will assist in finding the missing value. These relationships can also be used to solve application problems involving right triangles. Often, it is helpful to draw a figure to represent the problem to see what is missing.

Circles

Circle Theorems

The formula for area of a circle is $A = \pi r^2$ and therefore, formula for area of a **sector** is $\pi r^2 \frac{A}{360}$, a fraction of the entire area of the circle. If the radius of a circle and arc length is known, the central angle measurement in degrees can be found by using the formula $\frac{360 \cdot arclength}{2\pi r}$. If the desired central angle measurement is in radians, the formula for the central angle measurement is much simpler as $\frac{arc\ length}{r}$.

The Center, Radius, Central Angle, a Sector, and an Arc of a Circle

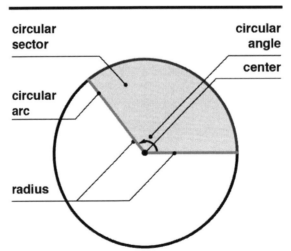

A **chord** of a circle is a straight-line segment that connects any two points on a circle. The line segment does not have to travel through the center, as the diameter does. Also, note that the chord stops at the circumference of the circle. If it did not stop and extended toward infinity, it would be known as a **secant line.** The following shows a diagram of a circle with a chord shown by the dotted line. The radius is *r* and the central angle is *A*:

A Circle with a Chord

$$\text{Chord Length} = 2\,r\,\sin\frac{A}{2}$$

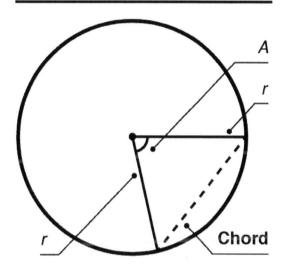

One formula for chord length can be seen in the diagram and is equal to $2r \sin\frac{A}{2}$, where *A* is the central angle. Another formula for chord length is: chord length = $2\sqrt{r^2 - D^2}$, where *D* is equal to the distance from the chord to the center of the circle. This formula is basically a version of the Pythagorean Theorem.

Formulas for chord lengths vary based on what type of information is known. If the radius and central angle are known, the first formula listed above should be used by plugging the radius and angle in directly. If the radius and the distance from the center to the chord are known, the second formula listed previously (chord length = $2\sqrt{r^2 - D^2}$) should be used.

Many theorems exist between arc lengths, angle measures, chord lengths, and areas of sectors. For instance, when two chords intersect in a circle, the product of the lengths of the individual line segments are equal. For instance, in the following diagram, $A \times B = C \times D$.

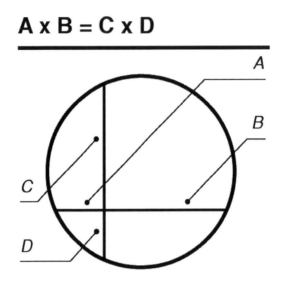

Geometric Measurement and Dimension

Problems Involving Angle Measure, Area, Perimeter, Surface Area, and Volume

Geometric figures can be identified by matching the definition with the object. For example, a line segment is made up of two connected endpoints. A **ray** is made up of one endpoint and one extending side that goes on forever. A line has no endpoints and two sides that extend forever. These three geometric figures are shown below. What happens at A and B determines the name of each figure.

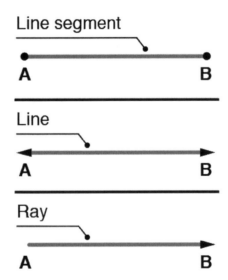

A set of lines can be parallel, perpendicular, or neither, depending on how the two lines interact. Parallel lines run alongside each other but never intersect. **Perpendicular** lines intersect at a 90-degree, or a right, angle. An example of these two sets of lines is shown below. Also shown in the figure are non-examples of these two types of lines. Because the first set of lines, in the top left corner, will eventually intersect if they continue, they are not parallel. In the second set, the lines run in the same direction and will never intersect, making them parallel. The third set, in the bottom left corner, intersect at an angle that is not right, or not 90 degrees. The fourth set is perpendicular because the lines intersect at exactly a right angle.

Lines

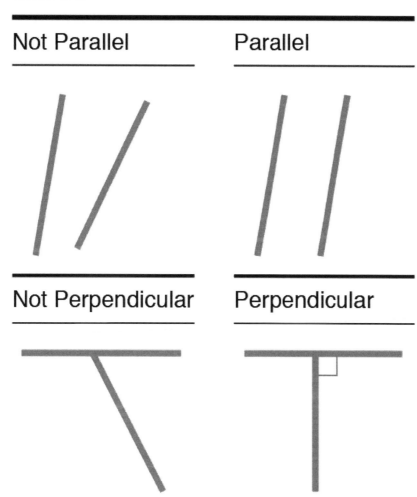

Classifying Angles Based on Their Measure

When two rays join together at their endpoints, they form an angle. Angles can be described based on their measure. An angle whose measure is ninety degrees is a right angle. Ninety degrees is a standard to which other angles are compared. If an angle is less than ninety degrees, it is an **acute angle**. If it is greater than ninety degrees, it is an **obtuse angle**. If an angle is equal to twice a right angle, or 180 degrees, it is a **straight angle**.

Examples of these types of angles are shown below:

Acute Angle

Less than 90°

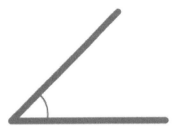

Right Angle

Exactly 90°

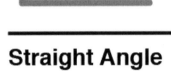

Obtuse Angle

Greater than 90° but less than 180°

Straight Angle

Exactly 180°

A **straight angle** is equal to 180 degrees, or a straight line. If the line continues through the **vertex,** or point where the rays meet, and does not change direction, then the angle is straight. This is shown in Figure 1 below. The second figure shows an obtuse angle. Its measure is greater than ninety degrees, but less than that of a straight angle. An estimate for its measure may be 175 degrees. Figure 3 shows an acute angle because it is just less than that of a right angle. Its measure may be estimated to be 80 degrees.

The last image, Figure 4, shows another acute angle. This measure is much smaller, at approximately 35 degrees, but it is still classified as acute because it is between zero and 90 degrees.

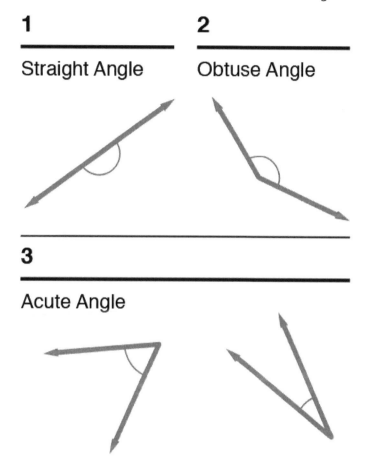

Perimeter and Area

Perimeter and **area** are geometric quantities that describe objects' measurements. **Perimeter** is the distance around an object. The perimeter of an object can be found by adding the lengths of all sides. Perimeter may be used in problems dealing with lengths around objects such as fences or borders. It may also be used in finding missing lengths or working backwards. If the perimeter is given, but a length is missing, subtraction can be used to find the missing length. Given a square with side length s, the formula for perimeter is $P = 4s$. Given a rectangle with length l and width w, the formula for perimeter is:

$$P = 2l + 2w$$

The perimeter of a triangle is found by adding the three side lengths, and the perimeter of a trapezoid is found by adding the four side lengths. The units for perimeter are always the original units of length, such as meters, inches, miles, etc. When discussing a circle, the distance around the object is referred to as its **circumference,** not perimeter. The formula for the circumference of a circle is $C = 2\pi r$, where r

represents the radius of the circle. This formula can also be written as $C = d\pi$, where d represents the diameter of the circle.

Area is the two-dimensional space covered by an object. These problems may include the area of a rectangle, a yard, or a wall to be painted. Finding the area may require a simple formula or multiple formulas used together. The units for area are square units, such as square meters, square inches, and square miles. Given a square with side length s, the formula for its area is $A = s^2$. The table below shows some other common shapes and their area formulas:

Shape	Formula	Graphic
Rectangle	$Area = length \times width$	
Triangle	$Area = \dfrac{1}{2} \times base \times height$	
Circle	$Area = \pi \times radius^2$	

The following formula, not as widely used as those shown on the previous page, but very important, is the area of a trapezoid:

Area of a Trapezoid

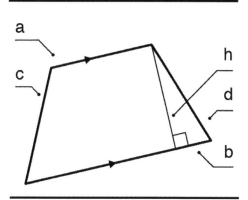

$$A = \frac{1}{2}(a+b)h$$

To find the area of the shapes above, use the given dimensions of the shape in the formula. Complex shapes might require more than one formula. To find the area of the figure below, break the figure into two shapes. The rectangle's dimensions are 6 cm by 7 cm. The triangle has a base of 4 cm and a height of 6 cm. Plug the dimensions into the rectangle formula:

$$A = 6 \times 7$$

Multiplication yields an area of 42 cm². The triangle's area can be found using the formula:

$$A = \frac{1}{2} \times 4 \times 6$$

Multiplication yields an area of 12 cm2. Add the two areas to find the total area of the figure, which is 54 cm2.

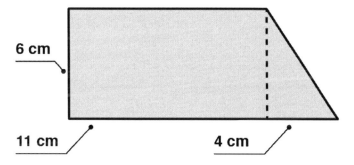

Instead of combining areas, some problems may require subtracting them, or finding the difference.

To find the area of the shaded region in the figure below, determine the area of the whole figure. Then subtract the area of the circle from the whole.

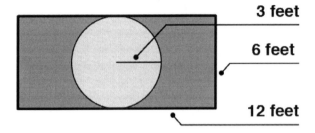

3 feet

6 feet

12 feet

The following formula shows the area of the outside rectangle:

$$A = 12 \times 6 = 72 \text{ ft}^2$$

The area of the inside circle can be found by the following formula:

$$A = \pi(3)^2 = 9\pi = 28.3 \text{ ft}^2$$

As the shaded area is outside the circle, the area for the circle can be subtracted from the area of the rectangle to yield an area of 43.7 ft^2.

Geometric figures may be shown as pictures or described in words. If a rectangular playing field with dimensions 95 meters long by 50 meters wide is measured for perimeter, the distance around the field must be found. The perimeter includes two lengths and two widths to measure the entire outside of the field. This quantity can be calculated using the following equation:

$$P = 2(95) + 2(50) = 290 \, m$$

The distance around the field is 290 meters.

Perimeter and area are two-dimensional descriptions; volume is three-dimensional. Volume describes the amount of space that an object occupies, but it differs from area because it has three dimensions instead of two. The units for volume are cubic units, such as cubic meters, cubic inches, and cubic millimeters. Volume can be found by using formulas for common objects such as cylinders and boxes.

The following chart shows a formula and diagram for the volume of two objects:

Shape	Formula	Diagram
Rectangular Prism (box)	$V = length \times width \times height$	length / height / width
Cylinder	$V = \pi \times radius^2 \times height$	radius / height

Volume formulas of these two objects are derived by finding the area of the bottom two-dimensional shape, such as the circle or rectangle, and then multiplying times the height of the three-dimensional shape. Other volume formulas include the volume of a cube with side length s: $V = s^3$; the volume of a sphere with radius r: $V = \frac{4}{3}\pi r^3$; and the volume of a cone with radius r and height h:

$$V = \frac{1}{3}\pi r^2 h$$

If a soda can has a height of 5 inches and a radius on the top of 1.5 inches, the volume can be found using one of the given formulas. A soda can is a cylinder. Knowing the given dimensions, the formula can be completed as follows:

$$V = \pi(radius)^2 \times height$$

$$\pi(1.5 \text{ in})^2 \times 5 \text{ in} = 35.325 \text{ in}^3$$

Notice that the units for volume are inches cubed because it refers to the number of cubic inches required to fill the can.

With any geometric calculations, it's important to determine what dimensions are given and what quantities the problem is asking for. If a connection can be made between them, the answer can be found.

Other geometric quantities can include angles inside a triangle. The sum of the measures of any triangle's three angles is 180 degrees. Therefore, if only two angles are known, the third can be found by subtracting the sum of the two known quantities from 180. Two angles that add up to 90 degrees are known as complementary angles. For example, angles measuring 72 and 18 degrees are complementary. Finally, two angles that add up to 180 degrees are known as supplementary angles. To find the supplement of an angle, subtract the given angle from 180 degrees. For example, the supplement of an angle that is 50 degrees is 180 − 50 = 130 degrees.

These terms involving angles can be seen in many types of word problems. For example, consider the following problem: The measure of an angle is 60 degrees less than two times the measure of its complement. What is the angle's measure? To solve this, let x be the unknown angle. Therefore, its complement is $90 - x$. The problem gives that:

$$x = 2(90 - x) - 60$$

To solve for x, distribute the 2, and collect like terms. This process results in:

$$x = 120 - 2x$$

Then, use the addition property to add $2x$ to both sides to obtain:

$$3x = 120$$

Finally, use the multiplication properties of equality to divide both sides by 3 to get $x = 40$. Therefore, the angle measures 40 degrees. Also, its complement measures 50 degrees.

Solving for Missing Values in Triangles, Circles, and Other Figures
Solving for missing values in shapes requires knowledge of the shape and its characteristics. For example, a triangle has three sides and three angles that add up to 180 degrees. If two angle measurements are given, the third can be calculated. For the triangle below, the one given angle has a measure of 55 degrees. The missing angle is x. The third angle is labeled with a square, which indicates a measure of 90 degrees. Because all angles must add up to 180 degrees,, the following equation can be used to find the missing x-value:

$$55° + 90° + x = 180°$$

Adding the two given angles and subtracting the total from 180 gives an answer of 35 degrees.

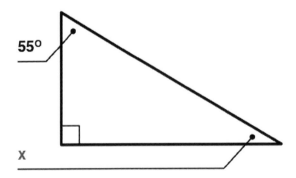

A similar problem can be solved with circles. If the radius is given but the circumference is unknown, the circumference can be calculated based on the formula $C = 2\pi r$. This example can be used in the figure below.

The radius can be substituted for r in the formula. Then the circumference can be found as:

$$C = 2\pi \times 8 = 16\pi = 50.24 \text{ cm}$$

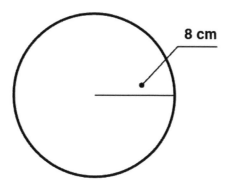

Other figures that may have missing values could be the length of a square, given the area, or the perimeter of a rectangle, given the length and width. All of the missing values can be found by first identifying all the characteristics that are known about the shape, then looking for ways to connect the missing value to the given information.

Determining Surface Area Measurements

Surface area is defined as the area of the surface of a figure. A **pyramid** has a surface made up of four triangles and one square. To calculate the surface area of a pyramid, the areas of each individual shape are calculated. Then the areas are added together. This method of decomposing the shape into two-dimensional figures to find area, then adding the areas, can be used to find surface area for any figure. Once these measurements are found, the area is described with square units. For example, the following figure shows a rectangular prism. The figure beside it shows the rectangular prism broken down into two-dimensional shapes, or rectangles. The area of each rectangle can be calculated by multiplying the length by the width. The area for the six rectangles can be represented by the following expression:

$$5 \times 6 + 5 \times 10 + 5 \times 6 + 6 \times 10 + 5 \times 10 + 6 \times 10$$

The total for all these areas added together is 280 m^2, or 280 square meters. This measurement represents the surface area because it is the area of all six surfaces of the rectangular prism.

The Net of a Rectangular Prism

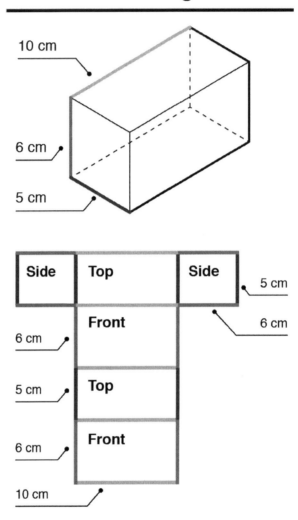

Another shape that has a surface area is a cylinder. The shapes used to make up the **cylinder** are two circles and a rectangle wrapped around between the two circles. A common example of a cylinder is a can. The two circles that make up the bases are obvious shapes. The rectangle can be more difficult to see, but the label on a can will help illustrate it. When the label is removed from a can and laid flat, the shape is a rectangle. When the areas for each shape are needed, there will be two formulas. The first is the area for the circles on the bases. This area is given by the formula $A = \pi r^2$. There will be two of these areas—one for the top and one for the bottom if the can (cylinder) is standing upright on a shelf. Then the area of the rectangle must be determined. The width of the rectangle is equal to the height of the can, h. The length of the rectangle is equal to the circumference of the base circle, $2\pi r$. The area for the rectangle can be found by using the formula:

$$A = 2\pi r \times h$$

By adding the two areas for the bases and the area of the rectangle, the surface area of the cylinder can be found, described in units squared.

Volume Formulas

Right rectangular prisms are those prisms in which all sides are rectangles, and all angles are right, or equal, to 90 degrees. The volume for these objects can be found by multiplying the length by the width by the height. The formula is $V = lwh$. For the following prism, the volume formula is:

$$V = 6\frac{1}{2} \times 3 \times 9$$

When dealing with fractional edge lengths, it is helpful to convert the length to an improper fraction. The length $6\frac{1}{2}$ cm becomes $\frac{13}{2}$ cm. Then the formula becomes:

$$V = \frac{13}{2} \times 3 \times 9 = \frac{13}{2} \times \frac{3}{1} \times \frac{9}{1} = \frac{351}{2}$$

This value for volume is better understood when turned into a mixed number, which would be $175\frac{1}{2}$ cm^3.

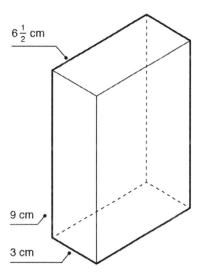

When dimensions for length are given with fractional parts, it can be helpful to turn the mixed number into an improper fraction, then multiply to find the volume, then convert back to a mixed number. When finding surface area, the conversion to improper fractions can also be helpful. The surface area can be found for the same prism above by breaking down the figure into basic shapes. These shapes are rectangles, made up of the two bases, two sides, and the front and back. The formula for surface area adds the areas for each of these shapes in the following equation:

$$SA = 6\frac{1}{2} \times 3 + 6\frac{1}{2} \times 3 + 3 \times 9 + 3 \times 9 + 6\frac{1}{2} \times 9 + 6\frac{1}{2} \times 9$$

Because there are so many terms in a surface area formula and because this formula contains a fraction, it can be simplified by combining groups that are the same. Each set of numbers is used twice, to represent areas for the opposite sides of the prism.

The formula can be simplified to:

$$SA = 2\left(6\frac{1}{2} \times 3\right) + 2(3 \times 9) + 2\left(6\frac{1}{2} \times 9\right)$$

$$2\left(\frac{13}{2} \times 3\right) + 2(27) + 2\left(\frac{13}{2} \times 9\right)$$

$$2\left(\frac{39}{2}\right) + 54 + 2\left(\frac{117}{2}\right)$$

$$39 + 54 + 117 = 210 \text{ cm}^2$$

Determining How Changes to Dimensions Change Area and Volume

When the dimensions of an object change, the area and volume are also subject to change. For example, the following rectangle has an area of 98 square centimeters:

$$A = 7 \times 14 = 98 \text{ cm}^2$$

If the length is increased by 2, becoming 16 cm, then the area becomes:

$$A = 7 \times 16 = 112 \text{ cm}^2$$

The area increased by 14 cm, or twice the width because there were two more widths of 7 cm.

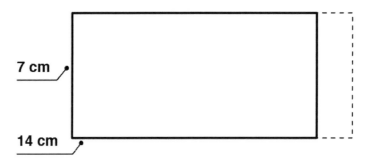

For the volume of an object, there are three dimensions. The given prism has a volume of:

$$V = 4 \times 12 \times 3 = 144 \text{ m}^3$$

If the height is increased by 3, the volume becomes:

$$V = 4 \times 12 \times 6 = 288 \text{ m}^3$$

When the height increased by 3, it doubled, which also resulted in the volume doubling. From the original, if the width was doubled, the volume would be:

$$V = 8 \times 12 \times 3 = 288 \text{ m}^3$$

The rectangle's dimensions are 6 cm by 7 cm. The same increase in volume would result if the length was doubled.

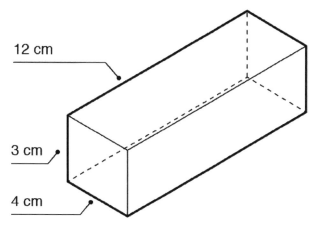

12 cm

3 cm

4 cm

Modeling with Geometry

Applying Geometric Concepts to Modeling Situations

The **net of a figure** is the resulting two-dimensional shapes when a three-dimensional shape is broken down. For example, the net of a cone is shown below. The base of the cone is a circle, shown at the bottom. The rest of the cone is a quarter of a circle. The bottom is the circumference of the circle, while the top comes to a point. If the cone is cut down the side and laid out flat, these would be the resulting shapes.

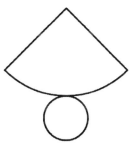

A net for a pyramid is shown in the figure below. The base of the pyramid is a square. The four shapes coming off the square are triangles. Bringing the triangles together at the top results in a pyramid:

The Net of a Pyramid

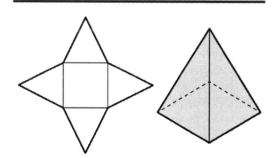

The net of a cylinder is shown below. When the cylinder is broken down, the bases are circles, and the side is a rectangle wrapped around the circles. The circumference of the circle turns into the length of the rectangle.

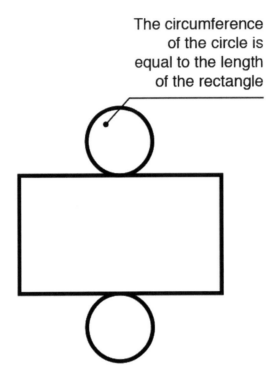

The circumference
of the circle is
equal to the length
of the rectangle

Nets can be used in calculating different values for given shapes. One useful way to calculate surface area is to find the net of the object, then find the areas of each shape and add them together. Nets are also useful when composing or decomposing shapes and when determining connections between objects.

Using Nets to Determine the Surface Area of Three-Dimensional Figures
The surface area of a three-dimensional figure is the total area of each of the figure's faces. Because nets lay out each face of an object, they make it easier to visualize and measure surface area. The image on the following page shows the dimensions for each face of the triangular prism. To determine the area for the two triangles, use the following formula:

$$A = \frac{1}{2}bh = \frac{1}{2} \times 8 \times 9 = 36 \text{ cm}^2$$

The rectangles' areas can be described by the equation:

$$A = lw = 8 \times 5 + 9 \times 5 + 10 \times 5 = 40 + 45 + 50 = 135 \text{ cm}^2$$

The area for the triangles can be multiplied by two, then added to the rectangle areas to yield a total surface area of 207 cm^2.

A Triangular Prism and Its Net

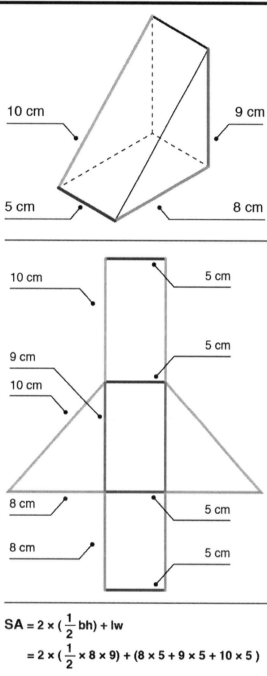

$$SA = 2 \times (\frac{1}{2} bh) + lw$$

$$= 2 \times (\frac{1}{2} \times 8 \times 9) + (8 \times 5 + 9 \times 5 + 10 \times 5)$$

$$= 207 cm^2$$

Other figures that have rectangles or triangles in their nets include pyramids, rectangular prisms, and cylinders. When the shapes of these three-dimensional objects are found, and areas are calculated, the sum will result in the surface area. The following picture shows the net for a rectangular prism and the dimensions for each shape making up the prism. As a formula, the surface area is the sum of each shape added together.

The following equation shows the formula:

$$SA = 5 \times 10 + 5 \times 6 + 6 \times 10 + 5 \times 6 + 5 \times 10 + 6 \times 10$$

$$SA = 50 + 30 + 60 + 30 + 50 + 60 = 280 \text{ m}^2$$

A Rectangular Prism and its Net

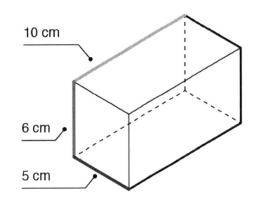

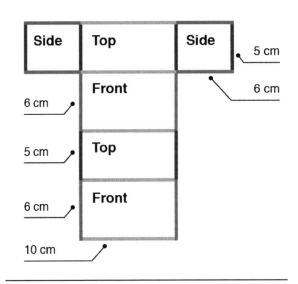

SA = 5×10 + 5×6 + 6×10 + 5×6 + 5×10 + 6×10

= 50 + 30 + 60 + 30 + 50 + 60

= 280cm²

Statistics and Probability

Basic Statistics and Probability

Statistical Variability

Statistics is the branch of mathematics that deals with the collection, organization, and analysis of data. A statistical question is one that can be answered by collecting and analyzing data. When collecting data, expect variability. For example, "How many pets does Yanni own?" is not a statistical question because it can be answered in one way. "How many pets do the people in a certain neighborhood own?" is a statistical question because, to determine this answer, one would need to collect data from each person in the neighborhood, and it is reasonable to expect the answers to vary.

Identify these as statistical or not statistical:

1. How old are you?

2. What is the average age of the people in your class?

3. How tall are the students in Mrs. Jones' sixth grade class?

4. Do you like Brussels sprouts?

The first and last questions are not statistical, but the two middle questions are.

Data collection can be done through surveys, experiments, observations, and interviews. A **census** is a type of survey that is done with a whole population. Because it can be difficult to collect data for an entire population, sometimes a **sample** is used. In this case, one would survey only a fraction of the population and make inferences about the data. Sample surveys are not as accurate as a census, but they are an easier and less expensive method of collecting data. An **experiment** is used when a researcher wants to explain how one variable causes changes in another variable. For example, if a researcher wanted to know if a particular drug affects weight loss, he or she would choose a **treatment group** that would take the drug, and another group, the **control group**, that would not take the drug. Special care must be taken when choosing these groups to ensure that bias is not a factor. **Bias** occurs when an outside factor influences the outcome of the research. In observational studies, the researcher does not try to influence either variable but simply observes the behavior of the subjects. Interviews are sometimes used to collect data as well. The researcher will ask questions that focus on her area of interest in order to gain insight from the participants. When gathering data through observation or interviews, it is important that the researcher is well trained so that he or she does not influence the results and the study remains reliable. A study is reliable if it can be repeated under the same conditions and the same results are received each time.

Describing Distributions

One way information can be interpreted from tables, charts, and graphs is through statistics. The three most common calculations for a set of data are the mean, median, and mode. These three are called **measures of central tendency**, which are helpful in comparing two or more different sets of data. The **mean** refers to the average and is found by adding up all values and dividing the total by the number of values. In other words, the mean is equal to the sum of all values divided by the number of data entries. For example, if you bowled a total of 532 points in 4 bowling games, your mean score was $\frac{532}{4} = 133$

points per game. Students can apply the concept of mean to calculate what score they need on a final exam to earn a desired grade in a class.

The **median** is found by lining up values from least to greatest and choosing the middle value. If there is an even number of values, then calculate the mean of the two middle amounts to find the median. For example, the median of the set of dollar amounts $5, $6, $9, $12, and $13 is $9. The median of the set of dollar amounts $1, $5, $6, $8, $9, $10 is $7, which is the mean of $6 and $8. The **mode** is the value that occurs the most. The mode of the data set {1, 3, 1, 5, 5, 8, 10} actually refers to two numbers: 1 and 5. In this case, the data set is **bimodal** because it has two modes. A data set can have no mode if no amount is repeated. Another useful statistic is range. The **range** for a set of data refers to the difference between the highest and lowest value.

In some cases, numbers in a list of data might have weights attached to them. In that case, a **weighted mean** can be calculated. A common application of a weighted mean is GPA. In a semester, each class is assigned a number of credit hours, its weight, and at the end of the semester each student receives a grade. To compute GPA, an A is a 4, a B is a 3, a C is a 2, a D is a 1, and an F is a 0. Consider a student that takes a 4-hour English class, a 3-hour math class, and a 4-hour history class and receives all B's. The weighted mean, GPA, is found by multiplying each grade times its weight, number of credit hours, and dividing by the total number of credit hours. Therefore, the student's GPA is:

$$\frac{3 \times 4 + 3 \times 3 + 3 \times 4}{11} = \frac{33}{11} = 3.0.$$

The following bar chart shows how many students attend a cycle class on each day of the week.

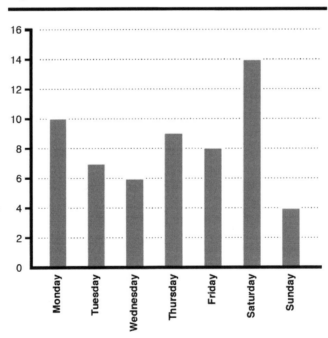

Cycle class attendance

To find the mean attendance for the week, each day's attendance can be added together:

$$10 + 7 + 6 + 9 + 8 + 14 + 4 = 58$$

The total is then divided by the number of days,

$$58 \div 7 = 8.3$$

The mean attendance for the week was 8.3 people. The median attendance can be found by putting the attendance numbers in order from least to greatest: 4, 6, 7, 8, 9, 10, 14, and choosing the middle number: 8 people. This set of data has no mode because no numbers repeat. The range is 10, which is found by finding the difference between the lowest number, 4, and the highest number, 14.

A **histogram** is a bar graph used to group data into "bins" that cover a range on the horizontal, or x-axis. Histograms consist of rectangles whose heights are equal to the frequency of a specific category. The horizontal axis represents the specific categories. Because they cover a range of data, these bins have no gaps between bars, unlike the bar graph above. In a histogram showing the heights of adult golden retrievers, the bottom axis would be groups of heights, and the y-axis would be the number of dogs in each range. Evaluating this histogram would show the height of most golden retrievers as falling within a certain range. It also provides information to find the average height and range for how tall golden retrievers may grow.

The following is a histogram that represents exam grades in a given class. The horizontal axis represents ranges of the number of points scored, and the vertical axis represents the number of students. For example, approximately 33 students scored in the 60 to 70 range.

Results of the exam

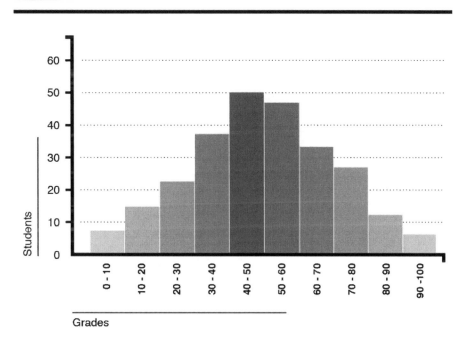

Certain measures of central tendency can be easily visualized with a histogram. If the points scored were shown with individual rectangles, the tallest rectangle would represent the mode. A bimodal set of data would have two peaks of equal height. Histograms can be classified as having data **skewed to the left, skewed to the right**, or **normally distributed**, which is also known as **bell-shaped**.

These three classifications can be seen in the following chart:

Measures of central tendency images

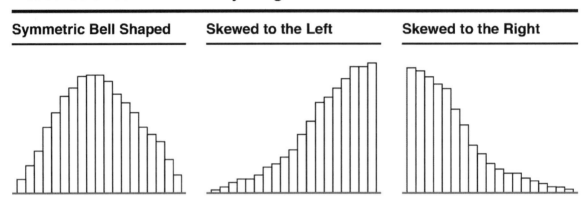

When the data is normal, the mean, median, and mode are very similar because they all represent the most typical value in the data set. In this case, the mean is typically considered the best measure of central tendency because it includes all data points. However, if the data is skewed, the mean becomes less meaningful because it is dragged in the direction of the skew. Therefore, the median becomes the best measure because it is not affected by any outliers.

The measures of central tendency and the range may also be found by evaluating information on a line graph.

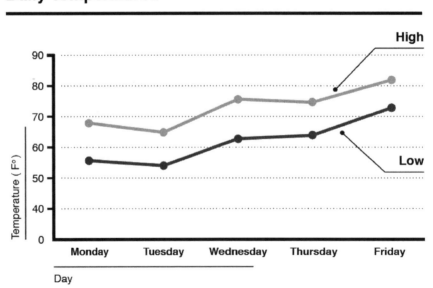

In the line graph above that shows the daily high and low temperatures, the average high temperature can be found by gathering data from each day on the triangle line. The days' highs are 69, 65, 75, 74, and 81. To find the average, add them together to get 364, then divide by 5 (because there are 5 temperatures). The average high for the five days is 72.8. If 72.8 degrees is found on the graph, it will fall in the middle of all the values. The average low temperature can be found in the same way.

Given a set of data, the **correlation coefficient**, r, measures the association between all the data points. If two values are **correlated**, there is an association between them. However, correlation does not necessarily mean causation, or that one value causes the other. There is a common mistake made that assumes correlation implies causation. Average daily temperature and number of sunbathers are both correlated and have causation. If the temperature increases, that change in weather causes more people to want to catch some rays. However, wearing plus-size clothing and having heart disease are two variables that are correlated but do not have causation. The larger someone is, the more likely he or she is to have heart disease. However, being overweight does not cause someone to have the disease.

The value of the correlation coefficient is between −1 and 1, where −1 represents a perfect negative linear relationship, 0 represents no relationship between the two data sets, and 1 represents a perfect positive linear relationship. A negative linear relationship means that as x-values increase, y-values decrease. A positive linear relationship means that as x-values increase, y-values increase. The formula for computing the correlation coefficient is:

$$r = \frac{n \sum xy - (\sum x)(\sum y)}{\sqrt{n(\sum x^2) - (\sum x)^2}\sqrt{n(\sum y^2) - (y)^2}}$$

where n is the number of data points. The closer r is to 1 or −1, the stronger the correlation. A correlation can be seen when plotting data. If the graph resembles a straight line, there is a correlation.

Solving Problems Involving Measures of Center and Range
As mentioned, a data set can be described by calculating the mean, median, and mode. These values allow the data to be described with a single value that is representative of the data set.

The most common measure of center is the **mean,** also referred to as the **average.**

To calculate the mean:

　　Add all data values together
　　Divide by the sample size (the number of data points in the set)

The **median** is middle data value, so that half of the data lies below this value and half lies above it.

To calculate the median:

　　Order the data from least to greatest
　　The point in the middle of the set is the median
　　If there is an even number of data points, add the two middle points and divide by 2

The **mode** is the data value that occurs most often.

To calculate the mode:

> Order the data from least to greatest
> Find the value that occurs most often

Example: Amelia is a leading scorer on the school's basketball team. The following data set represents the number of points that Amelia has scored in each game this season. Use the mean, median, and mode to describe the data.

> 16, 12, 26, 14, 28, 14, 12, 15, 25

Solution:

> Mean:
>
> $$16 + 12 + 26 + 14 + 28 + 14 + 12 + 15 + 25 = 162$$
>
> $$162 \div 9 = 18$$
>
> Amelia averages 18 points per game.
>
> Median:
>
> 12, 12, 14, 14, **15**, 16, 25, 26, 28
>
> Amelia's median score is 15.
>
> Mode:
>
> 12, 12, 14, 14, 15, 16, 25, 26, 28
>
> The numbers 12 and 14 each occur twice, so this data set has 2 modes: 12 and 14.

The **range** is the difference between the largest and smallest values in the set. In the example above, the range is 28 – 12 = 16.

Determining How Changes in Data Affect Measures of Center or Range

An **outlier** is a data point that lies an unusual distance from other points in the data set. Removing an outlier from a data set will change the measures of central tendency. Removing a large outlier (a high number) from a data set will decrease both the mean and the median. Removing a small outlier (a number much lower than most in the data set) from a data set will increase both the mean and the median. For example, in data set {3, 6, 8, 12, 13, 14, 60}, the data point 60, is an outlier because it is unusually far from the other points. In this data set, the mean is 16.6. Notice that this mean number is even larger than all other data points in the set except for 60. Removing the outlier changes the mean to 9.3, and the median goes from 12 to 10. Removing an outlier will also decrease the range. In the data set above, the range is 57 when the outlier is included, but it decreases to 11 when the outlier is removed.

Adding an outlier to a data set will also affect the measures of central tendency. When a larger outlier is added to a data set, the mean and median increase. When a small outlier is added to a data set, the mean and median decrease. Adding an outlier to a data set will increase the range.

This does not seem to provide an appropriate measure of center when considering this data set. What will happen if that outlier is removed? Removing the extremely large data point, 60, is going to reduce the

84

mean to 9.3. The mean decreased dramatically because 60 was much larger than any of the other data values. What would happen with an extremely low value in a data set like this one, {12, 87, 90, 95, 98, 100}? The mean of the given set is 80. When the outlier, 12, is removed, the mean should increase and fit more closely to the other data points. Removing 12 and recalculating the mean show that this is correct. After removing the outlier, the mean is 94. So, removing a large outlier will decrease the mean while removing a small outlier will increase the mean.

Using Random Sampling to Draw Inferences About a Population

In statistics, a **population** contains all subjects being studied. For example, a population could be every student at a university or all males in the United States. A **sample** consists of a group of subjects from an entire population. A sample would be 100 students at a university or 100,000 males in the United States. **Inferential statistics** is the process of using a sample to generalize information concerning populations. **Hypothesis testing** is the actual process used when evaluating claims made about a population based on a sample.

A **statistic** is a measure obtained from a sample, and a **parameter** is a measure obtained from a population. For example, the mean SAT score of the 100 students at a university would be a statistic, and the mean SAT score of all university students would be a parameter.

The beginning stages of hypothesis testing starts with formulating a **hypothesis,** a statement made concerning a population parameter. The hypothesis may be true, or it may not be true. The experiment will help answer that question. In each setting, there are two different types of hypotheses: the **null hypothesis**, written as H_0, and the **alternative hypothesis**, written as H_1. The null hypothesis represents verbally when there is not a difference between two parameters, and the alternative hypothesis represents verbally when there is a difference between two parameters. Consider the following experiment: A researcher wants to see if a new brand of allergy medication has any effect on drowsiness of the patients who take the medication. He wants to know if the average hours spent sleeping per day increases. The mean for the population under study is 8 hours, so $\mu = 8$. In other words, the population parameter is μ, the mean. The null hypothesis is $\mu = 8$ and the alternative hypothesis is $\mu > 8$. When using a smaller sample of a population, the **null hypothesis** represents the situation when the mean remains unaffected, and the **alternative hypothesis** represents the situation when the mean increases. The chosen statistical test will apply the data from the sample to actually decide whether the null hypothesis should or should not be rejected.

Chance Processes and Probability Models

Probability describes how likely it is that an event will occur. Probabilities are always a number from zero to 1. If an event has a high likelihood of occurrence, it will have a probability close to 1. If there is only a small chance that an event will occur, the likelihood is close to zero. A fair six-sided die has one of the numbers 1, 2, 3, 4, 5, and 6 on each side. When this die is rolled there is a one in six chance that it will land on 2. This is because there are six possibilities and only one side has a 2 on it. The probability then is $\frac{1}{6}$ or 0.167. The probability of rolling an even number from this die is three in six, which is $\frac{1}{2}$ or 0.5. This is because there are three sides on the die with even numbers (2, 4, 6), and there are six possible sides. The probability of rolling a number less than 10 is 1; since every side of the die has a number less than 6, it would be impossible to roll a number 10 or higher. On the other hand, the probability of rolling a number larger than 20 is zero. There are no numbers greater than 20 on the die, so it is certain that this will not occur, thus the probability is zero.

If a teacher says that the probability of anyone passing her final exam is 0.2, is it highly likely that anyone will pass? No, the probability of anyone passing her exam is low because 0.2 is closer to zero than to 1. If another teacher is proud that the probability of students passing his class is 0.95, how likely is it that a student will pass? It is highly likely that a student will pass because the probability, 0.95, is very close to 1.

Patterns of Association in Bivariate Data

Independent and dependent are two types of variables that describe how they relate to each other. The **independent variable** is the variable controlled by the experimenter. It stands alone and is not changed by other parts of the experiment. This variable is normally represented by x and is found on the horizontal, or x-axis, of a graph. The **dependent variable** changes in response to the independent variable. It reacts to, or depends on, the independent variable. This variable is normally represented by y and is found on the vertical, or y-axis of the graph.

The relationship between two variables, x and y, can be seen on a scatterplot.

The following scatterplot shows the relationship between weight and height. The graph shows the weight as x and the height as y. The first dot on the left represents a person who is 45 kg and approximately 150 cm tall. The other dots correspond in the same way. As the dots move to the right and weight increases, height also increases. A line could be drawn through the middle of the dots to move from bottom left to top right. This line would indicate a **positive correlation** between the variables. If the variables had a **negative correlation**, then the dots would move from the top left to the bottom right.

Height and Weight

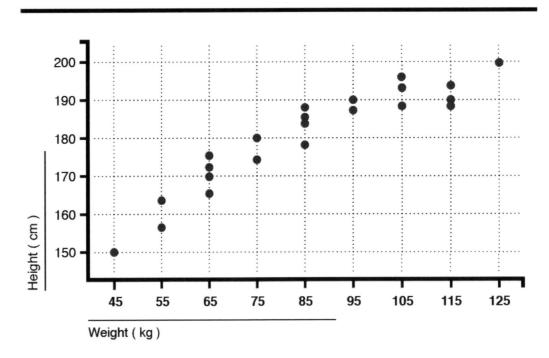

A scatterplot is useful in determining the relationship between two variables, but it is not required. Consider an example where a student scores a different grade on his math test for each week of the month. The independent variable would be the weeks of the month. The dependent variable would be the grades because they change depending on the week. If the grades trended up as the weeks passed, then the relationship between grades and time would be positive. If the grades decreased as the time passed, then the relationship would be negative. (As the number of weeks went up, the grades went down.)

The relationship between two variables can further be described as strong or weak. The relationship between age and height shows a strong positive correlation because children grow taller as they grow up. In adulthood, the relationship between age and height becomes weak, and the dots will spread out. People stop growing in adulthood, and their final heights vary depending on factors like genetics and health. The closer the dots on the graph are to the trend line, the stronger the relationship. As they spread apart, the relationship becomes weaker. If they are too spread out to determine a trend (and thus, correlation) up or down, then the variables are said to have no correlation.

Variables are values that change, so determining the relationship between them requires an evaluation of who changes them. If the variable changes because of a result in the experiment, then it's **dependent**. If the variable changes before the experiment, or is changed by the person controlling the experiment, then it's the **independent variable**. As they interact, one is manipulated by the other. The manipulator is the independent, and the manipulated is the dependent. Once the independent and dependent variable are determined, they can be evaluated to have a positive, negative, or no correlation.

Interpreting Categorical and Quantitative Data

Summarizing, Representing, and Interpreting Data on a Single Count or Measurement Variable

They all organize, categorize, and compare data, and they come in different shapes and sizes. Each type has its own way of showing information, whether through a column, shape, or picture. To answer a question relating to a table, chart, or graph, some steps should be followed. First, the problem should be read thoroughly to determine what is being asked to determine what quantity is unknown. Then, the title of the table, chart, or graph should be read. The title should clarify what data is actually being summarized in the table. Next, look at the key and labels for both the horizontal and vertical axes, if they are given. These items will provide information about how the data is organized. Finally, look to see if there is any more labeling inside the table. Taking the time to get a good idea of what the table is summarizing will be helpful as it is used to interpret information.

Tables are a good way of showing a lot of information in a small space. The information in a table is organized in columns and rows. For example, a table may be used to show the number of votes each candidate received in an election. By interpreting the table, one may observe which candidate won the election and which candidates came in second and third. In using a bar chart to display monthly rainfall amounts in different countries, rainfall can be compared between countries at different times of the year. Graphs are also a useful way to show change in variables over time, as in a line graph, or percentages of a whole, as in a pie graph.

The table below relates the number of items to the total cost. The table shows that one item costs $5. By looking at the table further, five items cost $25, ten items cost $50, and fifty items cost $250. This cost can be extended for any number of items. Since one item costs $5, then two items would cost $10. Though this information is not in the table, the given price can be used to calculate unknown information.

Number of Items	1	5	10	50
Cost ($)	5	25	50	250

A **bar graph** is a graph that summarizes data using bars of different heights. It is useful when comparing two or more items or when seeing how a quantity changes over time. It has both a horizontal and vertical axis. To interpret bar graphs, recognize what each bar represents and connect that to the two variables. The bar graph below shows the scores for six people during three different games. The different colors of the bars distinguish between the three games, and the height of the bar indicates their score for that game. William scored 25 on game 3, and Abigail scored 38 on game 3. By comparing the bars, it is obvious that Williams scored lower than Abigail.

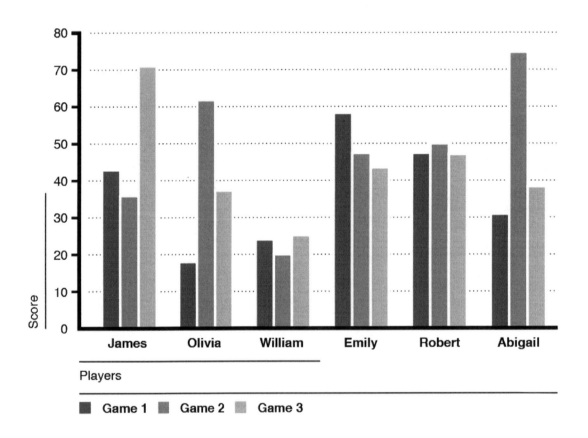

A line graph is a way to compare two variables that are plotted on opposite axes of a graph. The line indicates a continuous change as it rises or falls. The line's rate of change is known as its slope. The horizontal axis often represents a variable of time. Readers can quickly see if an amount has grown or decreased over time. The bottom of the graph, or the x-axis, shows the units for time, such as days, hours, months, etc. If there are multiple lines, a comparison can be made between what the two lines represent.

For example, the following line graph, shown previously, displays the change in temperature over five days. The top line represents the high, and the bottom line represents the low for each day. Looking at the top line alone, the high decreases for a day, then increases on Wednesday. Then it decreases on Thursday and increases again on Friday. The low temperatures have a similar trend, shown in the bottom line. The range in temperatures each day can also be calculated by finding the difference between the top line and bottom line on a particular day. On Wednesday, the range was 14 degrees, from 62 to 76° F.

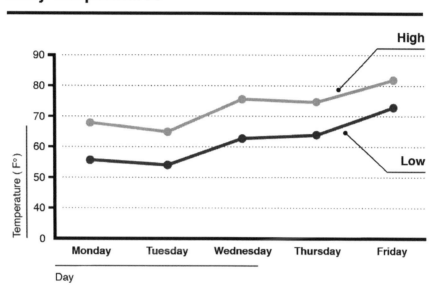

Pie charts show percentages of a whole; they are circular representations of data used to highlight numerical proportions. Each category represents a piece of the pie, and together, all of the pieces make up a whole. The size of each pie slice is proportional to the amount it represents; therefore, a reader can quickly make comparisons by visualizing the sizes of the pieces. They can be useful for comparison between different categories. The following pie chart is a simple example of three different categories shown in comparison to each other.

Light gray represents cats, dark gray represents dogs, and the medium shade of gray represents other pets. These three equal pieces each represent just more than 33 percent, or $\frac{1}{3}$ of the whole. Values 1 and 2 may be combined to represent $\frac{2}{3}$ of the whole. In an example where the total pie represents 75,000 animals, then cats would be equal to $\frac{1}{3}$ of the total, or 25,000. Dogs would equal 25,000 and other pets also equal 25,000.

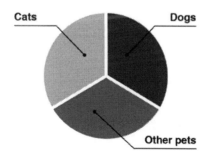

Since circles have 360 degrees, they are used to create pie charts. Because each piece of the pie is a percentage of a whole, that percentage is multiplied times 360 to get the number of degrees each piece represents. In the example above, each piece is $\frac{1}{3}$ of the whole, so each piece is equivalent to 120 degrees. Together, all three pieces add up to 360 degrees.

Stacked bar graphs are also used fairly frequently when comparing multiple variables at one time. They combine some elements of both pie charts and bar graphs, using the organization of bar graphs and the proportionality aspect of pie charts. The following is an example of a stacked bar graph that represents the number of students in a band playing drums, flute, trombone, and clarinet. Each bar graph is broken up further into girls and boys.

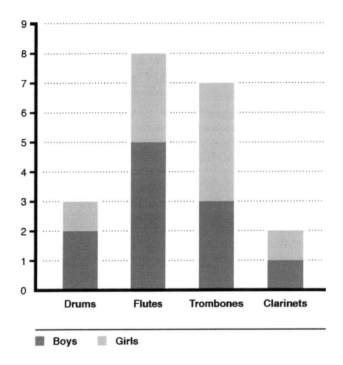

To determine how many boys play trombone, refer to the darker portion of the trombone bar, which indicates three boys.

As mentioned, a **scatterplot** is another way to represent paired data. It uses Cartesian coordinates, like a line graph, meaning it has both a horizontal and vertical axis. Each data point is represented as a dot on the graph. The dots are never connected with a line. For example, the following is a scatterplot showing the connection between people's ages and heights.

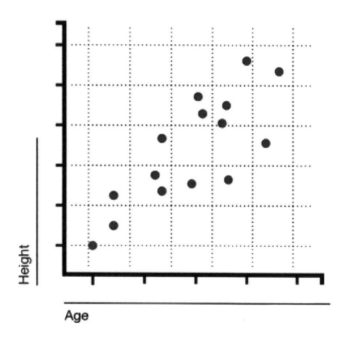

A scatterplot, also known as a **scattergram,** can be used to predict another value and to see if a correlation exists between two variables in a set of data. If the data resembles a straight line, then it is associated, or correlated. The following is an example of a scatterplot in which the data does not seem to have an association:

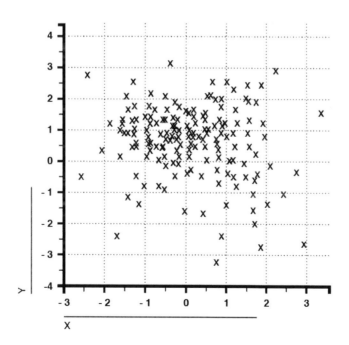

Sets of numbers and other similarly organized data can also be represented graphically. Venn diagrams are a common way to do so. A **Venn diagram** represents each set of data as a circle. The circles overlap, showing that each set of data is overlapping. A Venn diagram is also known as a *logic diagram* because it visualizes all possible logical combinations between two sets. Common elements of two sets are represented by the area of overlap. The following is an example of a Venn diagram of two sets A and B:

Parts of the Venn Diagram

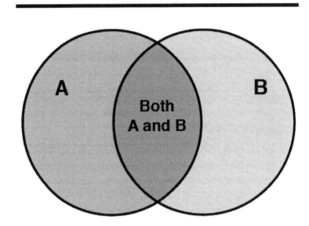

Another name for the area of overlap is the **intersection.** The intersection of A and B, written $A \cap B$, contains all elements that are in both sets A and B. The **union** of A and B, $A \cup B$, contains all elements in both sets A and B. Finally, the **complement** of $A \cup B$ is equal to all elements that are not in either set A or set B. These elements are placed outside of the circles.

The following is an example of a Venn diagram representing 24 students who were surveyed about their siblings. Ten students only had a brother, seven students only had a sister, and five had both a brother and a sister. Therefore, five is the intersection, represented by the section where the circles overlap. Two students did not have a brother or a sister. Therefore, two is the complement and is placed outside of the circles.

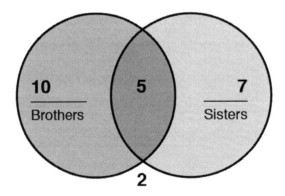

Venn diagrams can have more than two sets of data. The more circles, the more logical combinations are represented by the overlapping. The following is a Venn diagram that represents sock colors worn by a class of students. There were 30 students surveyed. The innermost region represents those students that had green, pink, and blue on their socks (perhaps in a striped pattern). Therefore, two students had all three colors.. In this example, all students had at least one color on their socks, so there is no complement.

30 students

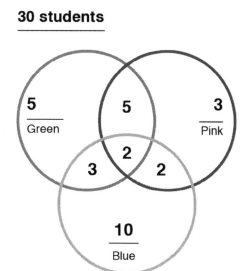

Venn diagrams are typically not drawn to scale; however, if they are, and if each circle's area is proportional to the amount of data it represents, then it is called an area-proportional Venn diagram.

Linear Regression Models

Graphs, equations, and tables are three different ways to represent linear relationships. The following graph shows a linear relationship because the relationship between the two variables is constant. Each time the distance increases by 25 miles, 1 hour passes. This pattern continues for the rest of the graph. The line represents a constant rate of 25 miles per hour. This graph can also be used to solve problems involving predictions for a future time. After 8 hours of travel, the rate can be used to predict the distance covered.

Eight hours of travel at 25 miles per hour covers a distance of 200 miles. The equation at the top of the graph corresponds to this rate also. The same prediction of distance in a given time can be found using the equation. For a time of 10 hours, the distance would be 250 miles, as the equation yields:

$$d = 25 \times 10 = 250 \; miles$$

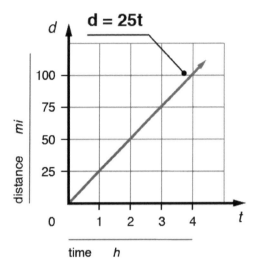

Another representation of a linear relationship can be seen in a table. The first thing to observe from the table is that the y-values increase by the same amount of 3 each time. As the x-values increase by 1, the y-values increase by 3. This pattern shows that the relationship is linear. If this table shows the money earned, y-value, for the hours worked, x-value, then it can be used to predict how much money will be earned for future hours. If 6 hours are worked, then the pay would be $19. For further hours and money to be determined, it would be helpful to have an equation that models this table of values. The equation will show the relationship between x and y. The y-value can each time be determined by multiplying the x-value by 3, then adding 1. The following equation models this relationship: $y = 3x + 1$. Now that there is an equation, any number of hours, x can be substituted into the equation to find the amount of money earned, y.

y = 3x + 1	
x	y
0	1
1	4
2	7
4	13
5	16

Identifying Relationships Between the Corresponding Terms of Two Numerical Patterns

Sets of numerical patterns can be found by starting with a number and following a given rule. If two sets are generated, the corresponding terms in each set can be found to relate to one another by one or more operations. For example, the following table shows two sets of numbers that each follow their own pattern. The first column shows a pattern of numbers increasing by 1. The second column shows the numbers increasing by 4. The numbers in the first column correspond to those in the second. A question to ask is, "How can the number in the first column turn into the number in the second column?"

1	4
2	8
3	12
4	16
5	20

This answer will lead to the relationship between the two sets. By recognizing the multiples of 4 in the right column and the counting numbers in order in the left column, the relationship of multiplying by four is determined. The first set is multiplied by 4 to get the second set of numbers. To confirm this relationship, check each pair of corresponding numbers. For any two sets of numerical patterns, the corresponding numbers can be lined up to find how each one relates to the other. In some cases, the relationship is simply addition or subtraction, multiplication or division. In other relationships, these operations are used in conjunction with each together. The relationship in the following table uses both multiplication and addition. The following expression shows this relationship: $3x + 2$. The x represents the numbers in the first column.

1	5
2	8
3	11
4	14

Making Inferences and Justifying Conclusions

The Random Processes Underlying Statistical Experiments

For researchers to make valid conclusions about population characteristics and parameters, the sample used to compare must be random. In a **random sample**, every member of the population must have an equal chance of being selected. In this situation, the sample is **unbiased** and is said to be a good representation of the population. If a sample is selected in an inappropriate manner, it is said to be **biased.** A sample can be biased if, for example, some subjects were more likely to be chosen than others. In order to have unbiased samples, the four main sampling methods used tend to be random, systematic, stratified, and cluster sampling.

Random sampling occurs when, given a sample size n, all possible samples of that size are equally likely to be chosen. Random numbers from calculators are typically used in this setting. Each member of a population is paired with a number, and then a set of random numbers is generated. Each person paired with one of those random numbers is selected. A **systematic sample** is when every fourth, seventh, tenth, etc., person from a population is selected to be in a sample. A **stratified sample** is when the population is divided into subgroups, or **strata**, using a characteristic, and then members from each stratum are randomly selected. For instance, university students could be divided into age groups and then selected from each age group. Finally, a **cluster sample** is when a sample is used from an already selected group, like city block or zip code. These four methods are used most frequently because they are most likely to yield unbiased results.

Once an unbiased sample is obtained, data need to be collected. Common data collection methods include surveys with questions that are unbiased, contain clear language, avoid double negatives, and do not contain compound sentences that ask two questions at once. When formulating these questions, the simpler verbiage, the better.

Using Probability to Make Decisions

Using Probability to Evaluate the Outcomes of Decisions

A **two-way frequency table** displays categorical data with two variables, and it highlights relationships that exist between those two variables. Such tables are used frequently to summarize survey results, and are also known as **contingency tables**. Each cell shows a count pertaining to that individual variable pairing, known as a **joint frequency**, and the totals of each row and column also are in the table.

Consider the following two-way frequency table:

Distribution of the Residents of a Particular Village

	70 or older	69 or younger	Totals
Women	20	40	60
Men	5	35	40
Total	25	75	100

The table shows the breakdown of ages and sexes of 100 people in a particular village. The end of each row or column displays the number of people represented by the corresponding data, and the total number of people is shown in the bottom right corner. For instance, there were 25 people aged 70 or older and 60 women in the data. The 20 in the first cell shows that out of 100 total villagers, 20 were women aged 70 or older. The 5 in the cell below shows that out of 100 total villagers, 5 were men aged 70 or older.

A two-way table can also show relative frequencies by indicating the percentages of people instead of the count. If each frequency is calculated over the entire total of 100, the first cell would be 20% or 0.2. However, the relative frequencies can also be calculated over row or column totals.

If row totals were used, the first cell would be:
$$\frac{20}{60} = 0.333 = 33.3\%$$

If column totals were used, the first cell would be:
$$\frac{20}{25} = 0.8 = 80\%$$

Such tables can be used to calculate **conditional probabilities**, which are probabilities that an event occurs, given another event. Consider a randomly-selected villager. The probability of selecting a male 70 years old or older is $\frac{5}{100} = 0.05$ because there are 5 males over the age of 70 and 100 total villagers.

Practice Questions

1. What is $\frac{12}{60}$ converted to a percentage?
   - a. 0.20
   - b. 20%
   - c. 25%
   - d. 12%
   - e. 1.2%

2. Which of the following is the correct decimal form of the fraction $\frac{14}{33}$ rounded to the nearest hundredth place?
   - a. 0.420
   - b. 0.14
   - c. 0.424
   - d. 0.140
   - e. 0.42

3. What is the correct sum of $\frac{14}{15}$ and $\frac{2}{5}$, in lowest possible terms?

   [ ]

4. What is the product of $\frac{5}{14}$ and $\frac{7}{20}$, in lowest possible terms?
   - a. $\frac{1}{8}$
   - b. $\frac{35}{280}$
   - c. $\frac{12}{34}$
   - d. $\frac{1}{2}$
   - e. $\frac{7}{140}$

5. What is the result of dividing 24 by $\frac{8}{5}$, in lowest possible terms?

   [ ]

6. Subtract $\frac{5}{14}$ from $\frac{5}{24}$. Which of the following is the correct result?

   a. $\frac{25}{168}$

   b. 0

   c. $-\frac{25}{168}$

   d. $\frac{1}{10}$

   e. $-\frac{1}{10}$

7. Which of the following is a correct mathematical statement?

   a. $\frac{1}{3} < -\frac{4}{3}$

   b. $-\frac{1}{3} > \frac{4}{3}$

   c. $\frac{1}{3} > \frac{4}{3}$

   d. $-\frac{1}{3} \geq \frac{4}{3}$

   e. $\frac{1}{3} > -\frac{4}{3}$

8. Which of the following is incorrect?

   a. $-\frac{1}{5} < \frac{4}{5}$

   b. $\frac{4}{5} > -\frac{1}{5}$

   c. $-\frac{1}{5} > \frac{4}{5}$

   d. $\frac{1}{5} > -\frac{4}{5}$

   e. $\frac{4}{5} > \frac{1}{5}$

9. What is the solution to the equation $3(x + 2) = 14x - 5$?

   a. $x = 1$

   b. $x = -1$

   c. $x = 0$

   d. All real numbers

   e. No solution

10. What is the solution to the equation $10 - 5x + 2 = 7x + 12 - 12x$?

   a. $x = 12$

   b. $x = 1$

   c. $x = 0$

   d. All real numbers

   e. No solution

11. Which of the following is the result when solving the equation $4(x + 5) + 6 = 2(2x + 3)$?

    a. $x = 6$

    b. $x = 1$

    c. $x = 26$

    d. All real numbers

    e. No solution

12. How many cases of cola can Lexi purchase if each case is $3.50 and she has $40?

    ☐

13. Two consecutive integers exist such that the sum of three times the first and two less than the second is equal to 411. What are those integers?

    a. 103 and 104

    b. 104 and 105

    c. 102 and 103

    d. 100 and 101

    e. 101 and 102

14. In a neighborhood, 15 out of 80 of the households have children under the age of 18. What percentage of the households have children under 18?

    a. 0.1875%

    b. 18.75%

    c. 1.875%

    d. 15%

    e. 1.50%

15. Gina took an algebra test last Friday. There were 35 questions, and she answered 60% of them correctly. How many correct answers did she have?

    a. 35

    b. 20

    c. 21

    d. 25

    e. 18

16. Paul took a written driving test, and he got 12 of the questions correct. If he answered 75% of the total questions correctly, how many problems were there in the test?

    ☐

17. If a car is purchased for $15,395 with a 7.25% sales tax, how much is the total price?

    ☐

18. A car manufacturer usually makes 15,412 SUVs, 25,815 station wagons, 50,412 sedans, 8,123 trucks, and 18,312 hybrids a month. About how many cars are manufactured each month?
   a. 120,000
   b. 200,000
   c. 300,000
   d. 12,000
   e. 20,000

19. Each year, a family goes to the grocery store every week and spends $105. About how much does the family spend annually on groceries?
   a. $10,000
   b. $50,000
   c. $500
   d. $5,000
   e. $1,200

20. Bindee is having a barbeque on Sunday and needs 12 packets of ketchup for every 5 guests. If 60 guests are coming, how many packets of ketchup should she buy?

   [   ]

21. A grocery store sold 48 bags of apples in one day, and 9 of the bags contained Granny Smith apples. The rest contained Red Delicious apples. What is the ratio of bags of Granny Smith to bags of Red Delicious that were sold?
   a. 48:9
   b. 39:9
   c. 9:48
   d. 9:39
   e. 39:48

22. If Oscar's bank account totaled $4,000 in March and $4,900 in June, what was the rate of change in his bank account total over those three months?
   a. $900 a month
   b. $300 a month
   c. $4,900 a month
   d. $100 a month
   e. $4,000 a month

23. Erin and Katie work at the same ice cream shop. Together, they always work less than 21 hours a week. In a week, if Katie worked two times as many hours as Erin, how many hours could Erin work?
   a. Less than 7 hours
   b. Less than or equal to 7 hours
   c. More than 7 hours
   d. Less than 8 hours
   e. More than 8 hours

24. From the chart below, which two are preferred by more men than women?

Preferred Movie Genres

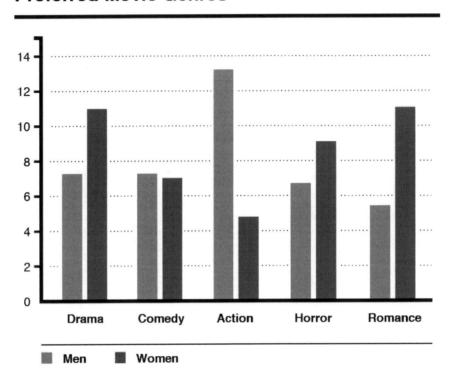

a. Comedy and Action
b. Drama and Comedy
c. Action and Horror
d. Action and Romance
e. Romance and Comedy

25. Which type of graph best represents a continuous change over a period of time?
a. Stacked bar graph
b. Bar graph
c. Pie graph
d. Histogram
e. Line graph

26. Using the graph below, what is the mean number of visitors for the first 4 hours?

Museum Visitors

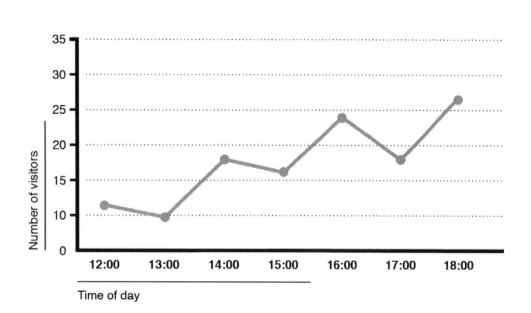

a. 12
b. 13
c. 14
d. 15
e. 16

27. What is the mode for the grades shown in the chart below?

Science Grades	
Jerry	65
Bill	95
Anna	80
Beth	95
Sara	85
Ben	72
Jordan	98

a. 65
b. 33
c. 95
d. 90
e. 84.3

28. What type of relationship is there between age and attention span as represented in the graph below?

Attention Span

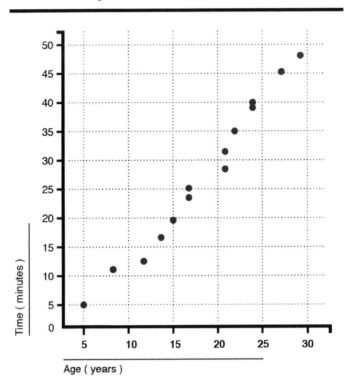

a. No correlation
b. Positive correlation
c. Negative correlation
d. Weak correlation
e. Inverse correlation

29. What is the area of the shaded region?

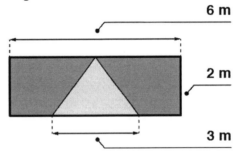

a. 9 m²
b. 12 m²
c. 6 m²
d. 8 m²
e. 4.5 m²

30. What is the volume of the cylinder below in cubic inches?

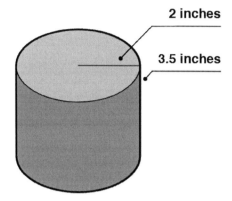

2 inches

3.5 inches

31. How many kiloliters are in 6 liters?
    a. 6,000
    b. 600
    c. 0.006
    d. 0.0006
    e. 0.06

32. How many centimeters are in 3 feet? (Note: 2.54cm = 1 inch)
    a. 0.635
    b. 1.1811
    c. 14.17
    d. 7.62
    e. 91.44

33. Which of the following relations is a function?
    a. {(1, 4), (1, 3), (2, 4), (5, 6)}
    b. {(-1, -1), (-2, -2), (-3, -3), (-4, -4)}
    c. {(0, 0), (1, 0), (2, 0), (1, 1)}
    d. {(1, 0), (1, 2), (1, 3), (1, 4)}
    e. {(-1, 1), (1, -3), (2, 7), (-1, 6)}

34. Find the indicated function value: $f(5)$ for $f(x) = x^2 - 2x + 1$.
    a. 16
    b. 1
    c. 5
    d. 8
    e. Does not exist

35. What is the domain of $f(x) = 4x^2 + 2x - 1$?

    a. $(0, \infty)$

    b. $(-\infty, 0)$

    c. $(-\infty, 4)$

    d. $(-1, 4)$

    e. $(-\infty, \infty)$

36. The function $f(x) = 3.1x + 240$ models the total U.S. population, in millions, x years after the year 1980. Use this function to answer the following question: What is the total U.S. population in 2011? Round to the nearest million.

    a. 336 people

    b. 336 million people

    c. 6,474 people

    d. 647 million people

    e. 64 million people

37. What is the domain of the logarithmic function $f(x) = \log_2(x - 2)$?

    a. 2

    b. $(-\infty, \infty)$

    c. $(0, \infty)$

    d. $(2, \infty)$

    e. $(-\infty, 2)$

38. The function $f(t) = \frac{20,000}{1 + 10e^{-2t}}$ represents the number of people who catch a disease t weeks after its initial outbreak in a population of 20,000 people. How many people initially had the disease at the time of the initial outbreak? Round to the nearest whole number.

    a. 20,000

    b. 1,818

    c. 2,000

    d. 0

    e. 18,181

39. What is the range of the polynomial function $f(x) = 2x^2 + 5$?

    a. $(-\infty, \infty)$

    b. $(2, \infty)$

    c. $(0, \infty)$

    d. $(-\infty, 5)$

    e. $[5, \infty)$

40. What is the perimeter of the following figure in meters?

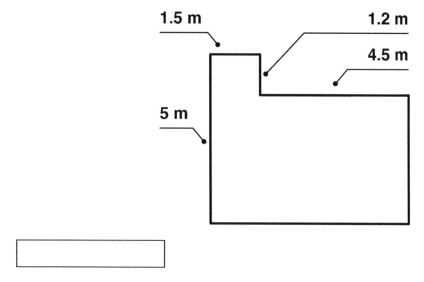

41. Which equation correctly shows how to find the surface area of a cylinder?

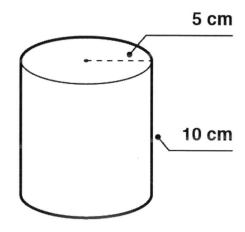

a. $SA = 2\pi \times 5 \times 10 + 2(\pi 5^2)$
b. $SA = 5 \times 2\pi \times 5$
c. $SA = 2\pi 5^2$
d. $SA = 2\pi \times 10 + \pi 5^2$
e. $SA = 2\pi \times 5 \times 10 + \pi 5^2$

42. Which shapes could NOT be used to compose a hexagon?

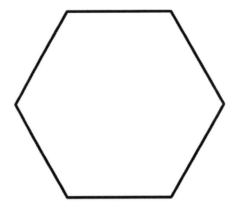

    a. Six triangles
    b. One rectangle and two triangles
    c. Two rectangles
    d. Two trapezoids
    e. One rectangle and four triangles

43. For which two values of x are the following functions equal? Select two answers.
$$f(x) = 4x + 4$$
$$g(x) = x^2 + 3x + 2$$

    a. -1
    b. 1
    c. 2
    d. -2
    e. 0

44. The population of coyotes in the local national forest has been declining since 2000. The population can be modeled by the function $y = -(x-2)^2 + 1600$, where y represents number of coyotes and x represents the number of years past 2000. When will there be no more coyotes?
    a. 2020
    b. 2040
    c. 2012
    d. 2064
    e. 2042

45. Given the linear function $g(x) = \frac{1}{4}x - 2$, which domain value corresponds to a range value of $\frac{1}{8}$?

    a. $\dfrac{17}{2}$

    b. $-\dfrac{63}{32}$

    c. 0

    d. $\dfrac{2}{17}$

    e. $\dfrac{15}{2}$

46. A ball is thrown up from a building that is 800 feet high. Its position s in feet above the ground is given by the function $s = -32t^2 + 90t + 800$, where t is the number of seconds since the ball was thrown. How long will it take for the ball to come back to its starting point? Round your answer to the nearest tenth of a second.

    a. 0 seconds

    b. 2.8 seconds

    c. 3 seconds

    d. 8 seconds

    e. 1.5 seconds

47. What are the zeros of the following cubic function? Select all that apply.
$$g(x) = x^3 - 2x^2 - 9x + 18$$

    a. -3

    b. -2

    c. 0

    d. 2

    e. 3

48. What is the domain of the following rational function?
$$f(x) = \frac{x^3 + 2x + 1}{2 - x}$$

    a. $(-\infty, -2) \cup (-2, \infty)$

    b. $(-\infty, 2) \cup (2, \infty)$

    c. $(2, \infty)$

    d. $(-2, \infty)$

    e. $(-2, 2)$

49. Given the function $f(x) = 4x - 2$, what is the correct form of the simplified difference quotient:
$$\frac{f(x + h) - f(x)}{h}$$

    a. $4x - 1$

    b. $4x$

    c. 4

    d. $4x + h$

    e. $2x - 1$

50. What type of units are used to describe surface area?

    a. Square

    b. Cubic

    c. Single

    d. Quartic

    e. Volumetric

51. Which expression is equivalent to $\sqrt[4]{x^6} - \frac{x}{x^3} + x - 2$?

a. $x^{\frac{3}{2}} - x^2 + x - 2$

b. $x^{\frac{2}{3}} - x^{-2} + x - 2$

c. $x^{\frac{3}{2}} - \frac{1}{x^2} + x - 2$

d. $x^{\frac{2}{3}} - \frac{1}{x^2} + x - 2$

e. $x^{\frac{1}{3}} - \frac{1}{x^2} + x - 2$

52. How many possible positive zeros does the polynomial function $f(x) = x^4 - 3x^3 + 2x + x - 3$ have?

53. Which of the following is equivalent to $16^{\frac{1}{4}} \times 16^{\frac{1}{2}}$?

a. 8
b. 16
c. 4
d. 4,096
e. 64

54. What is the solution to the following linear inequality?
$$7 - \frac{4}{5}x < \frac{3}{5}$$

a. $(-\infty, 8)$
b. $(8, \infty)$
c. $[8, \infty)$
d. $(-\infty, 8]$
e. $(-\infty, \infty)$

55. What is the solution to the following system of linear equations?
$$2x + y = 14$$
$$4x + 2y = -28$$

a. (0, 0)
b. (14, -28)
c. (-14, 28)
d. All real numbers
e. There is no solution

56. Triple the difference of five and a number is equal to the sum of that number and 5. What is the number?

57. Which of the following is perpendicular to the line $4x + 7y = 23$?

a. $y = -\frac{4}{7}x + 23$

b. $y = \frac{7}{4}x - 12$

c. $4x + 7y = 14$

d. $y = -\frac{7}{4}x + 11$

e. $y = \frac{4}{7}x - 12$

58. What is the solution to the following system of equations?
$$2x - y = 6$$
$$y = 8x$$

a. (1, 8)

b. (-1, -8)

c. (-1, 8)

d. All real numbers.

e. There is no solution.

59. The following set represents the test scores from a university class: {35, 79, 80, 87, 87, 90, 92, 95, 95, 98, 99}. If the outlier is removed from this set, which of the following is TRUE?

a. The mean and the median will decrease.

b. The mean and the median will increase.

c. The mean and the mode will increase.

d. The mean and the mode will decrease.

e. The mean, median, and mode will increase.

60. The mass of the moon is about 7.348×10^{22} kilograms and the mass of Earth is 5.972×10^{24} kilograms. How many times GREATER is Earth's mass than the moon's mass?

a. 8.127×10^{1}

b. 8.127

c. 812.7

d. 8.127×10^{-1}

e. 0.8127

61. What is the equation of the line that passes through the two points (-3, 7) and (-1, -5)?

a. $y = 6x + 11$

b. $y = 6x$

c. $y = -6x - 11$

d. $y = -6x$

e. $y = 6x - 11$

62. The percentage of smokers above the age of 18 in 2000 was 23.2 percent. The percentage of smokers above the age of 18 in 2015 was 15.1 percent. Find the average rate of change in the percent of smokers above the age of 18 from 2000 to 2015.

a. -.54 percent

b. -54 percent

c. -5.4 percent

d. -15 percent

e. -1.5 percent

63. A study of adult drivers finds that it is likely that an adult driver wears his seatbelt. Which of the following could be the probability that an adult driver wears his seat belt?

    a. 0.90

    b. 0.05

    c. 0.25

    d. 0

    e. 1.5

64. In order to estimate deer population in a forest, biologists obtained a sample of deer in that forest and tagged each one of them. The sample had 300 deer in total. They returned a week later and harmlessly captured 400 deer, and found that 5 were tagged. Use this information to estimate how many total deer were in the forest.

    a. 24,000 deer

    b. 30,000 deer

    c. 40,000 deer

    d. 100,000 deer

    e. 120,000 deer

65. Which of the following is the equation of a vertical line that runs through the point (1, 4)?

    a. $x = 1$

    b. $y = 1$

    c. $x = 4$

    d. $y = 4$

    e. $x = y$

66. What is the missing length x?

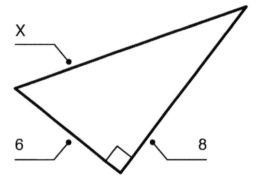

67. What is the correct factorization of the following binomial?
$$2y^3 - 128$$

    a. $2(y + 8)(y - 8)$

    b. $2(y - 4)(y^2 + 4y + 16)$

    c. $2(y + 4)(y - 4)^2$

    d. $2(y - 4)^3$

    e. $2(y - 4)(y^2 + 4y + 16)$

68. What is the simplified form of $(4y^3)^4(3y^7)^2$?

    a. $12y^{26}$

    b. $2,304y^{16}$

    c. $12y^{14}$

    d. $2,304y^{26}$

    e. $12y^{16}$

69. Use the graph below entitled "Projected Temperatures for Tomorrow's Winter Storm" to answer the question.

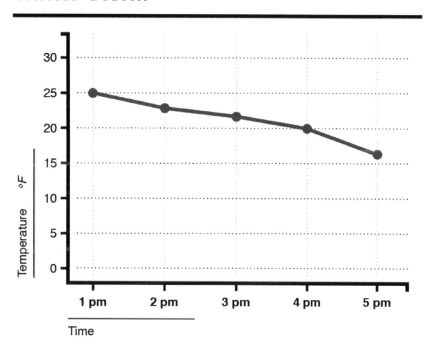

What is the expected temperature at 3:00 p.m.?

    a. 25 degrees

    b. 22 degrees

    c. 20 degrees

    d. 16 degrees

    e. 18 degrees

70. The number of members of the House of Representatives varies directly with the total population in a state. If the state of New York has 19,800,000 residents and has 27 total representatives, how many should Ohio have with a population of 11,800,000?

    a. 10
    b. 16
    c. 11
    d. 5
    e. 12

71. Which of the statements below is a statistical question?

    a. What was your grade on the last test?
    b. What were the grades of the students in your class on the last test?
    c. What kind of car do you drive?
    d. What was Sam's time in the marathon?
    e. What textbooks does Marty use this semester?

72. Eva Jane is practicing for an upcoming 5K run. She has recorded the following times (in minutes):
    25, 18, 23, 28, 30, 22.5, 23, 33, 20

Use the above information to answer the next three questions to the closest minute. What is Eva Jane's mean time?

73. What is the mode of Eva Jane's time in minutes?

74. What is Eva Jane's median score in minutes?

75. What is the area of the following figure?

4 cm

9 cm

114

76. What is the volume of the given figure?

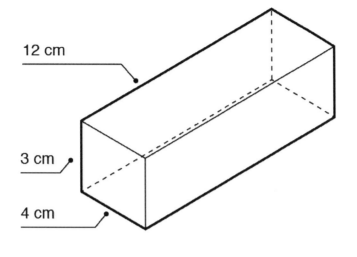

Answer Explanations

1. B: The fraction $\frac{12}{60}$ can be reduced to $\frac{1}{5}$, in lowest terms. First, it must be converted to a decimal. Dividing 1 by 5 results in 0.2. Then, to convert to a percentage, move the decimal point two units to the right and add the percentage symbol. The result is 20%.

2. E: If a calculator is used, divide 33 into 14 and keep two decimal places. If a calculator is not used, multiply both the numerator and denominator times 3. This results in the fraction $\frac{42}{99}$, and hence a decimal of 0.42.

3. $\frac{4}{3}$: Common denominators must be used. The LCD is 15, and $\frac{2}{5} = \frac{6}{15}$. Therefore, $\frac{14}{15} + \frac{6}{15} = \frac{20}{15}$, and in lowest terms, the answer is $\frac{4}{3}$. A common factor of 5 was divided out of both the numerator and denominator.

4. A: A product is found by multiplication. Multiplying two fractions together is easier when common factors are cancelled first to avoid working with larger numbers:

$$\frac{5}{14} \times \frac{7}{20} = \frac{5}{2 \times 7} \times \frac{7}{5 \times 4}$$

$$\frac{1}{2} \times \frac{1}{4} = \frac{1}{8}$$

5. 15: Division is completed by multiplying times the reciprocal. Therefore:

$$24 \div \frac{8}{5} = \frac{24}{1} \times \frac{5}{8}$$

$$\frac{3 \times 8}{1} \times \frac{5}{8} = \frac{15}{1} = 15$$

6. C: A common denominator must be used to subtract fractions. Remember that in order to find the least common denominator, the least common multiple of both of the denominators must be determined. The smallest multiple that 24 and 14 share is 168, which is 24×7 and 14×12. This means that the LCD is 168, so each fraction must be converted to have 168 as the denominator.

$$\frac{5}{24} - \frac{5}{14} = \frac{5}{24} \times \frac{7}{7} - \frac{5}{14} \times \frac{12}{12}$$

$$\frac{35}{168} - \frac{60}{168} = -\frac{25}{168}.$$

7. E: The correct mathematical statement is the one in which the number to the left on the number line is less than the number to the right on the number line. It is written in Choice E that $\frac{1}{3} > -\frac{4}{3}$, which is the same as $-\frac{4}{3} < \frac{1}{3}$, a correct statement.

8. C: $-\frac{1}{5} > \frac{4}{5}$ is an incorrect statement. The expression on the left is negative, which means that it is smaller than the expression on the right. As it is written, the inequality states that the expression on the left is greater than the expression on the right, which is not true.

9. A: First, the distributive property must be used on the left side. This results in:

$$3x + 6 = 14x - 5$$

The addition property is then used to add 5 to both sides, and then to subtract $3x$ from both sides, resulting in $11 = 11x$. Finally, the multiplication property is used to divide each side by 11. Therefore, $x = 1$ is the solution.

10. D: First, like terms are collected to obtain:

$$12 - 5x = -5x + 12$$

Then, if the addition principle is used to move the terms with the variable, $5x$ is added to both sides and the mathematical statement $12 = 12$ is obtained. This is always true; therefore, all real numbers satisfy the original equation.

11. E: The distributive property is used on both sides to obtain:

$$4x + 20 + 6 = 4x + 6$$

Then, like terms are collected on the left, resulting in:

$$4x + 26 = 4x + 6$$

Next, the addition principle is used to subtract $4x$ from both sides, and this results in the false statement $26 = 6$. Therefore, there is no solution.

12. 11: This is a one-step real-world application problem. The unknown quantity is the number of cases of cola to be purchased. Let x be equal to this amount. Because each case costs $3.50, the total number of cases multiplied by $3.50 must equal $40. This translates to the mathematical equation $3.5x = 40$. Divide both sides by 3.5 to obtain $x = 11.4286$, which has been rounded to four decimal places. Because cases are sold whole, and there is not enough money to purchase 12 cases, 11 cases is the correct answer.

13. A: First, the variables have to be defined. Let x be the first integer; therefore, $x + 1$ is the second integer. This is a two-step problem. The sum of three times the first and two less than the second is translated into the following expression:

$$3x + (x + 1 - 2)$$

Set this expression equal to 411 to obtain:

$$3x + (x + 1 - 2) = 411$$

The left-hand side is simplified to obtain:

$$4x - 1 = 411$$

The addition and multiplication properties are used to solve for x. First, add 1 to both sides and then divide both sides by 4 to obtain $x = 103$. The next consecutive integer is 104.

14. B: First, the information is translated into the ratio $\frac{15}{80}$. To find the percentage, translate this fraction into a decimal by dividing 15 by 80. The corresponding decimal is 0.1875. Move the decimal point two units to the right to obtain the percentage 18.75%.

15. C: Gina answered 60% of 35 questions correctly; 60% can be expressed as the decimal 0.60. Therefore, she answered $0.60 \times 35 = 21$ questions correctly.

16. 16: The unknown quantity is the number of total questions on the test. Let x be equal to this unknown quantity. Therefore, $0.75x = 12$. Divide both sides by 0.75 to obtain $x = 16$.

17. $16,511.14: If sales tax is 7.25%, the price of the car must be multiplied times 1.0725 to account for the additional sales tax. Therefore:

$$15,395 \times 1.0725 = 16,511.1375$$

This amount is rounded to the nearest cent, which is $16,511.14.

18. A: Rounding can be used to find the best approximation. All of the values can be rounded to the nearest thousand. 15,412 SUVs can be rounded to 15,000. 25,815 station wagons can be rounded to 26,000. 50,412 sedans can be rounded to 50,000. 8,123 trucks can be rounded to 8,000. Finally, 18,312 hybrids can be rounded to 18,000. The sum of the rounded values is 117,000, which is closest to 120,000.

19. D: There are 52 weeks in a year, and if the family spends $105 each week, that amount is close to $100. A good approximation is $100 a week for 50 weeks, which is found through the product:

$$50 \times 100 = \$5,000$$

20. 144 packets: This problem involves ratios and percentages. If 12 packets are needed for every 5 people, this statement is equivalent to the ratio $\frac{12}{5}$. The unknown amount x is the number of ketchup packets needed for 60 people. The proportion $\frac{12}{5} = \frac{x}{60}$ must be solved. Cross-multiply to obtain:

$$12 \times 60 = 5x$$

Therefore, $720 = 5x$. Divide each side by 5 to obtain $x = 144$.

21. D: There were 48 total bags of apples sold. If 9 bags were Granny Smith and the rest were Red Delicious, then $48 - 9 = 39$ bags were Red Delicious. Therefore, the ratio of Granny Smith to Red Delicious is 9:39.

22. B: The average rate of change is found by calculating the difference in dollars over the elapsed time. Therefore, the rate of change is equal to $(\$4,900 - \$4,000) \div 3$ months, which is equal to $\$900 \div 3$, or $300 per month.

23. A: Let x be the unknown, the number of hours Erin can work. We know Katie works $2x$, and the sum of all hours is less than 21.

Therefore, $x + 2x < 21$, which simplifies into $3x < 21$. Solving this results in the inequality $x < 7$ after dividing both sides by 3. Therefore, Erin can work less than 7 hours.

24. A: The chart is a bar chart showing how many men and women prefer each genre of movies. The dark gray bars represent the number of women, while the light gray bars represent the number of men. The light gray bars are higher and represent more men than women for the genres of Comedy and Action.

25. E: A line graph represents continuous change over time. The line on the graph is continuous and not broken, as on a scatter plot. Stacked bar graphs are used when comparing multiple variables at one time. They combine some elements of both pie charts and bar graphs, using the organization of bar graphs and the proportionality aspect of pie charts. A bar graph may show change but isn't necessarily continuous over time. A pie graph is better for representing percentages of a whole. Histograms are best used in grouping sets of data in bins to show the frequency of a certain variable.

26. C: The mean for the number of visitors during the first 4 hours is 14. The mean is found by calculating the average for the four hours. Adding up the total number of visitors during those hours gives:

$$12 + 10 + 18 + 16 = 56$$

Dividing total visitors by four hours gives average visitors per hour:

$$56 \div 4 = 14$$

27. C: The mode for a set of data is the value that occurs the most. The grade that appears the most is 95. It's the only value that repeats in the set. The mean is around 84.3.

28. B: The relationship between age and time for attention span is a positive correlation because the general trend for the data is up and to the right. As the age increases, so does attention span.

29. A: The area of the shaded region is calculated in a few steps. First, the area of the rectangle is found using the formula:

$$A = length \times width = 6 \times 2 = 12$$

Second, the area of the triangle is found using the formula:

$$A = \frac{1}{2} \times base \times height = \frac{1}{2} \times 3 \times 2 = 3$$

The last step is to take the rectangle area and subtract the triangle area. The area of the shaded region is:

$$A = 12 - 3 = 9m^2$$

30. 43.96 in^3: The volume for a cylinder is found by using the formula:

$$V = \pi r^2 h = \pi(2 \text{ in})^2 \times 3.5 \text{ in} = 43.96 \text{ in}^3$$

31. C: There are 0.006 kiloliters in 6 liters because 1 liter is 0.001 kiloliters. The conversion comes from the metric prefix -kilo which has a value of 1000. Thus, 1 kiloliter is 1000 liters, and 1 liter is 0.001 kiloliters.

32. E: The conversion between feet and centimeters requires a middle term. As there are 2.54 centimeters in 1 inch, the conversion between inches and feet must be found. As there are 12 inches in a foot, the fractions can be set up as follows:

$$3 \text{ ft} \times \frac{12 \text{ in}}{1 \text{ ft}} \times \frac{2.54 \text{ cm}}{1 \text{ in}}$$

The feet and inches cancel out to leave only centimeters for the answer. The numbers are calculated across the top and bottom to yield:

$$\frac{3 \times 12 \times 2.54}{1 \times 1} = 91.44$$

The number and units used together form the answer of 91.44 cm.

33. B: The only relation in which every *x*-value corresponds to exactly one *y*-value is the relation given in *B*, making it a function. The other relations have the same first component paired up to different second components, which goes against the definition of functions.

34. A: To find a function value, plug in the number given for the variable and evaluate the expression, using the order of operations (parentheses, exponents, multiplication, division, addition, subtraction). The function given is a polynomial function:

$$f(5) = 5^2 - 2 \times 5 + 1$$

$$f(5) = 25 - 10 + 1 = 16$$

35. E: The function given is a polynomial function. Anything can be plugged into a polynomial function to get an output. Therefore, its domain is all real numbers, which is expressed in interval notation as $(-\infty, \infty)$.

36. B: The variable *x* represents the number of years after 1980. The year 2011 was 31 years after 1980, so plug 31 into the function to obtain:

$$f(31) = 3.1 \times 31 + 240 = 336.1$$

This value rounds to 336 and represents 336 million people.

37. D: The argument of a logarithmic function has to be greater than or equal to zero. Basically, one cannot take the logarithm of a negative number or 0. Therefore, to find the domain, set the argument greater than 0 and solve the inequality. This results in $x - 2 > 0$, or $x > 2$. Therefore, in order to obtain an output of the function, the number plugged into the function must be greater than 2. This domain is represented as $(2, \infty)$.

38. B: The time of the initial outbreak corresponds to $t = 0$. Therefore, 0 must be plugged into the function. This results in:

$$\frac{20,000}{1 + 10e^0} = \frac{20,000}{1 + 10} = \frac{20,000}{11} = 1,818.182$$

which rounds to 1,818. Therefore, there were 1,818 people in the population that initially had the disease.

39. E: This is a parabola that opens up, as the coefficient on the x^2 term is positive. The smallest number in its range occurs when plugging 0 into the function $f(0) = 5$. Any other output is a number larger than 5, even when a positive number is plugged in. When a negative number gets plugged into the function, the output is positive, and same with a positive number. Therefore, the domain is written as $[5, \infty)$ in interval notation.

40. 22 meters: The perimeter is found by adding the length of all the exterior sides. When the given dimensions are added, the perimeter is 22 meters. The equation to find the perimeter can be:

$$P = 5 + 1.5 + 1.2 + 4.5 + 3.8 + 6 = 22$$

The last two dimensions can be found by subtracting 1.2 from 5, and adding 1.5 and 4.5, respectively.

41. A: The surface area for a cylinder is the sum of the two circle bases and the rectangle formed on the side. This is easily seen in the net of a cylinder.

The Net of a Cylinder

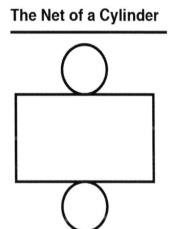

The area of a circle is found by multiplying pi times the radius squared. The rectangle's area is found by multiplying the circumference of the circle by the height. The equation:

$$SA = 2\pi \times 5 \times 10 + 2(\pi 5^2)$$

shows the area of the rectangle as $2\pi \times 5 \times 10$, which yields 314. The area of the bases is found by $\pi 5^2$, which yields 78.5, and then is multiplied by 2 for the two bases. Adding these together gives 471.

42. C: A hexagon can be formed by any combination of the given shapes except for two rectangles. There are no two rectangles that can make up a hexagon.

43. A and C: First set the functions equal to one another, resulting in:

$$x^2 + 3x + 2 = 4x + 4$$

This is a quadratic equation, so the best way to find the answer is to convert it to standard form by subtracting $4x + 4$ from both sides of the equation, setting it equal to 0:

$$x^2 - x - 2 = 0$$

Then, factor the equation:

$$(x - 2)(x + 1) = 0$$

Setting both factors equal to zero results in $x = 2$ and $x = -1$.

44. E: There will be no more coyotes when the population is 0, so set *y* equal to 0 and solve the quadratic equation:

$$0 = -(x - 2)^2 + 1600$$

Subtract 1600 from both sides, and divide through by -1. This results in:

$$1600 = (x - 2)^2$$

Then, take the square root of both sides. This process results in the following equation:

$$\pm 40 = x - 2$$

Adding 2 to both sides results in two solutions: $x = 42$ and $x = -38$.

Because the problem involves years after 2000, the only solution that makes sense is 42. Add 42 to 2000, so therefore in 2042 there will be no more coyotes.

45. A: The range value is given, and this is the output of the function. Therefore, the function must be set equal to $\frac{1}{8}$ and solved for x. Thus, $\frac{1}{8} = \frac{1}{4}x - 2$ needs to be solved. The fractions can be cleared by multiplying times the LCD 8. This results in:

$$1 = 2x - 16$$

Add 16 to both sides and divide by 2 to obtain $x = \frac{17}{2}$.

46. B: The ball is back at the starting point when the function is equal to 800 feet. Therefore, this results in solving the equation:
$$800 = -32t^2 + 90t + 800$$

Subtract 800 off of both sides and factor the remaining terms to obtain:

$$0 = 2t(-16t + 45)$$

Setting both factors equal to 0 results in $t = 0$, which is when the ball was thrown up initially, and:

$$t = \frac{45}{16} = 2.8 \text{ seconds}$$

Therefore, it will take the ball 2.8 seconds to come back down to its starting point.

47. A, D, and E: To find the zeros, set the function equal to 0 and factor the polynomial. Because there are four terms, it should be factored by grouping. Factor a common factor out of the first set of two terms, and then find a shared binomial factor in the second set of two terms. This results in:

$$x^2(x - 2) - 9(x - 2) = 0$$

The binomial can then be factored out of each set to get:

$$(x^2 - 9)(x - 2) = 0$$

This can be factored further as:

$$(x + 3)(x - 3)(x - 2) = 0$$

Setting each factor equal to zero and solving results in the three zeros -3, 3, and 2.

48. B: Given a rational function, the expression in the denominator can never be equal to 0. To find the domain, set the denominator equal to 0 and solve for x. This results in $2 - x = 0$, and its solution is $x = 2$. This value needs to be excluded from the set of all real numbers, and therefore the domain written in interval notation is $(-\infty, 2) \cup (2, \infty)$.

49. C: Plugging the function into the formula results in:

$$\frac{4(x + h) - 2 - (4x - 2)}{h}$$

Then, this is simplified to:

$$\frac{4x + 4h - 2 - 4x + 2}{h} = \frac{4h}{h} = 4$$

This value is also equal to the derivative of the given function. The derivative of a linear function is its slope.

50. A: Surface area is a type of area, which means it is measured in square units. Cubic units are used to describe volume, which has three dimensions multiplied by one another. Quartic units describe measurements multiplied in four dimensions.

51. C: By switching from a radical expression to rational exponents:

$$\sqrt[4]{x^6} = x^{\frac{6}{4}} = x^{\frac{3}{2}}$$

Also, properties of exponents can be used to simplify $\frac{x}{x^3}$ into:

$$x^{1-3} = x^{-2} = \frac{1}{x^2}$$

The other terms can be left alone, resulting in an equivalent expression:

$$x^{\frac{3}{2}} - \frac{1}{x^2} + x - 2$$

52. 3: Using Descartes' Rule of Signs, count the number of sign changes in coefficients in the polynomial. This results in the number of possible positive zeros. The coefficients are 1, -3, 2, 1, and -3, so the sign changes from 1 to -3, -3 to 2, and 1 to -3, a total of 3 times. Therefore, there are at most 3 positive zeros.

53. A: The first step is to simplify the expression. The second term, $16^{\frac{1}{2}}$, can be rewritten as $\sqrt{16}$, since fractional exponents represent roots. This can then be simplified to 4, because 16 is the perfect square of

4. The first term can be evaluated using the power rule for exponents: an exponent to a second exponent is multiplied by that second exponent. The first term can thus be rewritten as:

$$16^{\frac{1}{4}} = \left(16^{\frac{1}{2}}\right)^{\frac{1}{2}} = 4^{\frac{1}{2}} = 2$$

Combining these terms, the expression is evaluated as follows:

$$16^{\frac{1}{4}} \times 16^{\frac{1}{2}} = 2 \times 4 = 8$$

54. B: The goal is to first isolate the variable. The fractions can easily be cleared by multiplying the entire inequality by 5, resulting in $35 - 4x < 3$. Then, subtract 35 from both sides and divide by -4. This results in $x > 8$. Notice the inequality symbol has been flipped because both sides were divided by a negative number. The solution set, all real numbers greater than 8, is written in interval notation as $(8, \infty)$. A parenthesis shows that 8 is not included in the solution set.

55. E: This system can be solved using the method of substitution. Solving the first equation for y results in:

$$y = 14 - 2x$$

Plugging this into the second equation gives:

$$4x + 2(14 - 2x) = -28$$

which simplifies to $28 = -28$, an untrue statement. Therefore, this system has no solution because no x value will satisfy the system.

56. 2.5: Let x be the unknown number. The difference indicates subtraction, and sum represents addition. To triple the difference, it is multiplied by 3. The problem can be expressed as the following equation:

$$3(5 - x) = x + 5$$

Distributing the 3 results in:

$$15 - 3x = x + 5$$

Subtract 5 from both sides, add $3x$ to both sides, and then divide both sides by 4. This results in:

$$\frac{10}{4} = \frac{5}{2} = 2.5$$

57. B: The slopes of perpendicular lines are negative reciprocals, meaning their product is equal to -1. The slope of the line given needs to be found. Its equivalent form in slope-intercept form is $y = -\frac{4}{7}x + \frac{23}{7}$, so its slope is $-\frac{4}{7}$. The negative reciprocal of this number is $\frac{7}{4}$. The only line in the options given with this same slope is:

$$y = \frac{7}{4}x - 12$$

58. B: This system can be solved using substitution. Plug the second equation in for y in the first equation to obtain $2x - 8x = 6$, which simplifies to $-6x = 6$. Divide both sides by 6 to get $x = -1$, which is then substituted back into either original equation to obtain $y = -8$.

59. B: The outlier is 35. When a small outlier is removed from a data set, the mean and the median increase. The first step in this process is to identify the outlier, which is the number that lies away from the given set. Once the outlier is identified, the mean and median can be recalculated. The mean will be affected because it averages all of the numbers. The median will be affected because it finds the middle number, which is subject to change because a number is lost. The mode will most likely not change because it is the number that occurs the most, which will not be the outlier if there is only one outlier.

60. A: Division can be used to solve this problem. The division necessary is:

$$\frac{5.972 \times 10^{24}}{7.348 \times 10^{22}}$$

To compute this division, divide the constants first then use algebraic laws of exponents to divide the exponential expression.

This results in about 0.8127×10^2, which, written in scientific notation, is: 8.127×10^1.

61. C: First, the slope of the line must be found. This is equal to the change in y over the change in x, given the two points. Therefore, the slope is -6. The slope and one of the points are then plugged into the point-slope form of a line:

$$y - y_1 = m(x - x_1)$$

This results in:

$$y - 7 = -6(x + 3)$$

The -6 is simplified and the equation is solved for y to obtain:

$$y = -6x - 11$$

62. A: The formula for the rate of change is the same as slope: change in y over change in x. The y-value in this case is percentage of smokers and the x-value is year. The change in percentage of smokers from 2000 to 2015 was 8.1 percent. The change in x was 2000-2015 = -15. Therefore:

$$8.1\%/{-15} = -0.54\%$$

The percentage of smokers decreased 0.54 percent each year.

63. A: The probability of 0.9 is closer to 1 than any of the other answers. The closer a probability is to 1, the greater the likelihood that the event will occur. The probability of 0.05 shows that it is very unlikely that an adult driver will wear their seatbelt because it is close to zero. A zero probability means that it will not occur. The probability of 0.25 is closer to zero than to one, so it shows that it is unlikely an adult will wear their seatbelt. Choice *E* is wrong because probability must fall between 0 and 1.

64. A: A proportion should be used to solve this problem. The ratio of tagged to total deer in each instance is set equal, and the unknown quantity is a variable x. The proportion is:

$$\frac{300}{x} = \frac{5}{400}$$

Cross-multiplying gives $120,000 = 5x$, and dividing through by 5 results in 24,000.

65. A: A vertical line has the same x value for any point on the line. Other points on the line would be (1, 3), (1, 5), (1, 9), etc. Mathematically, this is written as $x = 1$. A vertical line is always of the form $x = a$ for some constant a.

66. 10: The Pythagorean Theorem can be used to find the missing length x because it is a right triangle. The theorem states that $6^2 + 8^2 = x^2$, which simplifies into $100 = x^2$. Taking the positive square root of both sides results in the missing value $x = 10$.

67. E: First, the common factor 2 can be factored out of both terms, resulting in:

$$2(y^3 - 64)$$

The resulting binomial is a difference of cubes that can be factored using the rule:

$$a^3 - b^3 = (a - b)(a^2 + ab + b^2)$$

$a = y$ and $b = 4$. Therefore, the result is:

$$2(y - 4)(y^2 + 4y + 16)$$

68. D: The exponential rules $(ab)^m = a^m b^m$ and $(a^m)^n = a^{mn}$ can be used to rewrite the expression as:

$$4^4 y^{12} \times 3^2 y^{14}$$

The coefficients are multiplied together and the exponential rule $a^m a^n = a^{m+n}$ is then used to obtain the simplified form $2304 y^{26}$.

69. B: Look on the horizontal axis to find 3:00 p.m. Move up from 3:00 p.m. to reach the dot on the graph. Move horizontally to the left to the horizontal axis to between 20 and 25; the best answer choice is 22. The answer of 25 is too high above the projected time on the graph, and the answers of 20, 16, and 18 degrees are too low.

70. B: The number of representatives varies directly with the population, so the equation necessary is $N = k \times P$, where N is number of representatives, k is the variation constant, and P is total population in millions. Plugging in the information for New York allows k to be solved for. This process gives $27 = k \times 19.8$, so $k = 1.36$. Therefore, the formula for number of representatives given total population in millions is $N = 1.36 \times P$. Plugging in $P = 11.8$ for Ohio results in $N = 16.05$, which rounds to 16 total representatives.

71. B: This is a statistical question because to determine this answer one would need to collect data from each person in the class and it is expected the answers would vary. The other answers do not require data to be collected from multiple sources, therefore the answers will not vary.

72. 25: The mean is found by adding all the times together and dividing by the number of times recorded.

$$25 + 18 + 23 + 28 + 30 + 22.5 + 23 + 33 + 20 = 222.5$$

$$\frac{222.5}{9} = 24.722$$

Rounding to the nearest minute, the mean is 25 minutes.

73. 23: The mode is the time from the data set that occurs most often. The number 23 occurs twice in the data set, while all others occur only once, so the mode is 23.

74. 23: To find the median of a data set, you must first list the numbers from smallest to largest, and then find the number in the middle. If there are two numbers in the middle, add the two numbers in the middle together and divide by 2. Putting this list in order from smallest to greatest yields 18, 20, 22.5, 23, 23, 25, 28, 30, and 33, where 23 is the middle number.

75. 36 cm²: The area for a rectangle is found by multiplying the length by the width. The area is also measured in square units.

76. 144 cm³: The volume of a rectangular prism is found by multiplying the length by the width by the height. This formula yields an answer of 144 cubic units. The answer must be in cubic units because volume involves all three dimensions.

Reading

Key Ideas and Details

Explicitly Stated Information vs. Implications

In the Reading Test of the Praxis Core Exam, test takers will be asked questions based on their direct knowledge of the passage. The information explicitly stated in the passage leaves the reader no room for confusion. Information is explicitly stated in the passage can be identified and used as text evidence. Additionally, test takers should consider if the information is an author's opinion or an objective fact, and whether the information contains bias or stereotypes. Also important to consider is the following question: Within the information stated, which words are directly stated and what words leave room for a connotative interpretation? Being cautious of the author's presentation of information will aid the test taker in determining the correct answer choice for the question stem.

Biases
Biases usually occur when someone allows their personal preferences or ideologies to interfere with what should be an objective decision. In personal situations, someone is biased towards someone if they favor them in an unfair way. In academic writing, being biased in your sources means leaving out objective information that would turn the argument one way or the other. The evidence of bias in academic writing makes the text less credible, so be sure to present all viewpoints when writing, not just your own, so to avoid coming off as biased. Being objective when presenting information or dealing with people usually allows the author to gain more credibility.

Stereotypes
Stereotypes are preconceived notions that place a particular rule or characteristics on an entire group of people. Stereotypes are usually offensive to the group they refer to or allies of that group and often have negative connotations. The reinforcement of stereotypes isn't always obvious. Sometimes stereotypes can be very subtle and are still widely used in order for people to understand categories within the world. For example, saying that women are more intuitive or nurturing than men is a stereotype, although this is still an assumption used by many in order to understand differences between one another.

Drawing Inferences and Implications from a Text

One technique authors often use to make their fictional stories more interesting is not giving away too much information easily; instead, they sprinkle in hints and descriptions. It is then up to the reader to draw a conclusion about the author's meaning by connecting textual clues with the reader's own pre-existing experiences and knowledge. Drawing conclusions is important as a reading strategy for understanding what is occurring in a text. Rather than directly stating who, what, where, when, or why, authors often describe story elements. Then, readers must draw conclusions to understand significant story components. As they go through a text, readers can think about the setting, characters, plot, problem, and solution; whether the author provided any clues for consideration; and combine any story clues with their existing knowledge and experiences to draw conclusions about what occurs in the text.

Making Predictions
Before and during reading, readers can apply the reading strategy of making predictions about what they think may happen next. For example, what plot and character developments will occur in fiction? What points will the author discuss in nonfiction? Making predictions about portions of text they have not yet

read prepares readers mentally for reading, and also gives them a purpose for reading. To inform and make predictions about text, the reader can do the following:

Consider the title of the text and what it implies
Look at the cover of the book
Look at any illustrations or diagrams for additional visual information
Analyze the structure of the text
Apply outside experience and knowledge to the text

Readers may adjust their predictions as they read. Reader predictions may or may not come true in the text but as readers become more experienced as consumers of different texts, their ability to make accurate predictions will likely improve.

Making Inferences

Authors describe settings, characters, characters' emotions, and events. Readers must infer to understand a text fully. Inferring enables readers to figure out meanings of unfamiliar words, make predictions about upcoming text, draw conclusions, and reflect on reading. Readers can infer about text before, during, and after reading. In everyday life, we use sensory information to infer. Readers can do the same with text. When authors do not answer all readers' questions, readers must infer by saying "I think . . . This could be . . . This is because . . . Maybe . . . This means . . . I guess . . ." etc. Looking at illustrations, considering characters' behaviors, and asking questions during reading facilitate inference. Taking clues from text and connecting text to prior knowledge help to draw conclusions. Readers can infer word meanings, settings, reasons for occurrences, character emotions, pronoun referents, author messages, and answers to questions unstated in text. To practice making inferences, students can read sentences written/selected by the instructor, discuss the setting and character, draw conclusions, and make predictions.

Making inferences and drawing conclusions involve skills that are quite similar: both require readers to fill in information the author has omitted. Authors may omit information as a technique for inducing readers to discover the outcomes themselves; or they may consider certain information unimportant; or they may assume their reading audience already knows certain information. To make an inference or draw a conclusion about text, readers should observe all facts and arguments the author has presented and consider what they already know from their own personal experiences. Reading students taking multiple-choice tests that refer to text passages can determine correct and incorrect choices based on the information in the passage. For example, from a text passage describing an individual's signs of anxiety while unloading groceries and nervously clutching their wallet at a grocery store checkout, readers can infer or conclude that the individual may not have enough money to pay for everything.

Determining Central Ideas or Themes of a Text

Themes are underlying meanings in literature. For example, if a story's main idea is a character succeeding against all odds, the theme is overcoming obstacles. If a story's main idea is one character wanting what another character has, the theme is jealousy. If a story's main idea is a character doing something they were afraid to do, the theme is courage. Themes differ from topics in that a **topic** is a subject matter; a theme is the author's opinion about it. For example, a work could have a topic of war and a theme that war is a curse. Authors present themes through characters' feelings, thoughts, experiences, dialogue, plot actions, and events. Themes function as "glue" holding other essential story elements together. They offer readers insights into characters' experiences, the author's philosophy, and how the world works.

Summaries of Main Points and Supporting Details

An important skill is the ability to read a complex text and then reduce its length and complexity by focusing on the key events and details. A **summary** is a shortened version of the original text, written by the reader in their own words. The summary should be shorter than the original text, and it must include the most critical points.

In order to effectively summarize a complex text, it's necessary to understand the original source and identify the major points covered. It may be helpful to outline the original text to get the big picture and avoid getting bogged down in the minor details. For example, a summary wouldn't include a statistic from the original source unless it was the major focus of the text. It is also important for readers to use their own words but still retain the original meaning of the passage. The key to a good summary is emphasizing the main idea without changing the focus of the original information.

Complex texts will likely be more difficult to summarize. Readers must evaluate all points from the original source, filter out the unnecessary details, and maintain only the essential ideas. The summary often mirrors the original text's organizational structure. For example, in a problem-solution text structure, the author typically presents readers with a problem and then develops solutions through the course of the text. An effective summary would likely retain this general structure, rephrasing the problem and then reporting the most useful or plausible solutions.

Paraphrasing is somewhat similar to summarizing. It calls for the reader to take a small part of the passage and list or describe its main points. Paraphrasing is more than rewording the original passage, though. Like a summary, it should be written in the reader's own words, while still retaining the meaning of the original source. The main difference between summarizing and paraphrasing is that a summary would be appropriate for a much larger text, while a paraphrase might focus on just a few lines of text. Effective paraphrasing will indicate an understanding of the original source, yet still help the readers expand on their interpretation. A paraphrase should neither add new information nor remove essential facts that change the meaning of the source.

Identifying the Topic, Main Idea, and Supporting Details

The **topic** of a text is the general subject matter. Text topics can usually be expressed in one word, or a few words at most. Additionally, readers should ask themselves what point the author is trying to make. This point is the **main idea** of the text—the one thing the author wants readers to know about the topic. Once the author has established the main idea, he or she will support the main idea with supporting details. **Supporting details** are evidence that support the main idea and include personal testimonies, examples, or statistics.

One analogy for these components and their relationships is that a text is like a well-designed house. The topic is the roof, covering all rooms. The main idea is the frame. The supporting details are the various rooms. To identify the topic of a text, readers can ask themselves what or who the author is writing about in the paragraph. To locate the main idea, readers can ask themselves what one idea the author wants readers to know about the topic. To identify supporting details, readers can put the main idea into question form and ask, "what does the author use to prove or explain their main idea?"

Let's look at an example. An author is writing an essay about the Amazon rainforest and trying to convince the audience that more funding should go into protecting the area from deforestation. The author makes the argument stronger by including evidence of the benefits of the rainforest: it provides habitats to a variety of species, it provides much of the earth's oxygen which in turn cleans the atmosphere, and it is the home to medicinal plants that are useful against some of the world's deadliest diseases. Here is an outline of the essay looking at topic, main idea, and supporting details:

Topic: Amazon rainforest
Main Idea: The Amazon rainforest should receive more funding to protect it from deforestation.
Supporting Details:
1. It provides habitats to a variety of species
2. It provides much of the earth's oxygen which in turn cleans the atmosphere
3. It is home to medicinal plants that are useful against some of the deadliest diseases.

Notice that the topic of the essay is listed in a few key words: "Amazon rainforest." The main idea tells us what about the topic is important: that the topic should be funded to prevent deforestation. Finally, the supporting details are what author relies on to convince the audience to act or to believe in the truth of the main idea.

Determining How Ideas or Details Inform the Author's Argument

When authors want to strengthen the support for an argument, evidence-based data in the form of statistics or concrete examples can be used. Statistics and examples are often accompanied by detailed explanations to help increase the audience's understanding and shape their ideas. Expert opinions are another way to strengthen an argument. But all this effort toward supporting a given argument does not necessarily make the argument absolute. After all, the word "argument" implies that there is more than one way to think about the subject. Arguments are meant to be challenged, questioned, and analyzed.

Authors will generally use one of two argument models: deductive or inductive. **Deductive arguments** require two general statements to support the argument. **Inductive arguments** employ specific data, examples, or facts to support the argument.

Deductive	Inductive
All fruits contain seeds. Tomatoes contain seeds. Therefore, tomatoes are fruits.	9 out of 10 dentists prefer soft-bristled toothbrushes. Therefore, soft-bristled toothbrushes are the best type of toothbrush for optimal dental health.

No matter what evidence is presented, readers should still challenge the argument. In any text, readers are encouraged to ask specific questions to evaluate the overall validity of the argument. Some important points to consider include:

Has the author employed logic in the argument?

Is the argument clearly explained?

Is the argument sufficiently supported?

Who conducted the research, and for what purpose?

Is the supporting data qualitative, quantitative, or a mixture of both?

Is the presented data representative of the typical cross-section of society or of the phenomenon being discussed?

Does the author present any bias?

Has the author overlooked anything that should be explored to form a well-rounded argument?

Although informational writing should be written objectively, such writing still constitutes the author's particular point of view or belief about a given subject. The author's main idea will likely be backed up with reasons, evidence, and supporting details, but it is important for the audience to question the main idea and evaluate the presented evidence. Although the author's ideas and shared details drive the overall argument, readers should feel compelled to explore the topic further, assess the evidence, and determine whether they agree with the overall message. Authors present the argument in order to convince their readers, but readers must strive to evaluate and assess the information to arrive at an informed opinion of the subject matter.

Craft, Structure, and Language Skills

Understanding the Effect of Word Choice

Denotation refers to a word's explicit definition, like that found in the dictionary. Denotation is often compared to connotation. **Connotation** is the emotional, cultural, social, or personal implication associated with a word. Denotation is more of an objective definition, whereas connotation can be more subjective, although many connotative meanings of words are similar for certain cultures. The denotative meanings of words are usually based on facts, and the connotative meanings of words are usually based on emotion. Here are some examples of words and their denotative and connotative meanings in Western culture:

Word	Denotative Meaning	Connotative Meaning
Home	A permanent place where one lives, usually as a member of a family.	A place of warmth; a place of familiarity; comforting; a place of safety and security. "Home" usually has a positive connotation.
Snake	A long reptile with no limbs and strong jaws that moves along the ground; some snakes have a poisonous bite.	An evil omen; a slithery creature (human or nonhuman) that is deceitful or unwelcome. "Snake" usually has a negative connotation.
Winter	A season of the year that is the coldest, usually from December to February in the northern hemisphere and from June to August in the southern hemisphere.	Circle of life, especially that of death and dying; cold or icy; dark and gloomy; hibernation, sleep, or rest. "Winter" can have a negative connotation, although many who have access to heat may enjoy the snowy season from their homes.

How an Author's Word Choice Conveys Attitude and Shapes Meaning, Style, and Tone

Words can be very powerful. When written words are used with the intent to make an argument or support a position, the words used—and the way in which they are arranged—can have a dramatic effect on the readers. Clichés, colloquialisms, run-on sentences, and misused words are all examples of ways that word choice can negatively affect writing quality. Unless the writer carefully considers word choice, a written work stands to lose credibility.

If a writer's overall intent is to provide a clear meaning on a subject, he or she must consider not only the exact words to use, but also their placement, repetition, and suitability. Academic writing should be intentional and clear, and it should be devoid of awkward or vague descriptions that can easily lead to misunderstandings. When readers find themselves reading and rereading just to gain a clear understanding of the writer's intent, there may be an issue with word choice. Although the words used in academic writing are different from those used in a casual conversation, they shouldn't necessarily be overly academic either. It may be relevant to employ key words that are associated with the subject, but struggling to inject these words into a paper just to sound academic may defeat the purpose. If the message cannot be clearly understood the first time, word choice may be the culprit.

Word choice also conveys the author's attitude and sets a tone. Although each word in a sentence carries a specific denotation, it might also carry positive or negative connotations—and it is the connotations that set the tone and convey the author's attitude. Consider the following similar sentences:

It was the same old routine that happens every Saturday morning—eat, exercise, chores.

The Saturday morning routine went off without a hitch—eat, exercise, chores.

The first sentence carries a negative connotation with the author's "same old routine" word choice. The feelings and attitudes associated with this phrase suggest that the author is bored or annoyed at the Saturday morning routine. Although the second sentence carries the same topic—explaining the Saturday morning routine—the choice to use the expression "without a hitch" conveys a positive or cheery attitude.

An author's writing style can likewise be greatly affected by word choice. When writing for an academic audience, for example, it is necessary for the author to consider how to convey the message by carefully considering word choice. If the author interchanges between third-person formal writing and second-person informal writing, the author's writing quality and credibility are at risk. Formal writing involves complex sentences, an objective viewpoint, and the use of full words as opposed to the use of a subjective viewpoint, contractions, and first- or second-person usage commonly found in informal writing.

Content validity, the author's ability to support the argument, and the audience's ability to comprehend the written work are all affected by the author's word choice.

An Author's Tone, Message, and Effect

Tone conveys the author's attitude toward the topic and the audience. The tone also reveals their level of confidence on the subject, and whether they intend to bring humor, emotion, or seriousness to the writing. Setting the tone ultimately determines how readers will receive the overall message.

In professional writing, it is imperative that authors maintain an appropriate and professional tone that strengthens the writing quality. Framing the writing ahead of time, determining the purpose of the paper, and even considering the author's own bias on the subject will help to set the appropriate tone. Why is the paper being written? What message does the author want to convey, and to whom? Why would the intended audience find this paper interesting, and how does the author expect the audience to react?

These are just some of the questions that can help to frame a piece of writing and develop an appropriate tone. To help develop the tone before writing, it sometimes helps to consider the intended audience's perspective.

When an author wishes to convey a clear message but does not want to compromise credibility by writing subjectively, using emphasis can be very effective. This is done by introducing and stressing the important points of the subject in the opening sentence or at the beginning of specific paragraphs. Consider the following:

> Music soothes the soul and captures our hearts. The following is a study on how music has affected North American society during the past five decades.

> The following is a study on how music has affected North American society during the past five decades. Music soothes the soul and captures our hearts.

Clearly, the author's attitude toward music is captured in the first sentence of the first example. When the sentences are rearranged in the second example, however, the emphasis is lost. With the subtle positioning of key words and phrases, an author can emphasize important points of the paper and set the tone.

Written tone can either capture readers' attention or turn them away. Considering the intended audience and how readers will perceive the message helps to develop the appropriate tone. In academic or professional writing, writers tend to employ a more serious tone, but serious does not mean dull or boring. Academic writing can engage readers by setting a tone that, although serious, also reveals a connection to readers. Authors who wish to connect with their audience on a more personal level might introduce their topic with a surprising or entertaining fact, or quote a famous individual who reinforces the paper's topic.

Analyzing the Structure of a Text

Text structure is the way in which the author organizes and presents textual information so readers can follow and comprehend it. One kind of text structure is sequence. This means the author arranges the text in a logical order from beginning to middle to end. There are three types of sequences:

Chronological: ordering events in time from earliest to latest

Spatial: describing objects, people, or spaces according to their relationships to one another in space

Order of Importance: addressing topics, characters, or ideas according to how important they are, from either least important to most important

Chronological sequence is the most common sequential text structure. Readers can identify sequential structure by looking for words that signal it, like *first, earlier, meanwhile, next, then, later, finally;* and specific times and dates the author includes as chronological references.

Transitional Words and Phrases

In writing, some sentences naturally lead to others, whereas in other cases, a new sentence expresses a new idea. Transitional phrases connect sentences and the ideas they convey, which makes the writing coherent. Transitional language also guides the reader from one thought to the next. For example, when pointing out an objection to the previous idea, starting a sentence with "However," "But," or "On the other hand" is transitional. When adding another idea or detail, writers use "Also," "In addition," "Furthermore,"

"Further," "Moreover," "Not only," etc. Readers have difficulty perceiving connections between ideas without such transitional wording.

The Organization and Structure of a Text

Problem-Solution Text Structure

Comparison identifies similarities between two or more things. **Contrast** identifies differences between two or more things. Authors typically employ both to illustrate relationships between things by highlighting their commonalities and deviations. For example, a writer might compare Windows and Linux as operating systems, and contrast Linux as free and open-source vs. Windows as proprietary. When writing an essay, sometimes it is useful to create an image of the two objects or events you are comparing or contrasting. Venn diagrams are useful because they show the differences as well as the similarities between two things. Once you've seen the similarities and differences on paper, it might be helpful to create an outline of the essay with both comparison and contrast. Every outline will look different because every two or more things will have a different number of comparisons and contrasts. Say you are trying to compare and contrast carrots with sweet potatoes.

Here is an example of a compare/contrast outline using those topics:

Introduction: Share why you are comparing and contrasting the foods. Give the thesis statement.
Body paragraph 1: Sweet potatoes and carrots are both root vegetables (similarity)
Body paragraph 2: Sweet potatoes and carrots are both orange (similarity)
Body paragraph 3: Sweet potatoes and carrots have different nutritional components (difference)
Conclusion: Restate the purpose of your comparison/contrast essay.

Of course, if there is only one similarity between your topics and two differences, you will want to rearrange your outline. Always tailor your essay to what works best with your topic.

Descriptive Text Structure

Description can be both a type of text structure and a type of text. Some texts are descriptive throughout entire books. For example, a book may describe the geography of a certain country, state, or region, or tell readers all about dolphins by describing many of their characteristics. Many other texts are not descriptive throughout but use descriptive passages within the overall text. The following are a few examples of descriptive text:

When the author describes a character in a novel
When the author sets the scene for an event by describing the setting
When a biographer describes the personality and behaviors of a real-life individual
When a historian describes the details of a particular battle within a book about a specific war
When a travel writer describes the climate, people, foods, and/or customs of a certain place

A hallmark of description is using sensory details, painting a vivid picture so readers can imagine it almost as if they were experiencing it personally.

Cause and Effect Text Structure

When using cause and effect to extrapolate meaning from text, readers must determine the cause when the author only communicates effects. For example, if a description of a child eating an ice cream cone includes details like beads of sweat forming on the child's face and the ice cream dripping down her hand faster than she can lick it off, the reader can infer or conclude it must be hot outside. A useful technique for making such decisions is wording them in "If...then" form, e.g. "If the child is perspiring and the ice cream melting, it may be a hot day." Cause and effect text structures explain why certain events or actions resulted in particular outcomes. For example, an author might describe America's historical large flocks of dodo birds, the fact that gunshots did not startle/frighten dodos, and that because dodos did not flee, settlers killed whole flocks in one hunting session, explaining how the dodo was hunted into extinction.

Recognizing Events in a Sequence

Sequence structure is the order of events in which a story or information is presented to the audience. Sometimes the text will be presented in chronological order, or sometimes it will be presented by displaying the most recent information first, then moving backwards in time. The sequence structure depends on the author, the context, and the audience. The structure of a text also depends on the genre in which the text is written. Is it literary fiction? Is it a magazine article? Is it instructions for how to complete a certain task? Different genres will have different purposes for switching up the sequence.

Narrative Structure

The structure presented in literary fiction, called **narrative structure**, is the foundation on which the text moves. The narrative structure comes from the plot and setting. The **plot** is the sequence of events in the narrative that move the text forward through cause and effect. The setting is the place or time period in which the story takes place. Narrative structure has two main categories: linear and nonlinear.

A narrative is linear when it is told in chronological order. Traditional linear narratives will follow the plot diagram below depicting the narrative arc. The narrative arc consists of the exposition, conflict, rising action, climax, falling action, and resolution.

- Exposition: The exposition is in the beginning of a narrative and introduces the characters, setting, and background information of the story. The exposition provides the context for the upcoming narrative. Exposition literally means "a showing forth" in Latin.

- Conflict: In a traditional narrative, the conflict appears toward the beginning of the story after the audience becomes familiar with the characters and setting. The conflict is a single instance between characters, nature, or the self, in which the central character is forced to make a decision or move forward with some kind of action. The conflict presents something for the main character, or protagonist, to overcome.

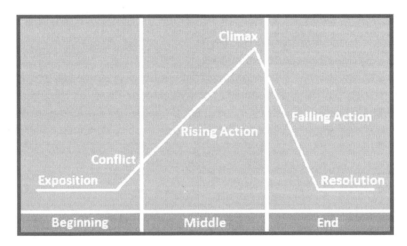

- Rising Action: The rising action is the part of the story that leads into the climax. The rising action will develop the characters and plot while creating tension and suspense that eventually lead to the climax.

- Climax: The climax is the part of the story where the tension produced in the rising action culminates. The climax is the peak of the story. In a traditional structure, everything before the climax builds up to it, and everything after the climax falls from it. It is the height of the narrative and is usually either the most exciting part of the story, or is marked by some turning point in the character's journey.

- Falling Action: The falling action happens as a result of the climax. Characters continue to develop, although there is a wrapping up of loose ends here. The falling action leads to the resolution.

- Resolution: The resolution is where the story comes to an end and usually leaves the reader with the satisfaction of knowing what happened within the story and why. However, stories do not always end in this fashion. Sometimes readers can be confused or frustrated at the end from the lack of information or the absence of a happy ending.

A **nonlinear narrative** deviates from the traditional narrative because it does not always follow the traditional plot structure of the narrative arc. Nonlinear narratives may include structures that are disjointed, circular, or disruptive, in the sense that they do not follow chronological order. **In medias res** is an example of a nonlinear structure. *In medias res* is Latin for "in the middle of things," which is how many ancient texts, especially epic poems, began their story, such as Homer's *Iliad*. Instead of having a clear exposition with a full development of characters, they would begin right in the middle of the action.

Many modernist texts in the late nineteenth and early twentieth centuries experimented with disjointed narratives, moving away from traditional linear narrative. Disjointed narratives are depicted in novels like *Catch 22*, where the author, Joseph Heller, structures the narrative based on free association of ideas rather than chronology. Another nonlinear narrative can be seen in the novel *Wuthering Heights*, written by Emily Brontë; after the first chapter, the narrative progresses retrospectively instead of chronologically. It seems that there are two narratives in *Wuthering Heights* working at the same time: a present narrative as well as a past narrative. Authors employ disrupting narratives for various reasons; some use it to create situational irony for the readers, while some use it to create a certain effect, such as excitement, discomfort, or fear.

How the Position and Purpose Shape the Text

Evaluating the Author's Purpose in a Given Text

Authors may have many purposes for writing a specific text. They could be imparting information, entertaining their audience, expressing their own feelings, or trying to persuade their readers of a particular position. Authors' purposes are their reasons for writing something. A single author may have one overriding purpose for writing or multiple reasons. An author may explicitly state his or her intention in the text, or the reader may need to infer that intention. When readers can identify the author's purpose, they are better able to analyze information in the text. By knowing why the author wrote the text, readers can glean ideas for how to approach it.

The following is a list of questions readers can ask in order to discern an author's purpose for writing a text:

Does the title of the text give you any clues about its purpose?
Was the purpose of the text to give information to readers?
Did the author want to describe an event, issue, or individual?
Was it written to express emotions and thoughts?

Did the author want to convince readers to consider a particular issue?
Do you think the author's primary purpose was to entertain?
Why do you think the author wrote this text from a certain point of view?
What is your response to the text as a reader?
Did the author state their purpose for writing it?

Rather than simply consuming the text, readers should attempt to interpret the information being presented. Being able to identify an author's purpose efficiently improves reading comprehension, develops critical thinking, and makes students more likely to consider issues in depth before accepting writer viewpoints. Authors of fiction frequently write to entertain readers. Another purpose for writing fiction is making a political statement; for example, Jonathan Swift wrote "A Modest Proposal" (1729) as a political satire. Another purpose for writing fiction as well as nonfiction is to persuade readers to take some action or further a particular cause. Fiction authors and poets both frequently write to evoke certain moods; for example, Edgar Allan Poe wrote novels, short stories, and poems that evoke moods of gloom, guilt, terror, and dread. Another purpose of poets is evoking certain emotions: love is popular, as in Shakespeare's sonnets and numerous others. In "The Waste Land" (1922), T.S. Eliot evokes society's alienation, disaffection, sterility, and fragmentation.

Authors seldom directly state their purposes in texts. Some students may be confronted with nonfiction texts such as biographies, histories, magazine and newspaper articles, and instruction manuals, among others. To identify the purpose in nonfiction texts, students can ask the following questions:

- Is the author trying to teach something?
- Is the author trying to persuade the reader?
- Is the author imparting factual information only?
- Is this a reliable source?
- Does the author have some kind of hidden agenda?

To apply author purpose in nonfictional passages, students can also analyze sentence structure, word choice, and transitions to answer the aforementioned questions and to make inferences. For example, authors wanting to convince readers to view a topic negatively often choose words with negative connotations.

Narrative Writing
Narrative writing tells a story. The most prominent type of narrative writing is the fictional novel. Here are some examples:

Mark Twain's *The Adventures of Tom Sawyer* and *The Adventures of Huckleberry Finn*
Victor Hugo's *Les Misérables*
Charles Dickens' *Great Expectations, David Copperfield,* and *A Tale of Two Cities*
Jane Austen's *Northanger Abbey, Mansfield Park, Pride and Prejudice*, and *Sense and Sensibility*
Toni Morrison's *Beloved, The Bluest Eye,* and *Song of Solomon*
Gabriel García Márquez's *One Hundred Years of Solitude* and *Love in the Time of Cholera*

Nonfiction works can also appear in narrative form. For example, some authors choose a narrative style to convey factual information about a topic, such as a specific animal, country, geographic region, and scientific or natural phenomenon.

Narrative writing tells a story, and the one telling the story is called the narrator. The narrator may be a fictional character telling the story from their own viewpoint. This narrator uses the first person (*I, me, my,* *mine* and *we, us, our,* and *ours*). The narrator may also be the author; for example, when Louisa May Alcott writes "Dear reader" in *Little Women*, she (the author) addresses us as readers. In this case, the novel is typically told in third person, referring to the characters as he, she, they, or them. Another more common technique is the omniscient narrator; in other words, the story is told by an unidentified individual who sees and knows everything about the events and characters—not only their externalized actions, but also their internalized feelings and thoughts. Second person narration, which addresses readers as you throughout the text, is more uncommon than the first and third person options.

Expository Writing

Expository writing is also known as informational writing. Its purpose is not to tell a story as in narrative writing, to paint a picture as in descriptive writing, or to persuade readers to agree with something as in argumentative writing. Rather, its point is to communicate information to the reader. As such, the point of view of the author will be more objective. Whereas other types of writing appeal to the reader's emotions, appeal to the reader's reason by using logic, or use subjective descriptions to sway the reader's opinion or thinking, expository writing seeks simply to provide facts, evidence, observations, and objective descriptions of the subject matter instead. Some examples of expository writing include research reports, journal articles, books about history, academic textbooks, essays, how-to articles, user instruction manuals, news articles, and other factual journalistic reports.

Technical Writing

Technical writing is similar to expository writing because it provides factual and objective information. Indeed, it may even be considered a subcategory of expository writing. However, technical writing differs from expository writing in two ways: (1) it is specific to a particular field, discipline, or subject, and (2) it uses technical terminology that belongs only to that area. Writing that uses technical terms is intended only for an audience familiar with those terms. An example of technical writing would be a manual on computer programming and use.

Persuasive Writing

Persuasive writing, or **argumentative writing**, attempts to convince the reader to agree with the author's position. Some writers may respond to other writers' arguments by making reference to those authors or texts and then disagreeing with them. However, another common technique is for the author to anticipate opposing viewpoints, both from other authors and from readers. The author brings up these opposing viewpoints, and then refutes them before they can even be raised, strengthening the author's argument. Writers persuade readers by appealing to the readers' reason and emotion, as well as to their own character and credibility. Aristotle called these appeals **logos**, **pathos**, and **ethos**, respectively.

Evaluating the Author's Point of View in a Given Text

When a writer tells a story using the first person, readers can identify this by the use of first-person pronouns, like *I, me, we, us,* etc. However, first-person narratives can be told by different people or from different points of view. For example, some authors write in the first person to tell the story from the main character's viewpoint, as Charles Dickens did in his novels *David Copperfield* and *Great Expectations.* Some authors write in the first person from the viewpoint of a fictional character in the story, but not necessarily the main character. For example, F. Scott Fitzgerald wrote *The Great Gatsby* as narrated by Nick Carraway, a character in the story, about the main characters, Jay Gatsby and Daisy Buchanan. Other authors write in the first person, but as the omniscient narrator—an often unnamed person who knows all of the characters' inner thoughts and feelings. Writing in first person as oneself is more common in nonfiction.

Third Person

The third-person narrative is probably the most prevalent voice used in fictional literature. While some authors tell stories from the point of view and in the voice of a fictional character using the first person, it is a more common practice to describe the actions, thoughts, and feelings of fictional characters in the third person using *he, him, she, her, they, them,* etc.

Although plot and character development are both necessary and possible when writing narrative texts from a first-person point of view, they are also more difficult, particularly for new writers and those who find it unnatural or uncomfortable to write from that perspective. Therefore, writing experts advise beginning writers to start out writing in the third person. A big advantage of third-person narration is that the writer can describe the thoughts, feelings, and motivations of every character in a story, which is not possible for the first-person narrator. Third-person narrative can impart information to readers that the characters do not know. On the other hand, beginning writers often regard using the third-person point of view as more difficult because they must write about the feelings and thoughts of every character, rather than only about those of the protagonist.

Second Person

Narrative texts written in the second person address someone else as "you." In novels and other fictional works, the second person is the narrative voice most seldom used. The primary reason for this is that it often reads in an awkward manner, which prevents readers from being drawn into the fictional world of the novel. The second person is more often used in informational text, especially in how-to manuals, guides, and other instructions.

First Person

First person uses pronouns such as *I, me, we, my, us, and our.* Some writers naturally find it easier to tell stories from their own points of view, so writing in the first person offers advantages for them. The first-person voice is better for interpreting the world from a single viewpoint, and for enabling reader immersion in one protagonist's experiences. However, others find it difficult to use the first-person narrative voice. Its disadvantages can include overlooking the emotions of characters, forgetting to include description, producing stilted writing, using too many sentence structures involving "I did. . .", and not devoting enough attention to the story's "here-and-now" immediacy.

Applying Knowledge of Language to Aid Comprehension

The English language is highly complex and writing in English can pose particular challenges. If an author makes repeated mistakes with spelling, grammar, or punctuation, the reader will likely experience difficulty with comprehension. Words with similar spellings can often be misused. Consider the words "affect" and "effect." The former is typically a verb and the latter is typically a noun. The words "except" and "accept" are also commonly misused. Another common error in writing is the misuse of pronouns, including "he," "she," "it," and "they." When pronouns are used to replace a singular noun, the pronouns, too, must remain singular.

Consider the two sentences below:

A bicycle is considered an antique if *they* were made prior to 1920.

A bicycle is considered an antique if *it* was made prior to 1920.

Because the passage is referring to "a bicycle," the pronoun that replaces this noun must be singular. Pronouns can also lead to ambiguity. Consider the following sentences:

The peaceful accord between the two nations led to an established truce. **It** was the beginning of a long-lasting alliance.

Does the pronoun "it" in the second sentence refer to the peaceful accord or the established truce? The author's word choice creates ambiguity. The following word choice avoids ambiguity by focusing on the clarity of the message:

The peaceful accord between the two nations not only led to an established truce but marked the beginning of a long-lasting alliance.

Having a command of the basics in the written structure of a language, however, is not enough to ensure a reader's comprehension. Academic writing requires a rich vocabulary and a logical order. In academic writing, the introduction should be compelling enough to draw in the audience. Within the first few sentences, the argument should be clearly stated, along with background information and subtle or overt reasons why the paper is worth reading. Once the introduction is complete, a well-organized academic paper will begin to unfold the evidence, data, and information that supports the argument. The importance of evidence cannot be overstated because the audience will immediately begin to weigh the evidence. The more objective the data, the more credible the argument. It isn't enough for the author to simply unfold the data. The data should be clearly explained and analyzed in a way that supports the argument, leaving little doubt in the reader's mind about the argument's strength. Concluding the academic paper with a concise summary, restating the evidence, and reasserting the argument without sounding redundant will add strength to the overall message and will leave the audience with a sense of closure.

Discerning Fact Vs. Opinion in a Text

A fact is a statement that is true empirically or an event that has actually occurred in reality and can be proven or supported by evidence; it is generally objective. In contrast, an **opinion** is subjective, representing something that someone believes rather than something that exists in the absolute. People's individual understandings, feelings, and perspectives contribute to variations in opinion. Though facts are typically objective in nature, in some instances, a statement of fact may be both factual and yet also subjective. For example, emotions are individual subjective experiences. If an individual says that he or she feels happy or sad, the feeling is subjective, but the statement is factual; hence, it is a subjective fact. In contrast, if one person tells another that the other is feeling happy or sad—whether this is true or not—it is an assumption or an opinion.

Using Context Clues to Determine a Word's Meaning

When readers encounter an unfamiliar word in text, they can use the surrounding context to help determine the word's meaning. The text's overall subject matter, the specific chapter or section, and the immediate sentence context can all provide clues to help the reader understand the word. Among others, one category of context clues is grammar. For example, the position of a word in a sentence and its relationship to the other words can help the reader establish whether the unfamiliar word is a verb, a noun, an adjective, an adverb, etc. This narrows down the possible meanings of the word to one part of speech. However, this may be insufficient. In the sentence, "Many birds migrate twice yearly," the reader can determine that the italicized word is a verb. While it probably does not mean eat or drink (because birds would need to do those actions more than twice each year), it could mean travel, mate, lay eggs, hatch, molt, etc.

Some words can have a number of different meanings depending on how they are used. For example, the word *fly* has a different meaning in each of the following sentences:

"His trousers have a fly on them."
"He swatted the fly on his trousers."
"Those are some fly trousers."
"They went fly fishing."
"She hates to fly."
"If humans were meant to fly, they would have wings."

As strategies, readers can try substituting a familiar word for an unfamiliar one and see whether it makes sense in the sentence. They can also identify other words in a sentence, offering clues to an unfamiliar word's meaning.

Figurative Language

Figurative language is not meant to be taken literally, but it is useful when the author wants to produce an emotional effect in the reader or add heightened complexity to the text's meaning. Figurative language is used more heavily in texts such as literary fiction, poetry, critical theory, and speeches. It goes beyond literal language, allowing readers to form associations they wouldn't normally form. Using language in a figurative sense appeals to the imagination of the reader. It is important to remember that words signify objects and ideas and are not the objects and ideas themselves. Figurative language can highlight this detachment by creating multiple associations, but it also points to the fact that language is fluid and capable of creating a world full of linguistic possibilities. It can be argued that figurative language is the heart of communication even outside of fiction and poetry. People connect through humor, metaphors, cultural allusions, puns, and symbolism in their everyday rhetoric. The following are terms associated with figurative language:

Simile

A simile is a comparison of two things using *like*, *than*, or *as*. A simile usually takes objects that have no apparent connection, such as a mind and an orchid, and compares them:

His mind was as complex and rare as a field of ghost orchids.

Similes encourage new, fresh perspectives on objects or ideas that would not otherwise occur. Unlike similes, metaphors are comparisons that do not use *like*, *than*, or *as*. So, a metaphor from the above example would be:

His mind was a field of ghost orchids.

Thus, similes highlight the comparison by focusing on the figurative side of the language, elucidating the author's intent. Metaphors, however, provide a beautiful yet somewhat equivocal comparison.

Metaphor

A popular use of figurative language, metaphors compare objects or ideas directly, asserting that something *is* a certain thing, even if it isn't. The following is an example of a metaphor used by writer Virginia Woolf:

> Books are the mirrors of the soul.

Metaphors have a vehicle and a tenor. The tenor is "books" and the vehicle is "mirrors of the soul." That is, the tenor is what is meant to be described, and the vehicle is that which carries the weight of the comparison. In this metaphor, perhaps the author means to say that written language (books) reflect a person's most inner thoughts and desires.

Dead metaphors are phrases that have been overused to the point where the figurative language has taken on a literal meaning, like "crystal clear." This phrase is in such popular use that the meaning seems literal ("perfectly clear") even when it is not.

Finally, an extended metaphor is one that goes on for several paragraphs,, or even an entire text. "On First Looking into Chapman's Homer," a poem by John Keats, begins, "Much have I travell'd in the realms of gold," and goes on to explain the first time he hears Chapman's translation of Homer's writing. We see the extended metaphor begin in the first line. Keats is comparing travelling into "realms of gold" and exploration of new lands to the act of hearing a certain kind of literature for the first time. The extended metaphor goes on until the end of the poem where Keats stands "Silent, upon a peak in Darien," having heard the end of Chapman's translation. Keats has gained insight into new lands (new text) and is the richer for it.

The following are brief definitions and examples of popular figurative language:

Onomatopoeia: A word that, when spoken, imitates the sound to which it refers. For example: "We heard a loud *boom* while driving to the beach yesterday."

Personification: When human characteristics are given to animals, inanimate objects, or abstractions. An example would be in William Wordsworth's poem "Daffodils" where he sees a "crowd . . . / of golden daffodils . . . / Fluttering and dancing in the breeze." Dancing is usually a characteristic attributed solely to humans, but Wordsworth personifies the daffodils here as a crowd of people dancing.

Juxtaposition: Juxtaposition places two objects side by side for comparison or contrast. For example, Milton juxtaposes God and Satan in "Paradise Lost."

Paradox: A paradox is a statement that is self-contradictory but will, nonetheless, be found to be true. One example of a paradox is when Socrates said,, "I know one thing; that I know nothing." Seemingly, if Socrates knew nothing, he wouldn't know that he knew nothing. However, he is using figurative language not to say that he literally knows nothing, but that true wisdom begins with casting all presuppositions about the world aside.

Hyperbole: A hyperbole is an exaggeration. For example: "I'm so tired I could sleep for centuries."

Allusion: An allusion is a reference to a character or event that happened in the past. T.S. Eliot's "The Waste Land" is a poem littered with allusions, including, "I will show you fear in a handful of dust," alluding to Genesis 3:19: "For you are dust, and to dust you shall return."

Pun: Puns are used in popular culture to invoke humor by exploiting the meanings of words. They can also be used in literature to give hints of meaning in unexpected places. In "Romeo and Juliet," Mercutio makes a pun after he is stabbed by Tybalt: "look for me tomorrow and you will find me a grave man."

Imagery: This is a collection of images given to the reader by the author. If a text is rich in imagery, it is easier for the reader to imagine themselves in the author's world. One example of a poem that relies on imagery is William Carlos Williams' "The Red Wheelbarrow":

> so much depends
> upon
>
> a red wheel
> barrow
>
> glazed with rain
> water
>
> beside the white
> chickens

To some readers, the starkness of the imagery and the placement of the words in the poem throw the poem into a meditative state where, indeed, the world of this poem is made up solely of images of a purely simple life. Through its imagery, this poem tells a story in just sixteen words.

Symbolism: A symbol is used to represent an idea or belief system. For example, poets in Western civilization have been using the symbol of a rose for hundreds of years to represent love. In Japan, poets have used the firefly to symbolize passionate love, and sometimes even spirits of those who have died. Symbols can also express powerful political commentary and can be used in propaganda.

Irony: There are three types of irony: verbal, dramatic, and situational. **Verbal irony** is when a person states one thing and means the opposite. For example, a person is probably using irony when they say, "I can't wait to study for this exam next week." **Dramatic irony** occurs in a narrative and happens when the audience knows something that the characters do not. In the modern TV series Hannibal, the audience knows that Hannibal Lecter is a serial killer, but most of the main characters do not. This is dramatic irony. Finally, **situational irony** is when one expects something to happen, and the opposite occurs. For example, we can say that a fire station burning down would be an instance of situational irony.

Understanding a Range of Words and Phrases to Improve Comprehension and Read at the College Level

The first three years of a child's life are arguably the most intensive in terms of speech acquisition and language development. There seems to be a direct correlation between a child's vocabulary and a childhood environment rich in sights, sounds, and positive social interaction. In those beginning years, a child's **receptive vocabulary**—the words he or she can comprehend—will undoubtedly be more expansive than the child's **expressive vocabulary,** or the words he or she can use to communicate. During a child's educational career, certain language milestones need to be achieved, each building on the previous one. Children who develop a command of English language conventions, including grammar, usage, and mechanics, will be in a better position to develop more sophisticated ways to use language later.

However, continuously expanding a child's vocabulary requires much more than a command of conventions. As children grow, so does their vocabulary, especially with the introduction to reading. An environment that encourages reading and offers a variety of reading material has been shown to strengthen comprehension and expand a child's vocabulary base. An effective reading program provides increasingly more challenging texts, including informational texts, stories, poems, and historical fiction, as well as specialized texts that focus on specific disciplines. The more students are exposed to such a reading program, the greater the likelihood that they will build a foundation of knowledge in various fields of study and strengthen comprehension of the often complex structures and elements of different texts.

Introducing students to effective reading comprehension skills is key to reading at the college level. Reading comprehension and vocabulary can be improved by encouraging students to build reading stamina and a determination to read through a text no matter the challenges it presents. Consider the following reading skills that help to improve reading comprehension and prepare students to college-level texts:

Reading Stamina	Identification of Main Idea	Paraphrasing	Annotation	Consistent Reading
Students are encouraged to read through complex texts, even if confronted with unfamiliar vocabulary.	Once the main idea has been identified, the rest of the text will begin to make more sense.	Students are encouraged to write out sections of the text in their own words. This strengthens comprehension and allows for reflection.	Students are encouraged to underline interesting ideas, circle unknown words, and use a dictionary to define the words that impede understanding.	Students who read complex and varied reading material on a regular basis are more likely to advance their reading skills and expand their expressive and receptive vocabulary.

It is clear that the more students read on a regular basis, the more prepared they will be for college-level reading, but this doesn't mean that a student has to read informational texts exclusively. Reading material that interests students also works to increase their vocabulary knowledge. When students are interested in the material, they are more likely to continue reading and will likely be motivated to learn the unfamiliar words in the text. But it isn't just about reading. Since reading, writing, listening, and speaking are all intimately connected, when students write regularly and intentionally practice writing newly-acquired words and phrases, this practice will undoubtedly reinforce their reading skills.

Integration of Knowledge and Ideas

Interpreting Media and Non-Print Text

Books as Resources

When a student has an assignment to research and write a paper, one of the first steps after determining the topic is to select research sources. The student may begin by conducting an Internet or library search of the topic, may refer to a reading list provided by the instructor, or may use an annotated bibliography of works related to the topic. To evaluate the worth of the book for the research paper, the student should first consider the book title to get an idea of its content. Then the student can scan the book's table of contents for chapter titles and topics to get further ideas of the book's applicability to the topic. The student may also turn to the end of the book to look for an alphabetized index. Most academic textbooks and scholarly works have these; students can look up key topic terms to see how many are included and how many pages are devoted to them.

Journal Articles

Like books, journal articles are primary or secondary sources the student may need to use for researching any topic. To assess whether a journal article will be a useful source for a particular paper topic, a student can first get some idea about the content of the article by reading its title and subtitle, if any exists. Many journal articles, particularly scientific ones, include abstracts. These are brief summaries of the content. The student should read the abstract to get a more specific idea of whether the experiment, literature review, or other work documented is applicable to the paper topic. Students should also check the references at the end of the article, which today often contain links to related works for exploring the topic further.

Encyclopedias and Dictionaries

Dictionaries and encyclopedias are both reference books for looking up information alphabetically. **Dictionaries** are more exclusively focused on vocabulary words. They include each word's correct spelling, pronunciation, variants, part(s) of speech, definitions of one or more meanings, and examples used in a sentence. Some dictionaries provide illustrations of certain words when these inform the meaning. Some dictionaries also offer synonyms, antonyms, and related words under a word's entry. **Encyclopedias**, like dictionaries, often provide word pronunciations and definitions. However, they have broader scopes: one can look up entire subjects in encyclopedias, not just words, and find comprehensive, detailed information about historical events, famous people, countries, disciplines of study, and many other things. Dictionaries are for finding word meanings, pronunciations, and spellings; encyclopedias are for finding breadth and depth of information on a variety of topics.

Card Catalogs

A **card catalog** is a means of organizing, classifying, and locating the large numbers of books found in libraries. Without being able to look up books in library card catalogs, it would be virtually impossible to find them on library shelves. Card catalogs may be on traditional paper cards filed in drawers, or electronic catalogs accessible online; some libraries combine both. Books are shelved by subject area; subjects are coded using formal classification systems—standardized sets of rules for identifying and labeling books by subject and author. These assign each book a **call number**: a code indicating the classification system, subject, author, and title. Call numbers also function as bookshelf "addresses" where books can be located. Most public libraries use the Dewey Decimal Classification System. Most university, college, and research libraries use the Library of Congress Classification. Nursing students will also encounter the National Institute of Health's National Library of Medicine Classification System, which major collections of health sciences publications utilize.

Databases

A **database** is a collection of digital information organized for easy access, updating, and management. Users can sort and search databases for information. One way of classifying databases is by content, i.e. full-text, numerical, bibliographical, or images. Another classification method used in computing is by organizational approach. The most common approach is a relational database, which is tabular and defines data so they can be accessed and reorganized in various ways. A **distributed database** can be reproduced or interspersed among different locations within a network. An **object-oriented database** is organized to be aligned with object classes and subclasses defining the data. Databases usually collect files like product inventories, catalogs, customer profiles, sales transactions, student bodies, and resources. An associated set of application programs is a database management system or database manager. It enables users to specify which reports to generate, control access to reading and writing data, and analyze database usage. **Structured Query Language (SQL)** is a standard computer language for updating, querying, and otherwise interfacing with databases.

Identifying Primary Sources in Various Media

A **primary source** is a piece of original work. This can include books, musical compositions, recordings, movies, works of visual art (paintings, drawings, photographs), jewelry, pottery, clothing, furniture, and other artifacts. Within books, primary sources may be of any genre. Whether nonfiction based on actual events or a fictional creation, the primary source relates the author's firsthand view of some specific event, phenomenon, character, place, process, ideas, field of study or discipline, or other subject matter. Whereas primary sources are original treatments of their subjects, secondary sources are a step removed from the original subjects; they analyze and interpret primary sources. These include journal articles, newspaper or magazine articles, works of literary criticism, political commentaries, and academic textbooks.

In the field of history, primary sources frequently include documents that were created around the same time period that they were describing, and most often produced by someone who had direct experience or knowledge of the subject matter. In contrast, **secondary sources** present the ideas and viewpoints of other authors about the primary sources; in history, for example, these can include books and other written works about the particular historical periods or eras in which the primary sources were produced. Primary sources pertinent in history include diaries, letters, statistics, government information, and original journal articles and books. In literature, a primary source might be a literary novel, a poem or book of poems, or a play. Secondary sources addressing primary sources may be criticism, dissertations, theses, and journal articles. Tertiary sources, typically reference works referring to primary and secondary sources, include encyclopedias, bibliographies, handbooks, abstracts, and periodical indexes.

In scientific fields, when scientists conduct laboratory experiments to answer specific research questions and test hypotheses, lab reports and reports of research results constitute examples of primary sources. When researchers produce statistics to support or refute hypotheses, those statistics are primary sources. When a scientist is studying some subject longitudinally or conducting a case study, they may keep a journal or diary. For example, Charles Darwin kept diaries of extensive notes on his studies during sea voyages on the *Beagle*, visits to the Galápagos Islands, etc.; Jean Piaget kept journals of observational notes for case studies of children's learning behaviors. Many scientists, particularly in past centuries, shared and discussed discoveries, questions, and ideas with colleagues through letters, which also constitute primary sources. When a scientist seeks to replicate another's experiment, the reported results, analysis, and commentary on the original work is a secondary source, as is a student's dissertation if it analyzes or discusses others' work rather than reporting original research or ideas.

Business Memos

Whereas everyday office memos were traditionally typed on paper, photocopied, and distributed, today they are more often typed on computers and distributed via e-mail, both interoffice and externally. Technology has thus made these communications more immediate. It is also helpful for people to read carefully and be familiar with memo components. For example, e-mails automatically provide the same "To:, From:, and Re:" lines traditionally required in paper memos, and in corresponding places—the top of the page/screen. Readers should observe whether "To: names/positions" include all intended recipients in case of misdirection errors or omitted recipients. "From:" informs sender level, role, and who will receive responses when people click "Reply." Users must be careful not to click "Reply All" unintentionally. They should also observe the "CC:" line, typically below "Re:," showing additional recipients.

Classified Ads

Classified advertisements include "Help Wanted" ads informing readers of positions open for hiring, real estate listings, cars for sale, and home and business services available. Traditional ads in newspapers had to save space, and this necessity has largely transferred to online ads. Because of needing to save space, advertisers employ many abbreviations. For example, here are some examples of abbreviations:

FT=full-time
PT=part-time
A/P=accounts payable
A/R=accounts receivable
Asst.=assistant
Bkkg.=bookkeeping
Comm.=commission
Bet.=between
EOE=equal opportunity employer
G/L=general ledger
Immed.=immediately
Exc.=excellent
Exp.=experience
Eves.=evenings
Secy.=secretary
Temp=temporary
Sal=salary
Req=required
Refs=references
Wk=week or work
WPM=words per minute

Classified ads frequently use abbreviations to take up less space, both on paper and digitally on websites. Those who read these ads will find it less confusing if they learn some common abbreviations used by businesses when advertising job positions. Here are some examples:

Mgt.=management
Mgr.=manager
Mfg.=manufacturing
Nat'l=national
Dept.=department
Min.=minimum
Yrs.=years
Nec=necessary
Neg=negotiable
Oppty=opportunity
O/T=overtime
K=1,000

Readers of classified ads may focus on certain features to the exclusion of others. For example, if a reader sees the job title or salary they are seeking, or notices the experience, education, degree, or other credentials required match their own qualifications perfectly, they may fail to notice other important information, like "No benefits." This is important because the employers are disclosing that they will not provide health insurance, retirement accounts, paid sick leave, paid maternity/paternity leave, paid vacation, etc. to any employee whom they hire. Someone expecting a traditional 9 to 5 job who fails to observe that an ad states "Evenings" or just the abbreviation "Eves" will be disappointed, as will the applicant who overlooks a line saying, "Some evenings and weekends reqd." Applicants overlooking information like "Apply in person" may e-mail or mail their resumes and receive no response. The job hopeful with no previous experience and one reference must attend to information like "Minimum 5 yrs. exp, 3 refs," meaning they likely will not qualify.

Employment Ads

Job applicants should pay attention to the information included in classified employment ads. On one hand, they do need to believe and accept certain statements, such as "Please, no phone calls," which is frequently used by employers posting ads on Craigslist and similar websites. New applicants just graduated from or still in college will be glad to see "No exp necessary" in some ads, indicating they need no previous work experience in that job category. "FT/PT" means the employer offers the options of working full-time or part-time, another plus for students. On the other hand, ad readers should also take into consideration the fact that many employers list all the attributes of their *ideal* employee, but they do not necessarily expect to find such a candidate. If a potential applicant's education, training, credentials, and experience are not exactly the same as what the employer lists as desired but are not radically different either, it can be productive to apply anyway, while honestly representing one's actual qualifications.

Atlases

A **road atlas** is a publication designed to assist travelers who are driving on road trips rather than taking airplanes, trains, ships, etc. Travelers use road atlases to determine which routes to take and places to stop; how to navigate specific cities, locate landmarks, estimate mileages and travel times; see photographs of places they plan to visit; and find other travel-related information. One familiar, reputable road atlas is published by the National Geographic Society. It includes detailed, accurate maps of the United States, Canada, and Mexico; historic sites, scenic routes, recreation information, and points of interest; and its Adventure Edition spotlights 100 top U.S. adventure destinations and most popular national parks. The best-selling road atlas in the United States, also probably the best-known and most trusted, is published annually by Rand McNally, which has published road atlases for many years. It includes maps, mileage charts, information on tourism and road construction, maps of individual city details, and the editor's favorite road trips (in the 2016 edition) including recommended points of interest en route.

Owners' Manuals

An **owner's manual** is typically a booklet, but may also be as short as a page or as long as a book, depending on the individual instance. The purpose of an owner's manual is to give the owner instructions, usually step-by-step, for how to use a specific product or a group or range of products. Manuals accompany consumer products as diverse as cars, computers, tablets, smartphones, printers, home appliances, shop machines, and many others. In addition to directions for operating products, they include important warnings of things *not* to do that pose safety or health hazards or can damage the product and void the manufacturer's product warranty, like immersion in water, exposure to high temperatures, operating something for too long, dropping fragile items, or rough handling. Manuals teach correct operating practices, sequences, precautions, and cautions, averting many costly and/or dangerous mishaps.

Food Labels

When reading the labels on food products, it is often necessary to interpret the nutrition facts and other product information. Without the consumer's being aware and informed of this, much of this information can be very misleading. For example, a popular brand name of corn chips lists the calories, fat, etc. per serving in the nutrition facts printed on the bag, but on closer inspection, it defines a serving size as six chips—far fewer than most people would consume at a time. Serving sizes and the number of servings per container can be unrealistic. For example, a jumbo muffin's wrapper indicates it contains three servings. Not only do most consumers not divide a muffin and eat only part; but it is moreover rather difficult to cut a muffin into equal thirds. A king-sized package of chili cheese-flavored corn chips says it contains 4.5 servings per container. This is not very useful information, since people cannot divide the package into equal servings and are unlikely to eat four servings and then ½ a serving.

Product Packaging

Consumers today cannot take product labels at face value. While many people do not read or even look at the information on packages before eating their contents, those who do must use more consideration and analysis than they might expect to understand it. For example, a well-known brand of strawberry-flavored breakfast toaster pastry displays a picture of four whole strawberries on the wrapper. While this looks appealing, encouraging consumers to infer the product contains wholesome fruit—and perhaps even believe it contains four whole strawberries—reading the ingredients list reveals it contains only 2 percent or less of dried strawberries. A consumer must be detail-oriented (and curious or motivated enough) to read the full ingredients list, which also reveals unhealthy corn syrup and high fructose corn syrup high on the list after enriched flour. Consumers must also educate themselves about euphemistically misleading terms: "enriched" flour has vitamins and minerals added, but it is refined flour without whole grain, bran, or fiber.

While manufacturers generally provide extensive information printed on their package labels, it is typically in very small print—many consumers do not read it—and even consumers who do read all the information must look for small details to discover that the information is often not realistic. For example, a box of brownie mix lists grams of fat, total calories, and calories from fat. However, by paying attention to small details like asterisks next to this information, and finding the additional information referenced by the asterisks, the consumer discovers that these amounts are for only the dry mix—not the added eggs, oil, or milk. Consumers typically do not eat dry cake mixes, and having to determine and add the fat and calories from the additional ingredients is inconvenient. In another example, a box of macaroni and cheese mix has an asterisk by the fat grams indicating this value is for the macaroni only without the cheese, butter, or milk required, which contributes 6.4 times more fat.

Ingredients' Lists

Consumers can realize the importance of reading drug labeling through an analogy: What might occur if they were to read only part of the directions on a standardized test? Reading only part of the directions on medications can have similar, even more serious consequences. Prescription drug packages typically contain inserts, which provide extremely extensive, thorough, detailed information, including results of clinical trials and statistics showing patient responses and adverse effects. Some over-the-counter medications include inserts, and some do not. "Active ingredients" are those ingredients making medication effective. "Inactive ingredients" including flavorings, preservatives, stabilizers, and emulsifiers have purposes, but not to treat symptoms. "Uses" indicates which symptoms a medication is meant to treat. "Directions" tell the dosage, frequency, maximum daily amount, and other requirements, like "Take with food," "Do not operate heavy machinery while using," etc. Drug labels also state how to store the product, like at what temperature or away from direct sunlight or humidity.

Many drugs which were previously available only by doctor prescription have recently become available over the counter without a prescription. While enough years of testing may have determined that these substances typically do not cause serious problems, consumers must nevertheless thoroughly read and understand all the information on the labels before taking them. If they do not, they could still suffer serious harm. For example, some individuals have allergies to specific substances. Both prescription and over-the-counter medication products list their ingredients, including warnings about allergies. Allergic reactions can include anaphylactic shock, which can be fatal if not treated immediately. Also, consumers must read and follow dosing directions: taking more than directed can cause harm, and taking less can be ineffective to treat symptoms. Some medication labels warn not to mix them with certain other drugs to avoid harmful drug interactions. Additionally, without reading ingredients, some consumers take multiple products including the same active ingredients, resulting in overdoses.

Using Text Features
Table of Contents and Index
When examining a book, a journal article, a monograph, or other publication, the table of contents is in the front. In books, it is typically found following the title page, publication information (often on the facing side of the title page), and dedication page, when one is included. In shorter publications, the table of contents may follow the title page, or the title on the same page. The table of contents in a book lists the number and title of each chapter and its beginning page number. An index, which is most common in books but may also be included in shorter works, is at the back of the publication. Books, especially academic texts, frequently have two: a subject index and an author index. Readers can look alphabetically for specific subjects in the subject index. Likewise, they can look for specific authors cited, quoted, discussed, or mentioned in the author index.

The index in a book offers particular advantages to students. For example, college course instructors typically assign certain textbooks, but do not expect students to read the entire book from cover to cover immediately. They usually assign specific chapters to read in preparation for specific lectures and/or discussions in certain upcoming classes. Reading portions at a time, some students may find references they either do not fully understand or want to know more about. They can look these topics up in the book's subject index to find them in later chapters. When a text author refers to another author, students can also look up the name in the book's author index to find all page numbers of all other references to that author. College students also typically are assigned research papers to write. A book's subject and author indexes can guide students to pages that may help inform them of other books to use for researching paper topics.

Headings
Headings and subheadings concisely inform readers what each section of a paper contains, and show how its information is organized both visually and verbally. Headings are typically up to about five words long. They are not meant to give in-depth analytical information about the topic of their section, but rather an idea of its subject matter. Text authors should maintain consistent style across all headings. Readers should not expect headings if there is not material for more than one heading at each level, just as a list is unnecessary for a single item. Subheadings may be a bit longer than headings because they expand upon them. Readers should skim the subheadings in a paper to use them as a map of how the content is arranged. Subheadings are in smaller fonts than headings to mirror relative importance. Subheadings are not necessary for every paragraph. They should enhance content, not substitute for topic sentences.

When a heading is brief, simple, and written in the form of a question, it can have the effect of further drawing readers into the text. An effective author will also answer the question in the heading soon in the following text. Question headings and their text answers are particularly helpful for engaging readers with average reading skills. Both headings and subheadings are most effective with more readers when they are obvious, simple, and get to their points immediately. Simple headings attract readers; simple subheadings allow readers a break, during which they also inform reader decisions whether to continue reading or not. Headings stand out from other text through boldface, but also italicizing and underlining them would be excessive. Uppercase-lowercase headings are easier for readers to comprehend than all capitals. More legible fonts are better. Some experts prefer serif fonts in text, but sans-serif fonts in headings. Brief subheadings that preview upcoming chunks of information reach more readers.

Text Features

Textbooks that are designed well employ varied text features for organizing their main ideas, illustrating central concepts, spotlighting significant details, and signaling evidence that supports the ideas and points conveyed. When a textbook uses these features in recurrent patterns that are predictable, it makes it easier for readers to locate information and come up with connections. When readers comprehend how to make use of text features, they will take less time and effort deciphering how the text is organized, leaving them more time and energy for focusing on the actual content in the text. Instructional activities can include not only previewing text through observing main text features, but moreover, through examining and deconstructing the text and ascertaining how the text features can aid them in locating and applying text information for learning.

Included among various text features are a table of contents, headings, subheadings, an index, a glossary, a foreword, a preface, paragraphing spaces, bullet lists, footnotes, sidebars, diagrams, graphs, charts, pictures, illustrations, captions, italics, boldface, colors, and symbols. A **glossary** is a list of key vocabulary words and/or technical terminology and definitions. This helps readers recognize or learn specialized terms used in the text before reading it. A **foreword i**s typically written by someone other than the text's author and appears at the beginning to introduce, inform, recommend, and/or praise the work. A *preface* is often written by the author and also appears at the beginning, to introduce or explain something about the text, like new additions. A **sidebar** is a box with text and sometimes graphics at the left or right side of a page, typically focusing on a more specific issue, example, or aspect of the subject. *Footnotes* are additional comments/notes at the bottom of the page, signaled by superscript numbers in the text.

Text Features on Websites

On the Internet or in computer software programs, text features include URLs, home pages, pop-up menus, drop-down menus, bookmarks, buttons, links, navigation bars, text boxes, arrows, symbols, colors, graphics, logos, and abbreviations. URLs (Universal Resource Locators) indicate the internet "address" or location of a website or web page. They often start with www. (world wide web) or http:// (hypertext transfer protocol) or https:// (the "s" indicates a secure site) and appear in the Internet browser's top address bar. Clickable buttons are often links to specific pages on a website or other external sites. Users can click on some buttons to open pop-up or drop-down menus, which offer a list of actions or departments from which to select. Bookmarks are the electronic versions of physical bookmarks. When users bookmark a website/page, a link is established to the site URL and saved, enabling returning to the site in the future without having to remember its name or URL by clicking the bookmark.

Readers can more easily navigate websites and read their information by observing and utilizing their various text features. For example, most fully developed websites include search bars, where users can type in topics, questions, titles, or names to locate specific information within the large amounts stored on many sites. Navigation bars (software developers frequently use the abbreviation term "navbar") are graphical user interfaces (GUIs) that facilitate visiting different sections, departments, or pages within a website, which can be difficult or impossible to find without these. Typically, they appear as a series of links running horizontally across the top of each page. Navigation bars displayed vertically along the left side of the page are also called sidebars. Links, i.e. hyperlinks, enable hyperspeed browsing by allowing readers to jump to new pages/sites. They may be URLs, words, phrases, images, buttons, etc. They are often but not always underlined and/or blue, or other colors.

Answering Questions Using Information from Informational Graphics

Line Graphs

Line graphs are useful for visually representing data that vary continuously over time, like an individual student's test scores. The horizontal or x-axis shows dates/times; the vertical or y-axis shows point values. A dot is plotted on the point where each horizontal date line intersects each vertical number line, and then these dots are connected, forming a line. Line graphs show whether changes in values over time exhibit trends like ascending, descending, flat, or more variable, like going up and down at different times. For example, suppose a student's scores on the same type of reading test were 75% in October, 80% in November, 78% in December, 82% in January, 85% in February, 88% in March, and 90% in April.

A line graph of these scores, which helps visualize the trends, would look like this:

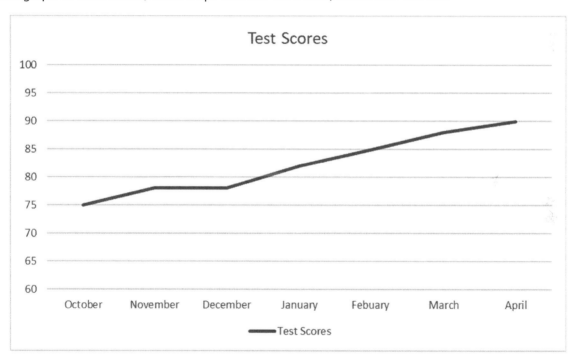

Bar Graphs

Bar graphs feature equally spaced, horizontal or vertical rectangular bars representing numerical values. They can show changes over time as line graphs do, but unlike line graphs, bar graphs can also show differences and similarities among values at a single point in time. Bar graphs are also helpful for visually representing data from different categories, especially when the horizontal axis displays some value that is not numerical, like various countries with inches of annual rainfall.

From the following is a bar graph that compares different classes and how many books they read, it can be seen that the fewest books were read by the students in Class D:

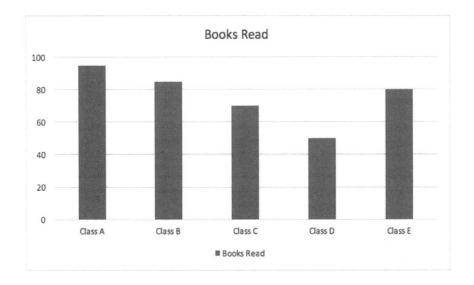

Pie Charts

Pie charts, also called **circle graphs**, are good for representing percentages or proportions of a whole quantity because they represent the whole as a circle or "pie," with the various proportion values shown as "slices" or wedges of the pie. This gives viewers a clear idea of how much of a total each item occupies. To calculate central angles to make each portion the correct size, each percentage is multiplied by 3.6 (because this is 360/100). For example, biologists may have information that 60% of Americans have brown eyes, 20% have hazel eyes, 15% have blue eyes, and 5% have green eyes. A pie chart of these distributions would look like this:

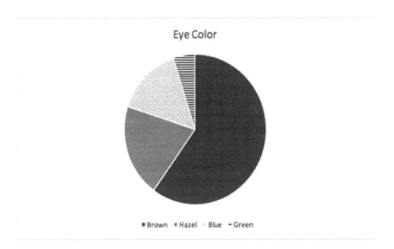

Line Plots

Rather than showing trends or changes over time like line graphs, line plots show the frequency with which a value occurs in a group. Line plots are used for visually representing data sets that total 50 or fewer values. They make visible features like gaps between some data points, clusters of certain numbers/number ranges, and outliers (data points with significantly smaller or larger values than others).

For example, the age ranges in a class of nursing students might appear like this in a line plot:

XXXXXXXXX	XXXXX	XX	X	XXX	XX	X
18	23	28	33	38	43	48

Pictograms

Magazines, newspapers, and other similar publications designed for consumption by the general public often use pictograms to represent data. Pictograms feature icons or symbols that look like whatever category of data is being counted, such as little silhouettes shaped like human beings commonly used to represent people. If the data involve large numbers, like populations, one person symbol might represent one million people, or one thousand, etc. For smaller values, such as how many individuals out of ten fit a given description, one symbol might equal one person. Male and female silhouettes are used to differentiate gender, and child shapes for children. Little clock symbols are used to represent amounts of time, such as a given number of hours; calendar pages might depict months; suns and moons could show days and nights; hourglasses might represent minutes. While pictogram symbols are easily recognizable and appealing to general viewers, one disadvantage is that it is difficult to precisely display and interpret partial symbols for in-between quantities.

Evaluating Arguments and Claims

When authors write text for the purpose of persuading others to agree with them, they assume a position with the subject matter about which they are writing. Rather than presenting information objectively, the author treats the subject matter subjectively so that the information presented supports his or her position. In their argumentation, the author presents information that refutes or weakens opposing positions. Another technique authors use in persuasive writing is to anticipate arguments against the position. When students learn to read subjectively, they gain experience with the concept of persuasion in writing, and learn to identify positions taken by authors. This enhances their reading comprehension and develops their skills for identifying pro and con arguments and biases.

The Relationship Among Ideas Presented in a Text

There are five main parts of the classical argument that writers employ in a well-designed stance:

Introduction: In the introduction to a classical argument, the author establishes goodwill and rapport with the reading audience, warms up the readers, and states the thesis or general theme of the argument.

Narration: In the narration portion, the author gives a summary of pertinent background information, informs the readers of anything they need to know regarding the circumstances and environment surrounding and/or stimulating the argument, and establishes what is at risk or the stakes in the issue or topic. Literature reviews are common examples of narrations in academic writing.

Confirmation: The confirmation states all claims supporting the thesis and furnishes evidence for each claim, arranging this material in logical order—e.g. from most obvious to most subtle or strongest to weakest.

Refutation and Concession: The refutation and concession discuss opposing views and anticipate reader objections without weakening the thesis, yet permitting as many oppositions as possible.

Summation: The summation strengthens the argument while summarizing it, supplying a strong conclusion and showing readers the superiority of the author's solution.

Introduction

A classical argument's introduction must pique reader interest, get readers to perceive the author as a writer, and establish the author's position. Shocking statistics, new ways of restating issues, or quotations or anecdotes focusing the text can pique reader interest. Personal statements, parallel instances, or analogies can also begin introductions—so can bold thesis statements if the author believes readers will agree. Word choice is also important for establishing author image with readers.

The introduction should typically narrow down to a clear, sound thesis statement. If readers cannot locate one sentence in the introduction explicitly stating the writer's position or the point they support, the writer probably has not refined the introduction sufficiently.

Narration and Confirmation

The narration part of a classical argument should create a context for the argument by explaining the issue to which the argument is responding, and by supplying any background information that influences the issue. Readers should understand the issues, alternatives, and stakes in the argument by the end of the narration to enable them to evaluate the author's claims equitably. The confirmation part of the classical argument enables the author to explain why they believe in the argument's thesis. The author builds a chain of reasoning by developing several individual supporting claims and explaining why that evidence supports each claim and also supports the overall thesis of the argument.

Refutation and Concession and Summation

The classical argument is the model for argumentative/persuasive writing, so authors often use it to establish, promote, and defend their positions. In the refutation aspect of the refutation and concession part of the argument, authors disarm reader opposition by anticipating and answering their possible objections, persuading them to accept the author's viewpoint. In the concession aspect, authors can concede those opposing viewpoints with which they agree. This can avoid weakening the author's thesis while establishing reader respect and goodwill for the author: all refutation and no concession can antagonize readers who disagree with the author's position. In the conclusion part of the classical argument, a less skilled writer might simply summarize or restate the thesis and related claims; however, this does not provide the argument with either momentum or closure. More skilled authors revisit the issues and the narration part of the argument, reminding readers of what is at stake.

Determining the Logical Assumptions Upon Which an Argument or Conclusion is Based

In the structure of an argument, an **assumption** is an unstated premise. Some questions on the Reading test will ask you to identify the assumption within arguments, and you must find something that the argument is relying on that the author is not stating explicitly. Many strengthening and weakening questions deal with unstated assumptions, as well as necessary and sufficient assumption questions. Let's take a look at what an unstated assumption looks like:

All restaurants in the Seattle area serve vegan food. *Haile's Seafood* must serve vegan food.

Let's identify all parts of the argument, including the unstated assumption. The conclusion of this argument is the last sentence: *Haile's Seafood* must serve vegan food. The premise we are given is the first sentence: All restaurants in the Seattle area serve vegan food. Now let's ask ourselves if there's a missing link. How did the author reach this conclusion? The author reached this conclusion with an unstated assumption, which might look like this: *Haile's Seafood* is in the Seattle area. Now we have the argument:

Premise: All restaurants in the Seattle area serve vegan food.

Unstated Assumption: *Haile's Seafood* is in the Seattle area.

Conclusion: *Haile's Seafood* must serve vegan food

Another way to look at the missing link is like this: there is a connection between "Seattle area" and "vegan food," and one between *"Haile's Seafood"* and "vegan food", but there is no connection between "Seattle area" and *"Haile's Seafood."* The unstated assumption identifies this connection.

Drawing Conclusions

An inference is an educated guess or conclusion based on sound evidence and reasoning within the text. The test may include multiple-choice questions asking about the logical conclusion that can be drawn from reading a text, and you will have to identify the choice that unavoidably leads to that conclusion. In order to eliminate the incorrect choices, the test taker should come up with a hypothetical situation wherein an answer choice is true, but the conclusion is not true. Here is an example:

> Fred purchased the newest PC available on the market. Therefore, he purchased the most expensive PC in the computer store.
>
> What can one assume for this conclusion to follow logically?
>
> a. Fred enjoys purchasing expensive items.
> b. PCs are some of the most expensive personal technology products available.
> c. The newest PC is the most expensive one.

The premise of the text is the first sentence: Fred purchased the newest PC. The conclusion is the second sentence: Fred purchased the most expensive PC. Recent release and price are two different factors; the difference between them is the logical gap. To eliminate the gap, one must connect the new information from the conclusion with the pertinent information from the premise. In this example, there must be a connection between product recency and product price. Therefore, a possible bridge to the logical gap could be a sentence stating that the newest PCs always cost the most.

Connections Between Different Texts Addressing Similar Topics or Themes

The **theme** of a piece of text is the central idea the author communicates. Whereas the topic of a passage of text may be concrete in nature, by contrast the theme is always conceptual. For example, while the topic of Mark Twain's novel *The Adventures of Huckleberry Finn* might be described as something like the coming-of-age experiences of a poor, illiterate, functionally orphaned boy around and on the Mississippi River in 19th-century Missouri, one theme of the book might be that human beings are corrupted by society. Another might be that slavery and "civilized" society itself are hypocritical. Whereas the main idea in a text is the most important single point that the author wants to make, the theme is the concept or view around which the author centers the text.

Throughout time, humans have told stories with similar themes. Some themes are universal across time, space, and culture. These include themes of the individual as a hero, conflicts of the individual against nature, the individual against society, change vs. tradition, the circle of life, coming-of-age, and the complexities of love. Themes involving war and peace have featured prominently in diverse works, like Homer's *Iliad*, Tolstoy's *War and Peace* (1869), Stephen Crane's *The Red Badge of Courage* (1895), Hemingway's *A Farewell to Arms* (1929), and Margaret Mitchell's *Gone with the Wind* (1936). Another universal literary theme is that of the quest. These appear in folklore from countries and cultures worldwide, including the Gilgamesh Epic, Arthurian legend's Holy Grail quest, Virgil's *Aeneid*, Homer's *Odyssey*, and the *Argonautica*. Cervantes' *Don Quixote* is a parody of chivalric quests. J.R.R. Tolkien's *The Lord of the Rings* trilogy (1954) also features a quest.

Similar themes across cultures often occur in countries that share a border or are otherwise geographically close together. For example, a folklore story of a rabbit in the moon using a mortar and pestle is shared among China, Japan, Korea, and Thailand—making medicine in China, making rice cakes in Japan and Korea, and hulling rice in Thailand. Another instance is when cultures are more distant geographically, but their languages are related. For example, East Turkestan's Uighurs and people in Turkey share tales of folk hero Effendi Nasreddin Hodja. Another instance, which may either be called cultural diffusion or simply reflect commonalities in the human imagination, involves shared themes among geographically- and linguistically-different cultures: both Cameroon's and Greece's folklore tell of centaurs; Cameroon, India, Malaysia, Thailand, and Japan, of mermaids; Brazil, Peru, China, Japan, Malaysia, Indonesia, and Cameroon, of underwater civilizations; and China, Japan, Thailand, Vietnam, Malaysia, Brazil, and Peru, of shape-shifters.

Two prevalent literary themes are love and friendship, which can end happily, sadly, or both. William Shakespeare's *Romeo and Juliet*, Emily Brontë's *Wuthering Heights*, Leo Tolstoy's *Anna Karenina*, and both *Pride and Prejudice* and *Sense and Sensibility* by Jane Austen are famous examples. Another theme recurring in popular literature is of revenge, an old theme in dramatic literature, e.g. Elizabethans Thomas Kyd's *The Spanish Tragedy* and Thomas Middleton's *The Revenger's Tragedy*. Some more well-known instances include Shakespeare's tragedies *Hamlet* and *Macbeth*, Alexandre Dumas' *The Count of Monte Cristo*, John Grisham's *A Time to Kill*, and Stieg Larsson's *The Girl Who Kicked the Hornet's Nest*.

Recognizing or Predicting Ideas or Situations that are Extensions of or Similar to What Has Been Presented in a Reading Selection

In its most basic form, an analogy compares two different things. An analogy question is a situation that parallels the principles or foundations given in another situation. The source will require you to pick out the most apt target in a set of particular events.

Analogy questions may look like the following:

Based on the hypothetical situation given in paragraph 4, which of the following is most closely analogous?

The answer choices will consist of particular situations that attempt to mirror the hypothetical situation given in the passage. In order to find the correct answer, it might be helpful to know the basics of what an analogy is. The following is a list of different types of analogies:

Analogous Relationships	
Category	Example
Part to whole	"All screwdrivers are considered tools." Tools is the whole, and screwdrivers is the part to that whole. Be careful of reversing this logic, though. It would be an error to say "Likewise, all tools are considered screwdrivers." In simplified terms, saying "All A are B" is not the same as saying "All B are A."
Confusing causation with correlation	"The number of traffic accidents in Florida has gone up this past summer. The temperature has also increased this summer by 10 degrees. I bet the heat is making drivers more irritable." This logic confuses causation (the heat is causing accidents) with correlation. Traffic accidents have gone up and so has the heat, but that doesn't necessarily mean that one is causing the other. A new iPhone could have been released, creating distracted drivers. Or, there could have been more rain in the summer, causing dangerous driving conditions.
Performer to related action	"A lawyer passes the bar exam after finishing law school." "A student passes the SAT after finishing high school." Performer to related action requires a test taker to make an association between actions and their performers. Here, we see a performer passing some kind of exam after they've gone through years of training. In this way, the student and their actions are analogous to the lawyer and their actions.
Cause and effect	"A restaurant was shut down because it had an infestation problem." "A company went out of business because it couldn't produce enough inventory." In the analogy above, we see something shutting down because of a problem. The cause and effect analogy presents an unequivocal effect to an action and requires no effort to make something happen.
Unintended consequence	"Two parents enter therapy with the purpose of finding help for their son, who is struggling with substance abuse and behavioral problems at school. As a result, they find that they also are dealing with unresolved issues in the past and learn ways to cope with these issues." Here, a group of people set out to do one thing, and receive another in return. In this situation, there is an unintended consequence beside an intended consequence. In some situations, the intended consequence might not happen at all, and the unintended consequence will have the opposite effect of the intended consequence, creating an ironic situation.

Let's look at an example of an analogy question. This is a passage from *Ten Great Events in History* by James Johonnot.

> Meantime, in the Church of England a spirit of criticism had grown up. Stricter thinkers disliked the imposing ceremonies which the English church still retained: some of the ministers ceased to wear gowns in preaching, performed the marriage ceremony without using a ring, and were in favor of simplifying all the church service. Unpretentious workers began to tire of the everlasting quarreling, and to long for a religion simple and quiet. These soon met trouble, for the rulers had decided that salvation was by the Church of England, as the sovereign, its head, should order. Dissent was the two-fold guilt of heresy and revolution—sin against God and crime against the king and English law. They were forbidden to preach at all if they would not wear a gown during service, and the people who went to hear them were punished. This treatment caused serious thought among the "non-conformists," as they were called, and, once thinking, they soon concluded that the king had no such supreme right to order the church, and the church had over its ministers no such right of absolute dictation.

Given Johonnot's account of the criticism of the Church of England in the Middle Ages, which one of the following is most analogous to the situation of the ministers' refusal to wear gowns and the workers' resistance of fighting leading to problems with the church?
　　a. A church body meets resistance from an outside secular entity for issues related to social injustice.
　　b. Three members of a sorority refuse to do the hazing ritual, so they are kicked out of the sorority by the other members.
　　c. A group of kids at school who create an exclusive club that says anyone can join as long as they are in second grade and live on Magnolia Street.
　　d. A book club that finds it is no longer useful to its members, and thus attempts to change the group to a film club instead.

What we have in the original source are members part of a group refusing to participate in a tradition, so as a result, they are punished by the group. The ministers and workers are refusing to participate in church traditions, so they are punished or banished by the church.

Choice *B* is the correct answer to this analogy question. We have members of a group refusing to participate in a tradition (a hazing ritual), so they are punished by the other members of the group. This target fits the original analogy source the closest.

Choice *A* is incorrect. Although we are dealing with a church, the structure of the analogy is not the same. In this situation, the group is experiencing external problems rather than internal problems depicted in the original source.

Choice *C* is incorrect because this analogy depicts a creation of a group and the rules for joining it. In the original analogy, the group is already established with its laws and traditions.

Choice *D* is incorrect because this group is able to adapt to dissent as a whole, and is not in disagreement about traditions that are no longer working.

Applying Ideas Presented in a Reading Selection to Other Situations

There may be questions that give a scenario with a general conclusion and ask you to apply that general conclusion to a new context. Skills for making inferences and drawing conclusions will be helpful in the first portion of this question type. Reading the initial scenario carefully and finding the general concept, or the bigger picture, is necessary for when the test taker attempts to apply this general concept to the new context the question provides. Here is an example of a test question that asks the test taker to apply information in a selection to a new context:

> The placebo effect is a phenomenon used in clinical trial studies to test the effectiveness of new medications. A group of people are given either the new medication or the placebo but are not told which. Interestingly, about one-third of people who are given the placebo in clinical trials will report a cessation of their symptoms. In one trial in 1925, a group of people were given sugar pills and told their migraines should dissipate as a result of the pills. Forty-two percent noticed that in the following six months, their weekly migraines evaporated. Researchers believe that human belief and expectation might be a reason that the placebo will work in some patients.

Considering the phenomenon of the placebo effect, what would probably happen to someone who is given a shot with no medication and told their arm should go numb from it?

  a. The patient might experience some burning in their arm, but then they would feel nothing.
  b. The patient would feel their arm going numb, as the placebo effect is certain to work.
  c. Nothing would happen because the shot does not actually have any medication in it.
  d. The individual might actually experience a numbing sensation in their arm, as the placebo works on some people by simply being told the placebo will have certain effects.

The answer is Choice *D*. The individual might actually experience a numbing sensation in their arm, as the placebo works on some people by simply being told the placebo will have certain effects. Choices *B* and *C* are too absolute to be considered correct—watch out for words like "never" or "always" in the answer choices so you can rule them out if possible. Choice *A* is incorrect because we don't know what the initial sensation of the shot would feel like for this individual. The placebo effect would have a chance of working with the shot, just like it would have a chance of working in the above example with the pill. The patient's belief in an effect is what can possibly manifest the desired result of the placebo.

Practice Questions

Questions 1-6 are based on the following passage from *The Life, Crime, and Capture of John Wilkes Booth* by George Alfred Townsend:

The box in which the President sat consisted of two boxes turned into one, the middle partition being removed, as on all occasions when a state party visited the theater. The box was on a level with the dress circle; about twelve feet above the stage. There were two entrances—the door nearest to the wall having been closed and locked; the door nearest the balustrades of the dress circle, and at right angles with it, being open and left open, after the visitors had entered. The interior was carpeted, lined with crimson paper, and furnished with a sofa covered with crimson velvet, three arm chairs similarly covered, and six cane-bottomed chairs. Festoons of flags hung before the front of the box against a background of lace.

President Lincoln took one of the arm-chairs and seated himself in the front of the box, in the angle nearest the audience, where, partially screened from observation, he had the best view of what was transpiring on the stage. Mrs. Lincoln sat next to him, and Miss Harris in the opposite angle nearest the stage. Major Rathbone sat just behind Mrs. Lincoln and Miss Harris. These four were the only persons in the box.

The play proceeded, although "Our American Cousin," without Mr. Sothern, has, since that gentleman's departure from this country, been justly esteemed a very dull affair. The audience at Ford's, including Mrs. Lincoln, seemed to enjoy it very much. The worthy wife of the President leaned forward, her hand upon her husband's knee, watching every scene in the drama with amused attention. Even across the President's face at intervals swept a smile, robbing it of its habitual sadness.

About the beginning of the second act, the mare, standing in the stable in the rear of the theater, was disturbed in the midst of her meal by the entrance of the young man who had quitted her in the afternoon. It is presumed that she was saddled and bridled with exquisite care.

Having completed these preparations, Mr. Booth entered the theater by the stage door; summoned one of the scene shifters, Mr. John Spangler, emerged through the same door with that individual, leaving the door open, and left the mare in his hands to be held until he (Booth) should return. Booth who was even more fashionably and richly dressed than usual, walked thence around to the front of the theater, and went in. Ascending to the dress circle, he stood for a little time gazing around upon the audience and occasionally upon the stage in his usual graceful manner. He was subsequently observed by Mr. Ford, the proprietor of the theater, to be slowly elbowing his way through the crowd that packed the rear of the dress circle toward the right side, at the extremity of which was the box where Mr. and Mrs. Lincoln and their companions were seated. Mr. Ford casually noticed this as a slightly extraordinary symptom of interest on the part of an actor so familiar with the routine of the theater and the play.

1. Which of the following best describes the author's attitude toward the events leading up to the assassination of President Lincoln?
    a. Excitement, due to the setting and its people
    b. Sadness, due to the death of a beloved president
    c. Anger, due to the impending violence
    d. Neutrality, due to the style of the report
    e. Apprehension, due to the crowd and their ignorance

2. What does the author mean by the last sentence in the passage?
    a. Mr. Ford was suspicious of Booth and assumed he was making his way to Mr. Lincoln's box.
    b. Mr. Ford assumed Booth's movement throughout the theater was due to being familiar with the theater.
    c. Mr. Ford thought that Booth was making his way to the theater lounge to find his companions.
    d. Mr. Ford thought that Booth was elbowing his way to the dressing room to get ready for the play.
    e. Mr. Ford thought that Booth was coming down with an illness due to the strange symptoms he displayed.

3. Given the author's description of the play "Our American Cousin," which one of the following is most analogous to Mr. Sothern's departure from the theater?
    a. A ballet dancer who leaves the New York City Ballet just before they go on to their final performance.
    b. A basketball player leaves an NBA team and the next year they make it to the championship but lose.
    c. A lead singer leaves their band to begin a solo career, and the band's sales on their next album drop by 50 percent.
    d. A movie actor who dies in the middle of making a movie and the movie is made anyway by actors who resemble the deceased.
    e. A professor who switches to the top-rated university for their department only to find the university they left behind has surpassed his new department's rating.

4. Which of the following texts most closely relates to the organizational structure of the passage?
    a. A chronological account in a fiction novel of a woman and a man meeting for the first time.
    b. A cause-and-effect text ruminating on the causes of global warming.
    c. An autobiography that begins with the subject's death and culminates in his birth.
    d. A text focusing on finding a solution to the problem of the Higgs boson particle.
    e. A text contrasting the realities of life on Mars versus life on Earth.

5. Which of the following words, if substituted for the word *festoons* in the first paragraph, would LEAST change the meaning of the sentence?
    a. Feathers
    b. Armies
    c. Adornments
    d. Buckets
    e. Boats

6. What is the primary purpose of the passage?
   a. To persuade the audience that John Wilkes Booth killed Abraham Lincoln
   b. To inform the audience of the setting wherein Lincoln was shot
   c. To narrate the bravery of Lincoln and his last days as President
   d. To recount in detail the events that led up to Abraham Lincoln's death
   e. To disprove the popular opinion that John Wilkes Booth is the person who killed Abraham Lincoln

Questions 7-13 are based on the following passage from The Story of Germ Life *by Herbert William Conn:*

The first and most universal change effected in milk is its souring. So universal is this phenomenon that it is generally regarded as an inevitable change that cannot be avoided, and, as already pointed out, has in the past been regarded as a normal property of milk. To-day, however, the phenomenon is well understood. It is due to the action of certain of the milk bacteria upon the milk sugar which converts it into lactic acid, and this acid gives the sour taste and curdles the milk. After this acid is produced in small quantity its presence proves deleterious to the growth of the bacteria, and further bacterial growth is checked. After souring, therefore, the milk for some time does not ordinarily undergo any further changes.

Milk souring has been commonly regarded as a single phenomenon, alike in all cases. When it was first studied by bacteriologists it was thought to be due in all cases to a single species of micro-organism which was discovered to be commonly present and named *Bacillus acidi lactici.* This bacterium has certainly the power of souring milk rapidly, and is found to be very common in dairies in Europe. As soon as bacteriologists turned their attention more closely to the subject it was found that the spontaneous souring of milk was not always caused by the same species of bacterium. Instead of finding this *Bacillus acidi lactici* always present, they found that quite a number of different species of bacteria have the power of souring milk, and are found in different specimens of soured milk. The number of species of bacteria that have been found to sour milk has increased until something over a hundred are known to have this power. These different species do not affect the milk in the same way. All produce some acid, but they differ in the kind and the amount of acid, and especially in the other changes which are effected at the same time that the milk is soured, so that the resulting soured milk is quite variable. In spite of this variety, however, the most recent work tends to show that the majority of cases of spontaneous souring of milk are produced by bacteria which, though somewhat variable, probably constitute a single species, and are identical with the *Bacillus acidi lactici.* This species, found common in the dairies of Europe, according to recent investigations occurs in this country as well. We may say, then, that while there are many species of bacteria infesting the dairy which can sour the milk, there is one that is more common and more universally found than others, and this is the ordinary cause of milk souring.

When we study more carefully the effect upon the milk of the different species of bacteria found in the dairy, we find that there is a great variety of changes they produce when they are allowed to grow in milk. The dairyman experiences many troubles with his milk. It sometimes curdles without becoming acid. Sometimes it becomes bitter, or acquires an unpleasant "tainted" taste, or, again, a "soapy" taste. Occasionally, a dairyman finds his milk becoming slimy, instead of souring and curdling in the normal fashion. At such times, after a number of hours, the milk becomes so slimy that it can be drawn into long threads. Such an infection proves very troublesome, for many a time it persists in spite of all attempts made to remedy it. Again, in other cases the milk will turn blue, acquiring about the time it becomes sour a beautiful sky-blue colour.

Or it may become red, or occasionally yellow. All of these troubles the dairyman owes to the presence in his milk of unusual species of bacteria which grow there abundantly.

7. The word *deleterious* in the first paragraph can be best interpreted as meaning which one of the following?
   a. Amicable
   b. Smoldering
   c. Luminous
   d. Ruinous
   e. Virtuous

8. Which of the following best explains how the passage is organized?
   a. The author begins by presenting the effects of a phenomenon, then explains the process of this phenomenon, and then ends by giving the history of the study of this phenomenon.
   b. The author begins by explaining a process or phenomenon, then gives the history of the study of this phenomenon, this ends by presenting the effects of this phenomenon.
   c. The author begins by giving the history of the study of a certain phenomenon, then explains the process of this phenomenon, then ends by presenting the effects of this phenomenon.
   d. The author begins by giving a broad definition of a subject, then presents more specific cases of the subject, then ends by contrasting two different viewpoints on the subject.
   e. The author begins by contrasting two different viewpoints, then gives a short explanation of a subject, then ends by summarizing what was previously stated in the passage.

9. What is the primary purpose of the passage?
   a. To inform the reader of the phenomenon, investigation, and consequences of milk souring
   b. To persuade the reader that milk souring is due to *Bacillus acidi lactici,* which is commonly found in the dairies of Europe
   c. To describe the accounts and findings of researchers studying the phenomenon of milk souring
   d. To discount the former researchers' opinions on milk souring and bring light to new investigations
   e. To narrate the story of one researcher who discovered the phenomenon of milk souring and its subsequent effects

10. What does the author say about the ordinary cause of milk souring?
   a. Milk souring is caused mostly by a species of bacteria called *Bacillus acidi lactici,* although former research asserted that it was caused by a variety of bacteria.
   b. The ordinary cause of milk souring is unknown to current researchers, although former researchers thought it was due to a species of bacteria called *Bacillus acidi lactici.*
   c. Milk souring is caused mostly by a species of bacteria identical to that of *Bacillus acidi lactici,* although there are a variety of other bacteria that cause milk souring as well.
   d. The ordinary cause of milk souring will sometimes curdle without becoming acidic, though sometimes it will turn colors other than white, or have strange smells or tastes.
   e. The ordinary cause of milk souring is from bacteria with a strange, "soapy" smell, usually the color of sky blue.

11. The author of the passage would most likely agree most with which of the following?

a. Milk researchers in the past have been incompetent and have sent us on a wild goose chase when determining what causes milk souring.

b. Dairymen are considered more expert in the field of milk souring than milk researchers.

c. The study of milk souring has improved throughout the years, as we now understand more of what causes milk souring and what happens afterward.

d. Any type of bacteria will turn milk sour, so it's best to keep milk in an airtight container while it is being used.

e. The effects of milk souring is a natural occurrence of milk, so it should not be dangerous to consume.

12. Given the author's account of the consequences of milk souring, which of the following is most closely analogous to the author's description of what happens after milk becomes slimy?

a. The chemical change that occurs when a firework explodes.

b. A rainstorm that overwaters a succulent plant.

c. Mercury inside of a thermometer that leaks out.

d. A child who swallows flea medication.

e. A large block of ice that melts into a liquid.

13. What type of paragraph would most likely come after the third?

a. A paragraph depicting the general effects of bacteria on milk.

b. A paragraph explaining a broad history of what researchers have found in regard to milk souring.

c. A paragraph outlining the properties of milk souring and the way in which it occurs.

d. A paragraph showing the ways bacteria infiltrate milk and ways to avoid this infiltration.

e. A paragraph naming all the bacteria in alphabetical order with a brief definition of what each does to milk.

Questions 14-20 are based on the following two passages, labeled "Passage A" and "Passage B":

Passage A

(from "Free Speech in War Time" by James Parker Hall, written in 1921, published in Columbia Law Review, Vol. 21 No. 6)

> In approaching this problem of interpretation, we may first put out of consideration certain obvious limitations upon the generality of all guaranties of free speech. An occasional unthinking malcontent may urge that the only meaning not fraught with danger to liberty is the literal one that no utterance may be forbidden, no matter what its intent or result; but in fact, it is nowhere seriously argued by anyone whose opinion is entitled to respect that direct and intentional incitations to crime may not be forbidden by the state. If a state may properly forbid murder or robbery or treason, it may also punish those who induce or counsel the commission of such crimes. Any other view makes a mockery of the state's power to declare and punish offences. And what the state may do to prevent the incitement of serious crimes that are universally condemned, it may also do to prevent the incitement of lesser crimes, or of those in regard to the bad tendency of which public opinion is divided. That is, if the state may punish John for burning straw in an alley, it may also constitutionally punish Frank for inciting John to do it, though Frank did so by speech or writing. And if, in 1857, the United States could punish John for helping a fugitive slave to escape, it could also punish Frank for inducing John to do this, even though a large section of public opinion might applaud John and condemn the Fugitive Slave Law.

Passage B

(from "Freedom of Speech in War Time" by Zechariah Chafee, Jr. written in 1919, published in Harvard Law Review Vol. 32 No. 8)

The true boundary line of the First Amendment can be fixed only when Congress and the courts realize that the principle on which speech is classified as lawful or unlawful involves the balancing against each other of two very important social interests, in public safety and in the search for truth. Every reasonable attempt should be made to maintain both interests unimpaired, and the great interest in free speech should be sacrificed only when the interest in public safety is really imperiled, and not, as most men believe, when it is barely conceivable that it may be slightly affected. In war time, therefore, speech should be unrestricted by the censorship or by punishment, unless it is clearly liable to cause direct and dangerous interference with the conduct of the war.

Thus our problem of locating the boundary line of free speech is solved. It is fixed close to the point where words will give rise to unlawful acts. We cannot define the right of free speech with the precision of the Rule against Perpetuities or the Rule in Shelley's Case, because it involves national policies which are much more flexible than private property, but we can establish a workable principle of classification in this method of balancing and this broad test of certain danger. There is a similar balancing in the determination of what is "due process of law." And we can with certitude declare that the First Amendment forbids the punishment of words merely for their injurious tendencies. The history of the Amendment and the political function of free speech corroborate each other and make this conclusion plain.

14. Which one of the following questions is central to both passages?
    a. Why is freedom of speech something to be protected in the first place?
    b. Do people want absolute liberty or do they only want liberty for a certain purpose?
    c. What is the true definition of freedom of speech in a democracy?
    d. How can we find an appropriate boundary of freedom of speech during wartime?
    e. What is the interpretation of the first amendment and its limitations?

15. The authors of the two passages would be most likely to disagree over which of the following?
    a. A man is thrown in jail due to his provocation of violence in Washington D.C. during a riot.
    b. A man is thrown in jail for stealing bread for his starving family, and the judge has mercy for him and lets him go.
    c. A man is thrown in jail for encouraging a riot against the U.S. government for the wartime tactics although no violence ensues.
    d. A man is thrown in jail because he has been caught as a German spy working within the U.S. army.
    e. A man is thrown in jail because he murdered a German-born citizen whom he thought was working for the Central Powers during World War I.

16. The relationship between Passage A and Passage B is most analogous to the relationship between the documents described in which of the following?

a. A research report that asserts water pollution in major cities in California has increased by thirty percent in the past five years; an article advocating the cessation of chicken farms in California near rivers to avoid pollution.

b. An article detailing the effects of radiation in Fukushima; a research report describing the deaths and birth defects as a result of the hazardous waste dumped on the Somali Coast.

c. An article that suggests that labor laws during times of war should be left up to the states; an article that showcases labor laws during the past that have been altered due to the current crisis of war.

d. A research report arguing that the leading cause of methane emissions in the world is from agriculture practices; an article citing that the leading cause of methane emissions in the world is from the transportation of coal, oil, and natural gas.

e. A journal article in the Netherlands about the law of euthanasia that cites evidence to support only the act of passive euthanasia as an appropriate way to die; a journal article in the Netherlands about the law of euthanasia that cites evidence to support voluntary euthanasia in any aspect.

17. The author uses the examples in the last lines of Passage A in order to do what?

a. To compare different types of crimes to see by which one the principle of freedom of speech would become objectionable

b. To demonstrate that anyone who incites a crime, despite the severity or magnitude of the crime, should be held accountable for that crime in some degree

c. To prove that the definition of "freedom of speech" is altered depending on what kind of crime is being committed

d. To show that some crimes are in the best interest of a nation and should not be punishable if they are proven to prevent harm to others

e. To suggest that the crimes mentioned should be reopened in order to punish those who incited the crimes

18. Which of the following, if true, would most seriously undermine the claim proposed by the author in Passage A that if the state can punish a crime, then it can punish the incitement of that crime?

a. The idea that human beings are able and likely to change their mind between the utterance and execution of an event that may harm others

b. The idea that human beings will always choose what they think is right based on their cultural upbringing

c. The idea that the limitation of free speech by the government during wartime will protect the country from any group that causes a threat to that country's freedom

d. The idea that those who support freedom of speech probably have intentions of subverting the government

e. The idea that if a man encourages a woman to commit a crime and she succeeds, the man is just as guilty as the woman

19. What is the primary purpose of the second passage?

    a. To analyze the First Amendment in historical situations in order to make an analogy to the current war at hand in the nation

    b. To demonstrate that the boundaries set during wartime are different from that when the country is at peace, and that we should change our laws accordingly

    c. To offer the idea that during wartime, the principle of freedom of speech should be limited to that of even minor utterances in relation to a crime

    d. To claim the interpretation of freedom of speech is already evident in the First Amendment and to offer a clear perimeter of the principle during war time

    e. To assert that any limitation on freedom of speech is a violation of human rights and that the circumstances of war do not change this violation

20. Which of the following words, if substituted for the word *malcontent* in Passage A, would LEAST change the meaning of the sentence?

    a. Regimen

    b. Cacophony

    c. Anecdote

    d. Residual

    e. Grievance

Questions 21-27 are based on the following passage from Rhetoric and Poetry in the Renaissance: A Study of Rhetorical Terms in English Renaissance Literary Criticism *by D.L. Clark:*

To the Greeks and Romans, rhetoric meant the theory of oratory. As a pedagogical mechanism, it endeavored to teach students to persuade an audience. The content of rhetoric included all that the ancients had learned to be of value in persuasive public speech. It taught how to work up a case by drawing valid inferences from sound evidence, how to organize this material in the most persuasive order, and how to compose in clear and harmonious sentences. Thus, to the Greeks and Romans, rhetoric was defined by its function of discovering means to persuasion and was taught in the schools as something that every free-born man could and should learn.

In both these respects the ancients felt that poetics, the theory of poetry, was different from rhetoric. As the critical theorists believed that the poets were inspired, they endeavored less to teach men to be poets than to point out the excellences which the poets had attained. Although these critics generally, with the exceptions of Aristotle and Eratosthenes, believed the greatest value of poetry to be in the teaching of morality, no one of them endeavored to define poetry, as they did rhetoric, by its purpose. To Aristotle, and centuries later to Plutarch, the distinguishing mark of poetry was imitation. Not until the renaissance did critics define poetry as an art of imitation endeavoring to inculcate morality . . .

The same essential difference between classical rhetoric and poetics appears in the content of classical poetics. Whereas classical rhetoric deals with speeches which might be delivered to convict or acquit a defendant in the law court, or to secure a certain action by the deliberative assembly, or to adorn an occasion, classical poetic deals with lyric, epic, and drama. It is a commonplace that classical literary critics paid little attention to the lyric. It is less frequently realized that they devoted almost as little space to discussion of metrics. By far the greater bulk of classical treatises on poetics is devoted to characterization and to the technique of plot construction, involving as it does narrative and dramatic unity and movement as distinct from logical unity and movement.

21. What does the author say about one way in which the purpose of poetry changed for later philosophers?

a. The author says that at first, poetry was not defined by its purpose but was valued for its ability to be used to teach morality. Later, some philosophers would define poetry by its ability to instill morality. Finally, during the renaissance, poetry was believed to be an imitative art, but was not necessarily believed to instill morality in its readers.

b. The author says that the classical understanding of poetry dealt with its ability to be used to teach morality. Later, philosophers would define poetry by its ability to imitate life. Finally, during the renaissance, poetry was believed to be an imitative art that instilled morality in its readers.

c. The author says that at first, poetry was thought to be an imitation of reality, then later, philosophers valued poetry more for its ability to instill morality.

d. The author says that the classical understanding of poetry was that it dealt with the search for truth through its content; later, the purpose of poetry would be through its entertainment value.

e. The author says that the initial understanding of the purpose of poetry was its entertainment value. Then, as poetry evolved into a more religious era, the renaissance, it was valued for its ability to instill morality through its teaching.

22. What does the author of the passage say about classical literary critics in relation to poetics?

a. That rhetoric was valued more than poetry because rhetoric had a definitive purpose to persuade an audience, and poetry's wavering purpose made it harder for critics to teach.

b. That although most poetry was written as lyric, epic, or drama, the critics were most focused on the techniques of lyric and epic and their performance of musicality and structure.

c. That although most poetry was written as lyric, epic, or drama, the critics were most focused on the techniques of the epic and drama and their performance of structure and character.

d. That the study of poetics was more pleasurable than the study of rhetoric due to its ability to assuage its audience, and the critics, therefore, focused on what poets did to create that effect.

e. That since poetics was made by the elite in Greek and Roman society, literary critics resented poetics for its obsession of material things and its superfluous linguistics.

23. What is the primary purpose of this passage?

a. To alert the readers to Greek and Roman culture regarding poetic texts and the focus on characterization and plot construction rather than lyric and meter.

b. To inform the readers of the changes in poetic critical theory throughout the years and to contrast those changes to the solidity of rhetoric.

c. To educate the audience on rhetoric by explaining the historical implications of using rhetoric in the education system.

d. To convince the audience that poetics is a subset of rhetoric as viewed by the Greek and Roman culture.

e. To contemplate the differences between classical rhetoric and poetry and to consider their purposes in a particular culture.

24. The word *inculcate* in the second paragraph can be best interpreted as meaning which one of the following?

a. Imbibe

b. Instill

c. Implode

d. Inquire

e. Idolize

25. Which of the following most closely resembles the way in which the passage is structured?

    a. The first paragraph presents an issue. The second paragraph offers a solution to the problem. The third paragraph summarizes the first two paragraphs.

    b. The first paragraph presents definitions and examples of a particular subject. The second paragraph presents a second subject in the same way. The third paragraph offers a contrast of the two subjects.

    c. The first paragraph presents an inquiry. The second paragraph explains the details of that inquiry. The last paragraph offers a solution.

    d. The first paragraph presents two subjects alongside definitions and examples. The second paragraph presents us a comparison of the two subjects. The third paragraph presents a contrast of the two subjects.

    e. The first paragraph offers a solution to a problem. The second paragraph questions the solution. The third paragraph offers a different solution.

26. Given the author's description of the content of rhetoric in the first paragraph, which one of the following is most analogous to what it taught? (The sentence is shown below.)

It taught how to work up a case by drawing valid inferences from sound evidence, how to organize this material in the most persuasive order, how to compose in clear and harmonious sentences.

    a. As a musician, they taught me that the end product of the music is everything—what I did to get there was irrelevant, whether it was my ability to read music or the reliance on my intuition to compose.

    b. As a detective, they taught me that time meant everything when dealing with a new case, that the simplest explanation is usually the right one, and that documentation is extremely important to credibility.

    c. As a writer, they taught me the most important thing about writing was consistently showing up to the page every single day, no matter where my muse was.

    d. As a football player, they taught me how to understand the logistics of the game, how my placement on the field affected the rest of the team, and how to run and throw with a mixture of finesse and strength.

    e. As a doctor, they taught me how to show compassion towards patients and how to take care of my own physical and mental health while running my own practice.

27. Which of the following words, if substituted for the word *treatises* in paragraph three, would LEAST change the meaning of the sentence?

    a. Thesauruses

    b. Encyclopedias

    c. Sermons

    d. Anthems

    e. Commentary

Questions 28–31 are based on the following passage. It is from Oregon, Washington, and Alaska. Sights and Scenes for the Tourist, *written by E.L. Lomax in 1890:*

> Portland is a very beautiful city of 60,000 inhabitants, and situated on the Willamette river twelve miles from its junction with the Columbia. It is perhaps true of many of the growing cities of the West, that they do not offer the same social advantages as the older cities of the East. But this is principally the case as to what may be called boom cities, where the larger part of the population is of that floating class which follows in the line of temporary growth for the purposes of speculation, and in no sense applies to those centers of trade whose prosperity is based on the

solid foundation of legitimate business. As the metropolis of a vast section of country, having broad agricultural valleys filled with improved farms, surrounded by mountains rich in mineral wealth, and boundless forests of as fine timber as the world produces, the cause of Portland's growth and prosperity is the trade which it has as the center of collection and distribution of this great wealth of natural resources, and it has attracted, not the boomer and speculator, who find their profits in the wild excitement of the boom, but the merchant, manufacturer, and investor, who seek the surer if slower channels of legitimate business and investment. These have come from the East, most of them within the last few years. They came as seeking a better and wider field to engage in the same occupations they had followed in their Eastern homes, and bringing with them all the love of polite life which they had acquired there, have established here a new society, equaling in all respects that which they left behind. Here are as fine churches, as complete a system of schools, as fine residences, as great a love of music and art, as can be found at any city of the East of equal size.

But while Portland may justly claim to be the peer of any city of its size in the United States in all that pertains to social life, in the attractions of beauty of location and surroundings it stands without its peer. The work of art is but the copy of nature. What the residents of other cities see but in the copy, or must travel half the world over to see in the original, the resident of Portland has at its very door.

The city is situated on a gently-sloping ground, with, on the one side, the river, and on the other a range of hills, which, within easy walking distance, rise to an elevation of a thousand feet above the river, affording a most picturesque building site. From the very streets of the thickly settled portion of the city, the Cascade Mountains, with the snow-capped peaks of Hood, Adams, St. Helens, and Rainier, are in plain view.

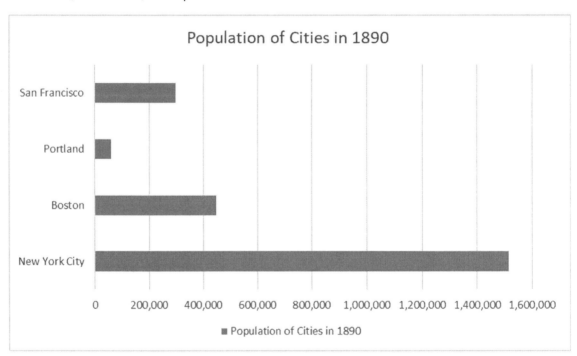

28. What is a characteristic of a "boom city," as indicated by the passage?

    a. A city that is built on a solid business foundation of mineral wealth and farming.

    b. An area of land on the west coast that quickly becomes populated by residents from the east coast.

    c. A city that, due to the hot weather and dry climate, catches fire frequently, resulting in a devastating population drop.

    d. A city whose population is made up of people who seek quick fortunes rather than building a solid business foundation.

    e. A city located on a river or river delta where the land is fertile and economic conditions are optimal.

29. By stating that "they do not offer the same social advantages as the older cities of the East" in the first paragraph, the author most likely intends to suggest which of the following?

    a. Inhabitants who reside in older cities in the East are much more social than inhabitants who reside in newer cities in the West because of background and experience.

    b. Cities in the West have no culture compared to the East because the culture in the East comes from European influence.

    c. Cities in the East are older than cities in the West, and older cities always have better culture than newer cities.

    d. Since cities in the West are newly established, it takes them a longer time to develop cultural roots and societal functions than those cities that are already established in the East.

    e. The culture in boom cities is likely to outpace previously-popular cities because they offer so much more.

30. Based on the information at the end of the first paragraph, what would the author say of Portland?

    a. It has twice as much culture as the cities in the East.

    b. It's amount of culture is dwindling as it becomes more business-oriented.

    c. It doesn't have as much culture as cities in the East.

    d. It doesn't have as much culture as cities in the West.

    e. It has as much culture as the cities in the East.

31. How many more citizens did San Francisco have than Portland in 1890?

    a. Approximately 110,000

    b. Approximately 240,000

    c. Approximately 500,000

    d. Approximately 1,000,000

    e. Approximately 1,500,000

Questions 32–35 are based on the excerpt from Variation of Animals and Plants *by Charles Darwin:*

> Peach (Amygdalus persica).—In the last chapter I gave two cases of a peach-almond and a double-flowered almond which suddenly produced fruit closely resembling true peaches. I have also given many cases of peach-trees producing buds, which, when developed into branches, have yielded nectarines. We have seen that no less than six named and several unnamed varieties of the peach have thus produced several varieties of nectarine. I have shown that it is highly improbable that all these peach-trees, some of which are old varieties, and have been propagated by the million, are hybrids from the peach and nectarine, and that it is opposed to all analogy to attribute the occasional production of nectarines on peach-trees to the direct action of pollen from some neighbouring nectarine-tree. Several of the cases are highly remarkable, because, firstly, the fruit thus produced has sometimes been in part a nectarine and in part a peach; secondly, because nectarines thus suddenly produced have reproduced themselves by seed; and

thirdly, because nectarines are produced from peach-trees from seed as well as from buds. The seed of the nectarine, on the other hand, occasionally produces peaches; and we have seen in one instance that a nectarine-tree yielded peaches by bud-variation. As the peach is certainly the oldest or primary variety, the production of peaches from nectarines, either by seeds or buds, may perhaps be considered as a case of reversion. Certain trees have also been described as indifferently bearing peaches or nectarines, and this may be considered as bud-variation carried to an extreme degree.

The grosse mignonne peach at Montreuil produced "from a sporting branch" the grosse mignonne tardive, "a most excellent variety," which ripens its fruit a fortnight later than the parent tree, and is equally good. This same peach has likewise produced by bud-variation the early grosse mignonne. Hunt's large tawny nectarine "originated from Hunt's small tawny nectarine, but not through seminal reproduction."

32. Which statement is NOT a detail from the passage?
    a. At least six named varieties of the peach have produced several varieties of nectarine.
    b. It is not probable that all of the peach-trees mentioned are hybrids from the peach and nectarine.
    c. An unremarkable case is the fact that nectarines are produced from peach-trees from seed as well as from buds.
    d. The production of peaches from nectarines might be considered a case of reversion.
    e. Some modern descendants of earlier plum trees now bear differently-colored fruit but are otherwise the same.

33. What is the meaning of the word *propagated* in the first paragraph of this passage?
    a. Multiplied
    b. Diminished
    c. Watered
    d. Uprooted
    e. Planted

34. Which of the following most closely reveals the author's tone in this passage?
    a. Enthusiastic
    b. Objective
    c. Critical
    d. Desperate
    e. Anxious

35. Which of the following is an accurate paraphrasing of the following phrase?

Certain trees have also been described as indifferently bearing peaches or nectarines, and this may be considered as bud-variation carried to an extreme degree.

a. Some trees are described as bearing peaches and some trees have been described as bearing nectarines, but individually, the buds are extreme examples of variation.

b. One way in which bud-variation is said to be carried to an extreme degree is when specific trees have been shown to casually produce peaches or nectarines.

c. Certain trees are indifferent to bud-variation, as recently shown in the trees that produce both peaches and nectarines in the same season.

d. Nectarines and peaches are known to have cross-variation in their buds, which indifferently bears other sorts of fruit to an extreme degree.

e. Although possible, it's extremely uncommon in this day and age to find trees that can bear peaches or nectarines.

Questions 36–39 are based on the excerpt from A Christmas Carol *by Charles Dickens:*

Meanwhile the fog and darkness thickened so, that people ran about with flaring links, proffering their services to go before horses in carriages, and conduct them on their way. The ancient tower of a church, whose gruff old bell was always peeping slyly down at Scrooge out of a Gothic window in the wall, became invisible, and struck the hours and quarters in the clouds, with tremulous vibrations afterwards as if its teeth were chattering in its frozen head up there. The cold became intense. In the main street, at the corner of the court, some labourers were repairing the gas-pipes, and had lighted a great fire in a brazier, round which a party of ragged men and boys were gathered: warming their hands and winking their eyes before the blaze in rapture. The water-plug being left in solitude, its overflowings sullenly congealed, and turned to misanthropic ice. The brightness of the shops where holly sprigs and berries crackled in the lamp heat of the windows, made pale faces ruddy as they passed. Poulterers' and grocers' trades became a splendid joke; a glorious pageant, with which it was next to impossible to believe that such dull principles as bargain and sale had anything to do. The Lord Mayor, in the stronghold of the mighty Mansion House, gave orders to his fifty cooks and butlers to keep Christmas as a Lord Mayor's household should; and even the little tailor, whom he had fined five shillings on the previous Monday for being drunk and bloodthirsty in the streets, stirred up to-morrow's pudding in his garret, while his lean wife and the baby sallied out to buy the beef.

Foggier yet, and colder. Piercing, searching, biting cold. If the good Saint Dunstan had but nipped the Evil Spirit's nose with a touch of such weather as that, instead of using his familiar weapons, then indeed he would have roared to lusty purpose. The owner of one scant young nose, gnawed and mumbled by the hungry cold as bones are gnawed by dogs, stopped down at Scrooge's keyhole to regale him with a Christmas carol: but at the first sound of

"God bless you, merry gentleman! May nothing you dismay"

Scrooge seized the ruler with such energy of action, that the singer fled in terror, leaving the keyhole to the fog and even more congenial frost.

36. In the context in which it appears, *congealed* most nearly means which of the following?
    a. Burst
    b. Loosened
    c. Shrank
    d. Thickened
    e. Pooled

37. Which of the following can NOT be inferred from the passage?
    a. The season of this narrative is in the winter time.
    b. The majority of the narrative is located in a bustling city street.
    c. This passage takes place during the night time.
    d. The Lord Mayor is a wealthy person within the narrative.
    e. Scrooge was not kind and receptive to the caroler.

38. According to the passage, which of the following regarding the poulterers and grocers is true?
    a. They were so poor in the quality of their products that customers saw them as a joke.
    b. They put on a pageant in the streets every year for Christmas to entice their customers.
    c. They did not believe in Christmas, so they refused to participate in the town parade.
    d. They worked tirelessly to convert non-believers and spread the Christmas spirit.
    e. They set their shops up to be entertaining public spectacles rather than a dull trade exchange.

39. The author's depiction of the scene in the last few paragraphs does all EXCEPT which of the following?
    a. Offer an allusion to religious affiliation in England.
    b. Attempt to evoke empathy for the character of Scrooge.
    c. Provide a palpable experience through the use of imagery and diction.
    d. Depict Scrooge as an uncaring, terrifying character to his fellows.
    e. Help readers visualize the setting and the adverse personality of Scrooge.

Questions 40–43 are based on the book On the Trail *by Lina Beard and Adelia Belle Beard:*

> For any journey, by rail or by boat, one has a general idea of the direction to be taken, the character of the land or water to be crossed, and of what one will find at the end. So it should be in striking the trail. Learn all you can about the path you are to follow. Whether it is plain or obscure, wet or dry; where it leads; and its length, measured more by time than by actual miles. A smooth, even trail of five miles will not consume the time and strength that must be expended upon a trail of half that length which leads over uneven ground, varied by bogs and obstructed by rocks and fallen trees, or a trail that is all up-hill climbing. If you are a novice and accustomed to walking only over smooth and level ground, you must allow more time for covering the distance than an experienced person would require and must count upon the expenditure of more strength, because your feet are not trained to the wilderness paths with their pitfalls and traps for the unwary, and every nerve and muscle will be strained to secure a safe foothold amid the tangled roots, on the slippery, moss-covered logs, over precipitous rocks that lie in your path. It will take time to pick your way over boggy places where the water oozes up through the thin, loamy soil as through a sponge; and experience alone will teach you which hummock of grass or moss will make a safe stepping-place and will not sink beneath your weight and soak your feet with hidden water. Do not scorn to learn all you can about the trail you are to take . . . It is not that you hesitate to encounter difficulties, but that you may prepare for them. In unknown regions take a responsible guide with you, unless the trail is short, easily followed, and a frequented one.

Do not go alone through lonely places; and, being on the trail, keep it and try no explorations of your own, at least not until you are quite familiar with the country and the ways of the wild.

Blazing the Trail

A woodsman usually blazes his trail by chipping with his axe the trees he passes, leaving white scars on their trunks, and to follow such a trail you stand at your first tree until you see the blaze on the next, then go to that and look for the one farther on; going in this way from tree to tree you keep the trail though it may, underfoot, be overgrown and indistinguishable.

If you must make a trail of your own, blaze it as you go by bending down and breaking branches of trees, underbrush, and bushes. Let the broken branches be on the side of bush or tree in the direction you are going, but bent down away from that side, or toward the bush, so that the lighter underside of the leaves will show and make a plain trail. Make these signs conspicuous and close together, for in returning, a dozen feet without the broken branch will sometimes confuse you, especially as everything has a different look when seen from the opposite side. By this same token it is a wise precaution to look back frequently as you go and impress the homeward-bound landmarks on your memory. If in your wanderings you have branched off and made ineffectual or blind trails which lead nowhere, and, in returning to camp, you are led astray by one of them, do not leave the false trail and strike out to make a new one, but turn back and follow the false trail to its beginning, for it must lead to the true trail again. Don't lose sight of your broken branches.

40. What part of the text is the girl most likely emulating in the image?
    a. Building a trap
    b. Setting up camp
    c. Blazing the trail
    d. Picking berries to eat
    e. Climbing an all uphill portion of a trail

41. According to the passage, what does the author say about unknown regions?
    a. You should try and explore unknown regions in order to learn the land better.
    b. Unless the trail is short or frequented, you should take a responsible guide with you.
    c. All unknown regions will contain pitfalls, traps, and boggy places.
    d. It's better to travel unknown regions by rail rather than by foot.
    e. It's wise to leave a false trail that you yourself know is false to deceive potential unwelcome people.

42. Which statement is NOT a detail from the passage?
    a. Learning about the trail beforehand is imperative.
    b. Time will differ depending on the land.
    c. Once you are familiar with the outdoors you can go places on your own.
    d. Be careful of wild animals on the trail you are on.
    e. Break branches on the side of bush or tree in the direction you are going.

43. In the last paragraph, which of the following does the author suggest when being led astray by a false trail?
    a. Bend down and break the branches off trees, underbrush, and bushes.
    b. Ignore the false trail and strike out to make a new one.
    c. Follow the false trail back to its beginning so that you can rediscover the real trail.
    d. Make the signs conspicuous so that you won't be confused when you turn around.
    e. Conceal the trail by bending the lighter side of the leaves downward to cover it.

Questions 44–47 are based on the following passage, which is from Poems by Alexander Pushkin *by Ivan Panin:*

> I do not believe there are as many as five examples of deviation from the literalness of the text. Once only, I believe, have I transposed two lines for convenience of translation; the other deviations are (*if* they are such) a substitution of an *and* for a comma in order to make now and then the reading of a line musical. With these exceptions, I have sacrificed *everything* to faithfulness of rendering. My object was to make Pushkin himself, without a prompter, speak to English readers. To make him thus speak in a foreign tongue was indeed to place him at a disadvantage; and music and rhythm and harmony are indeed fine things, but truth is finer still. I wished to present not what Pushkin would have said, or should have said, if he had written in English, but what he does say in Russian. That, stripped from all ornament of his wonderful melody and grace of form, as he is in a translation, he still, even in the hard English tongue, soothes and stirs, is in itself a sign that through the individual soul of Pushkin sings that universal soul whose strains appeal forever to man, in whatever clime, under whatever sky.
>
> I ask, therefore, no forgiveness, no indulgence even, from the reader for the crudeness and even harshness of the translation, which, I dare say, will be found in abundance by those who *look* for something to blame. Nothing of the kind is necessary. I have done the only thing there was to be done. Nothing more *could* be done (I mean by me, of course), and if critics still demand more,

they must settle it not with me, but with the Lord Almighty, who in his grim, yet arch way, long before critics appeared on the stage, hath ordained that it shall be impossible for a thing to be and not to be at the same time.

I have therefore tried neither for measure nor for rhyme. What I have done was this: I first translated each line word for word, and then by reading it aloud let mine ear arrange for me the words in such a way as to make some kind of rhythm. Where this could be done, I was indeed glad; where this could not be done, I was not sorry. It is idle to regret the impossible.

44. From clues in this passage, what type of work is the author doing?
   a. Translation work
   b. Criticism
   c. Historical validity
   d. Writing a biography
   e. Creating poetry

45. Where would you most likely find this passage in a text?
   a. Appendix
   b. Table of contents
   c. First chapter
   d. Preface
   e. After a graphic

46. According to the author, what is the most important aim of translation work?
   a. To retain the beauty of the work.
   b. To retain the truth of the work.
   c. To retain the melody of the work.
   d. To retain the form of the work.
   e. To retain the rhythm of the work.

47. What is the author trying to express in the second paragraph?
   a. The author is trying to say that he is not regretful for any crudeness on the part of the text because the translation was done to the best of the author's ability.
   b. The author is asking for forgiveness because his translation may be crude in some places, and it is not true to the meter or rhyme of the original text.
   c. The author wants to express that critics are cast out in the presence of God because their work is insincere and pointless.
   d. The author is saying that he is not afraid to fight somebody if they criticize his work or the work of his peers.
   e. The author is aiming to inform the audience how the process of translation is conducted.

Questions 48 – 49 are based off the following passage:

Rehabilitation, rather than punitive justice, is becoming much more popular in prisons around the world. Prisons in America, especially, where the recidivism rate is 67 percent, would benefit from mimicking prison tactics in Norway, which has a recidivism rate of only 20 percent. In Norway, the idea is that a rehabilitated prisoner is much less likely to offend than one harshly punished. Rehabilitation includes proper treatment for substance abuse, psychotherapy, healthcare and dental care, and education programs.

48. Which of the following best captures the author's purpose?
    a. To show the audience one of the effects of criminal rehabilitation by comparison
    b. To persuade the audience to donate to American prisons for education programs
    c. To convince the audience of the harsh conditions of American prisons
    d. To inform the audience of the incredibly lax system of Norwegian prisons
    e. To entertain the audience with interesting stories and anecdotes

49. Which of the following describes the word *recidivism* as it is used in the passage?
    a. The lack of violence in the prison system.
    b. The opportunity of inmates to receive therapy in prison.
    c. The event of a prisoner escaping the compound.
    d. The likelihood of a convicted criminal to reoffend.
    e. The propensity for a person to commit any sort of crime.

Nutrition Facts

8 servings per container

Serving size	2/3 cup (55g)

Amount per 2/3 cup

Calories   **230**

% DV*	
12%	**Total Fat** 8g
5%	Saturated Fat 1g
	Trans Fat 0g
0%	**Cholesterol** 0mg
7%	**Sodium** 160mg
12%	**Total Carbs** 37g
14%	Dietary Fiber 4g
	Sugars 1g
	Added Sugars 0g
	Protein 3g
10%	**Vitamin D** 2mcg
20%	**Calcium** 260mg
45%	**Iron** 8mg
5%	**Potassium** 235mg

* Footnote on Daily Values (DV) and calories reference to be inserted here.

50. A customer who eats two servings of the above food would consume how many carbohydrates?
   a. 74mg
   b. 17.5g
   c. 460g
   d. 8g
   e. 74g

51. Director: Movies require the audience to suspend their disbelief. As such, directors need to create a universe with consistent internal logic. When the subject matter is based on real events and communities, the director must closely mirror reality. For example, characters should talk like people from that specific region and historical period.

Critic: Movies hold immense power in our culture in defining what is and isn't socially acceptable. Consequently, directors have a responsibility not to use language that offends various groups, especially people in vulnerable positions. Censoring hate speech and racial slurs won't break the audience's disbelief.

Which one of the following best describes the main point in dispute between the director and critic?
   a. Movie audiences suspend their disbelief.
   b. Hate speech and racial slurs offend people.
   c. Movies should avoid offending people.
   d. Directors enjoy full creative control over their work.
   e. Movies have enormous cultural relevancy.

52. Businessman: My cardinal rule is to only invest in privately-held small businesses that exclusively sell tangible goods and have no debt.

Which one of the following is the best investment opportunity according to the businessman's cardinal rule?
   a. Jose owns his own grocery store. He's looking for a partner, because he fell behind on his mortgage and owes the bank three months' worth of payments.
   b. Elizabeth is seeking a partner with business expertise to help expand her standalone store that sells niche board games. The store isn't currently profitable, but it's never been in debt.
   c. A family-owned accounting firm with no outstanding debts is looking for its first outside investor. The firm has turned a profit every year since it opened
   d. A multinational corporation is selling high-yield bonds for the first time.
   e. A regional chain of liquor stores is selling the licensing rights for a new franchise to help repay its initial small business loan.

53. Ecologist: If we do not act now, more than one hundred animal species will be extinct by the end of the decade. The best way to save them is to sell hunting licenses for endangered species. Hunters can pay for the right to kill old and lame animals. Otherwise, there's no way to fund our conservation efforts.

Which one of the following assumptions does the ecologist's argument rely upon?
   a. Hunting licenses for non-endangered species aren't profitable.
   b. All one hundred animal species must be saved.
   c. The new hunting license revenue will fund conservation efforts.
   d. Conservation efforts should have begun last decade.
   e. It is physically impossible for old and lame animals to reproduce.

54. Politician: Every cigarette smoked costs the city more than $1,000. Smokers are bankrupting our healthcare system. Discarded filters pollute our waterways, and second-hand smoke poisons our airways, threatening all pedestrians. The city must ban tobacco smoking immediately.

Which one of the following, if true, would most strengthen the politician's argument?
- a. Placing a high tax on tobacco hasn't reduced smoking at all.
- b. Smoking cigarettes is already banned in bars and restaurants.
- c. The city's waterways and airways also suffer from heavy industrial pollution.
- d. Many tobacco substitutes are readily available.
- e. The state government is also considering a ban on tobacco.

Questions 55–57 are based on the passage from Many Marriages *by Sherwood Anderson:*

> There was a man named Webster who lived in a town of twenty-five thousand people in the state of Wisconsin. He had a wife named Mary and a daughter named Jane and he was himself a fairly prosperous manufacturer of washing machines. When the thing happened of which I am about to write, he was thirty-seven or thirty-eight years old and his one child, the daughter, was seventeen. Of the details of his life up to the time, a certain revolution happened within him it will be unnecessary to speak. He was however a rather quiet man inclined to have dreams which he tried to crush out of himself in order that he function as a washing machine manufacturer; and no doubt, at odd moments, when he was on a train going someplace or perhaps on Sunday afternoons in the summer when he went alone to the deserted office of the factory and sat several hours looking out at a window and along a railroad track, he gave way to dreams.

55. What does the author mean by the following sentence?

"Of the details of his life up to the time, a certain revolution happened within him it will be unnecessary to speak."

- a. The details of his external life don't matter; only the details of his internal life matter.
- b. Whatever happened in his life before he had a certain internal change is irrelevant.
- c. He had a traumatic experience earlier in his life which rendered it impossible for him to speak.
- d. Before the revolution, he was a lighthearted man who always wished to speak to others no matter who they were.
- e. He cannot talk about the events he witnessed and experienced during the revolution.

56. What Point Of View is this narrative told in?
- a. First person limited
- b. First person omniscient
- c. Second person
- d. Third person omniscient
- e. Third person limited

57. What did Webster do for a living?
    a. A foot soldier
    b. Train operator
    c. Leader of the revolution
    d. Stay-at-home husband
    e. Washing machine manufacturer

Use the following graph for question 58.

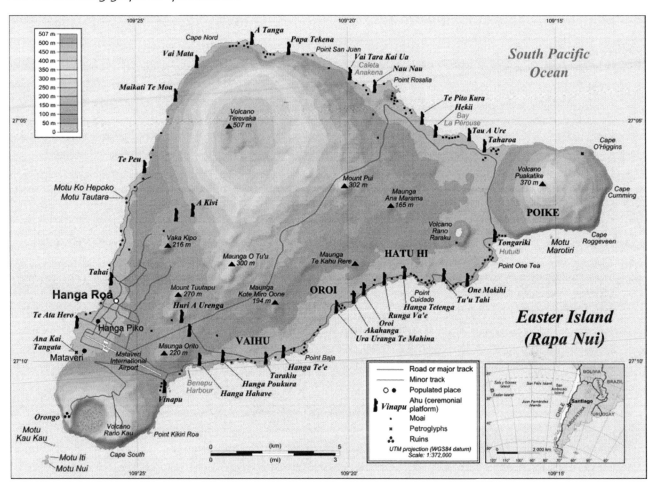

58. According to the map, which of the following is the highest points on the island?
    a. Volcano Terevaka
    b. Maunga Ana Marama
    c. Puakatike Volcano
    d. Vaka Kipo
    e. Mount Pui

Answer Explanations

1. D: Neutrality due to the style of the report. The report is mostly objective; we see very little language that entails any strong emotion whatsoever. The story is told almost as an objective documentation of a sequence of actions—we see the president sitting in his box with his wife, their enjoyment of the show, Booth's walk through the crowd to the box, and Ford's consideration of Booth's movements. There is perhaps a small amount of bias when the author mentions the president's "worthy wife." However, the word choice and style show no signs of excitement, sadness, anger, or apprehension from the author's perspective, so the best answer is Choice *D*.

2. B: Mr. Ford assumed Booth's movement throughout the theater was due to being familiar with the theater. Choice *A* is incorrect; although Booth does eventually make his way to Lincoln's box, Mr. Ford does not make this distinction in this part of the passage. Choice *C* is incorrect; although the passage mentions "companions," it mentions Lincoln's companions rather than Booth's companions. Choice *D* is incorrect; the passage mentions "dress circle," which means the first level of the theater, but this is different from a "dressing room." Finally, Choice *E* is incorrect; the passage mentions a "symptom" but does not signify a symptom from an illness.

3. C: A lead singer leaves their band to begin a solo career, and the band's sales on their next album drop by 50 percent. The original source of the analogy displays someone significant to an event who leaves, and then the event becomes the worst for it. We see Mr. Sothern leaving the theater company, and then the play becoming a "very dull affair." Choice *A* depicts a dancer who backs out of an event before the final performance, so this is incorrect. Choice *B* shows a basketball player leaving an event, and then the team makes it to the championship but then loses. This choice could be a contestant for the right answer; however, we don't know if the team has become the worst for his departure or the better for it. We simply do not have enough information here. Choice *D* is incorrect. The actor departs an event, but there is no assessment of the quality of the movie. It simply states what actors filled in instead. Choice *E* is incorrect because the opposite of the source happens; the professor leaves the entity, and the entity becomes better. Additionally, the betterment of the entity is not due to the individual leaving. Choice *E* is not analogous to the source.

4. A: A chronological account in a fiction novel of a woman and a man meeting for the first time. It's tempting to mark Choice A wrong because the genres are different. Choice *A* is a fiction text, and the original passage is not a fictional account. However, the question stem asks specifically for organizational structure. Choice *A* is a chronological structure just like the passage, so this is the correct answer. The passage does not have a cause and effect, problem/solution, or compare/contrast structure, making Choices *B*, *D*, and *E* incorrect. Choice *C* is tempting because it mentions an autobiography; however, the structure of this text starts at the end and works its way toward the beginning, which is the opposite structure of the original passage.

5. C: The word *adornments* would LEAST change the meaning of the sentence because it's the most closely related word to *festoons*. The other choices don't make sense in the context of the sentence. *Feathers* of flags, *armies* of flags, *buckets* of flags, and *boats* of flags are not as accurate as the phrase *adornments* of flags. The passage also talks about other décor in the setting, so the word *adornments* fits right in with the context of the paragraph.

6. D: The primary purpose of the passage is to recount in detail the events that led up to Abraham Lincoln's death. Choice *A* is incorrect; the author makes no claims and uses no rhetoric of persuasion towards the audience. Choice *B* is incorrect, though it's a tempting choice; the passage depicts the setting in exorbitant detail, but the setting itself is not the primary purpose of the passage. Choice *C* is incorrect; one could argue this is a narrative, and the passage is about Lincoln's last few hours, but this isn't the *best* choice. The best choice recounts the details that leads up to Lincoln's death. Finally, Choice *E* is incorrect. The author does not try to prove or disprove anything to the audience, and the passage does not even make it to when Lincoln gets shot, so this part of the story is irrelevant.

7. D: The word *deleterious* can be best interpreted as referring to the word *ruinous*. The first paragraph attempts to explain the process of milk souring, so the "acid" would probably prove "ruinous" to the growth of bacteria and cause souring. Choice *A*, *amicable*, means friendly, so this does not make sense in context. Choice *B*, *smoldering*, means to boil or simmer, so this is also incorrect. Choices *C* and *E*, *luminous* and *virtuous*, have positive connotations and don't make sense in the context of the passage. Luminous means shining or brilliant, and virtuous means to be honest or ethical.

8. B: The author begins by explaining a process or phenomenon, then gives the history of the study of this phenomenon, and ends by presenting the effects of this phenomenon. The author explains the process of souring in the first paragraph by informing the reader that "it is due to the action of certain of the milk bacteria upon the milk sugar which converts it into lactic acid, and this acid gives the sour taste and curdles the milk." In the second paragraph, we see how the phenomenon of milk souring was viewed when it was "first studied," and then we proceed to gain insight into "recent investigations" toward the end of the paragraph. Finally, the passage ends by presenting the effects of the phenomenon of milk souring. We see the milk curdling, becoming bitter, tasting soapy, turning blue, or becoming thread-like. All of the other answer choices are incorrect.

9: A: The primary purpose is to inform the reader of the phenomenon, investigation, and consequences of milk souring. Choice *B* is incorrect because the passage states that *Bacillus acidi lactici* is not the only cause of milk souring. Choice *C* is incorrect because, although the author mentions the findings of researchers, the main purpose of the text does not seek to describe their accounts and findings, as we are not even told the names of any of the researchers. Choice *D* is tricky. We do see the author present us with new findings in contrast to the first cases studied by researchers. However, this information is only in the second paragraph, so it is not the primary purpose of the *entire passage*. Finally, Choice *E* is incorrect because the genre of the passage is more informative than narrative, although the author does talk about the phenomenon of milk souring and its subsequent effects.

10. C: Milk souring is caused mostly by a species of bacteria identical to that of *Bacillus acidi lactici* although there are a variety of other bacteria that cause milk souring as well. Choice *A* is incorrect because it contradicts the assertion that the souring is still caused by a variety of bacteria. Choice *B* is incorrect because the ordinary cause of milk souring *is known* to current researchers. Choice *D* is incorrect because this names mostly the effects of milk souring, not the cause. Choice *E* is incorrect because the bacteria itself doesn't have a strange soapy smell or is a different color, but it eventually will cause the milk to produce these effects.

11. C: The study of milk souring has improved throughout the years, as we now understand more of what causes milk souring and what happens afterward. None of the choices here are explicitly stated, so we have to rely on our ability to make inferences. Choice *A* is incorrect because there is no indication from the author that milk researchers in the past have been incompetent—only that recent research has done a better job of studying the phenomenon of milk souring. Choice *B* is incorrect because the author refers to dairymen in relation to the effects of milk souring and their "troubles" surrounding milk souring, and does not compare them to milk researchers. Choice *D* is incorrect because we are told in the second paragraph that only certain types of bacteria are able to sour milk. Choice *E* is incorrect; although we are told that milk souring is a natural occurrence, the author makes no implication that soured milk is safe to consume. Choice *C* is the best answer choice here because although the author does not directly state that the study of milk souring has improved, we can see this might be true due to the comparison of old studies to newer studies, and the fact that the newer studies are being used as a reference in the passage.

12. A: It is most analogous to the chemical change that occurs when a firework explodes. The author tells us that after milk becomes slimy, "it persists in spite of all attempts made to remedy it," which means the milk has gone through a chemical change. It has changed its state from milk to sour milk by changing its odor, color, and material. After a firework explodes, there is little one can do to change the substance of a firework back to its original form—the original substance has combusted and released its energy as heat and light. Choice *B* is incorrect because, although the rain overwatered the plant, it's possible that the plant is able to recover from this. Choice *C* is incorrect because although mercury leaking out may be dangerous, the actual substance itself stays the same and does not alter into something else. Choice *D* is incorrect; this situation is not analogous to the alteration of a substance. Choice *E* is also incorrect. Ice melting into a liquid is a physical change, which means it can be undone. Milk turning sour, as the author asserts, cannot be undone.

13. D: It would most likely be a paragraph showing the ways bacteria infiltrate milk and ways to avoid this infiltration. Choices *A, B,* and *C* are incorrect because these are already represented in the third, second, and first paragraphs. Choice *E* is incorrect; this choice isn't impossible. There could be a glossary right after the third paragraph, but this would be an awkward place for a glossary. Choice *D* is the best answer because it follows a sort of problem/solution structure in writing.

14. E: A central question to both passages is: What is the interpretation of the first amendment and its limitations? Choice *A* is incorrect; this is a question for the first passage but it does not apply to the second. Choice *B* is incorrect; a quote mentions this at the end of the first passage, but this question is not found in the second passage. Choice *C* is incorrect, as the passages are not concerned with the definition of freedom of speech, but how to interpret it. Choice *D* is incorrect; this is a question for the second passage, but it is not found in the first passage.

15. C: The authors would most likely disagree over the man thrown in jail for encouraging a riot against the U.S. government for the wartime tactics although no violence ensued. The author of Passage A says that "If a state may properly forbid murder or robbery or treason, it may also punish those who induce or counsel the commission of such crimes." This statement tells us that the author of Passage A would support throwing the man in jail for encouraging a riot, although no violence ensues. The author of Passage B states that "And we can with certitude declare that the First Amendment forbids the punishment of words merely for their injurious tendencies." This is the best answer choice because we are clear on each author's stance in this situation. Choice *A* is tricky; the author of Passage A would definitely agree with this, but it's questionable whether the author of Passage B would also agree. Violence does ensue at the capitol as a result of this man's provocation, and the author of Passage B states "speech should be unrestricted by the censorship . . . unless it is clearly liable to cause direct . . . interference with the conduct of war." This answer is close, but it is not the *best* choice. Choice *B* is incorrect because we have no way of knowing what the authors' philosophies are in this situation. Choice *D* is incorrect because, again, we have no way of knowing what the authors would do in this situation, although it's assumed they would probably both agree with this. Choice *E* is something the authors would probably both agree on, because brutal violence ensued, but it has nothing to do with free speech, so we have no way of knowing for sure.

16. E: Choice *E* is the best answer. To figure out the correct answer choice we must find out the relationship between Passage A and Passage B. Between the two passages, we have a general principle (freedom of speech) that is questioned on the basis of interpretation. In Choice *E*, we see that we have a general principle (right to die, or euthanasia) that is questioned on the basis of interpretation as well. Should euthanasia only include passive euthanasia, or euthanasia in any aspect? Choice *A* is a problem/solution relationship; the first option outlines a problem, and the second option delivers a solution, so this choice is incorrect. Choice *B* is incorrect because it does not question the interpretation of a principle, but rather describes the effects of two events that happened in the past involving contamination of radioactive substances. Choice *C* begins with a principle—that of labor laws during wartime—but in the second option, the interpretation isn't questioned. The second option looks at the historical precedent of labor laws in the past during wartime. Choice *D* is incorrect because the two texts disagree over the cause of something rather than the interpretation of it.

17. B: Choice *B* is the best answer choice because the author is trying to demonstrate via the examples that anyone who incites a crime, despite the severity or magnitude of the crime, should be held accountable for that crime in some degree. Choice *A* is incorrect because the crimes mentioned are not being compared to each other, but they are being used to demonstrate a point. Choice *C* is incorrect because the author makes the same point using both of the examples and does not question the definition of freedom of speech but its ability to be limited. Choice *D* is incorrect because this sentiment goes against what the author has been arguing throughout the passage. Choice *E* is incorrect because the author does not suggest that the crimes mentioned be reopened anywhere in the passage.

18. A: The idea that human beings are able and likely to change their mind between the utterance and execution of an event that may harm others most seriously undermines the claim because it brings into question the tendency to commit a crime and points out the difference between utterance and action in moral situations. Choice *B* is incorrect; this idea does not undermine the claim at hand, but introduces an observation irrelevant to the claim. Choices *C, D,* and *E* are incorrect because they would actually strengthen the author's claim rather than undermine it.

19. D: The primary purpose is to call upon the interpretation of freedom of speech to be already evident in the First Amendment and to offer a clear perimeter of the principle during war time. Choice *A* is incorrect; the passage calls upon no historical situations as precedent in this passage. Choice *B* is incorrect; we can infer that the author would not agree with this, because the author states that "In war time, therefore, speech should be unrestricted . . . by punishment." Choice *C* is incorrect; this is more consistent with the main idea of the first passage. Choice *E* is incorrect; the passage states a limitation in saying that "speech should be unrestricted . . . unless it is clearly liable to cause direct and dangerous interference with the conduct of war."

20. E: The word that would least change the meaning of the sentence is *grievance. Malcontent* is a complaint or grievance, and in this context would be uttered in advocation of absolute freedom of speech. Choice *A, regimen,* means a pattern of living, and would not make sense in this context. Choice *B, cacophony,* means a harsh noise or mix of discordant noises; someone may express or "urge" a cacophony but it would be an awkward word in this context. Choice *C, anecdote,* is a short account of an amusing story. Since the word is a noun, it fits grammatically inside the sentence, but anecdotes are usually thought out, and this word is considered "unthinking." Choice *D, residual,* means to be something of an outcome, or what is left behind or remaining, which does not make sense within this context.

21. B: The author says that the classical understanding of poetry dealt with its ability to be used to teach morality. Later, philosophers would define poetry by its ability to imitate life. Finally, during the renaissance, poetry was believed to be an imitative art that instilled morality in its readers. The rest of the answer choices improperly interpret this explanation in the passage. Poetry was never mentioned for use in entertainment, which makes Choices *D* and *E* incorrect. Choices *A* and *C* are incorrect because they mix up the chronological order.

22. C: The author says that although most poetry was written as lyric, epic, or drama, the critics were most focused on the techniques of the epic and drama and their performance of structure and character. This is the best answer choice as portrayed by paragraph three. Choice *A* is incorrect because nowhere in the passage does it say rhetoric was more valued than poetry, although it did seem to have a more definitive purpose than poetry. Choice *B* is incorrect; this almost mirrors Choice *A*, but the critics were *not* focused on the lyric, as the passage indicates. Choice *D* is incorrect because the passage does not mention that the study of poetics was more pleasurable than the study of rhetoric. Choice *E* is incorrect because again, we do not see anywhere in the passage where poetry was reserved for the most elite in society.

23. E: The purpose is to contemplate the differences between classical rhetoric and poetry and to consider their purposes in a particular culture. Choice *A* is incorrect; this thought is discussed in the third paragraph, but it is not the main idea of the passage. Choice *B* is incorrect; although changes in poetics throughout the years is mentioned, this is not the main idea of the passage. Choice *C* is incorrect; although this is partly true—that rhetoric within the education system is mentioned—the subject of poetics is left out of this answer choice. Choice *D* is incorrect; the passage makes no mention of poetics being a subset of rhetoric.

24. B: The correct answer choice is Choice *B*, *instill*. Choice *A*, *imbibe*, means to drink heavily, so this choice is incorrect. Choice *C*, *implode*, means to collapse inward, which does not make sense in this context. Choice *D*, *inquire*, means to investigate. This option is better than the other options, but it is not as accurate as *instill*. Choice *E*, *idolize*, means to admire, which does not make sense in this context.

25. B: The first paragraph presents definitions and examples of a particular subject. The second paragraph presents a second subject in the same way. The third paragraph offers a contrast of the two subjects. In the passage, we see the first paragraph defining rhetoric and offering examples of how the Greeks and Romans taught this subject. In the second paragraph, poetics is defined and examples of its dynamic definition are provided. In the third paragraph, the contrast between rhetoric and poetry is characterized through how each of these were studied in a classical context.

26. D: The best answer is Choice *D:* As a football player, they taught me how to understand the logistics of the game, how my placement on the field affected the rest of the team, and how to run and throw with a mixture of finesse and strength. The content of rhetoric in the passage . . . "taught how to work up a case by drawing valid inferences from sound evidence, how to organize this material in the most persuasive order, and how to compose in clear and harmonious sentences. What we have here are three general principles: 1) it taught me how to understand logic and reason (drawing inferences parallels to understanding the logistics of the game), 2) it taught me how to understand structure and organization (organization of material parallels to organization on the field) and 3) it taught me how to make the end product beautiful (how to compose in harmonious sentences parallels to how to run with finesse and strength). Each part parallels by logic, organization, and style.

27. E: *Treatises* is most closely related to the word *commentary.* Choices *A* and *B* do not make sense because thesauruses and encyclopedias are not written about one single subject. Choice *C* is incorrect; sermons are usually given by religious leaders as advice or teachings. Choice *D* is incorrect; anthems are songs and do not fit within the context of this sentence.

28. D: A city whose population is made up of people who seek quick fortunes rather than building a solid business foundation. Choice *A* is a characteristic of Portland but not that of a boom city. Choice *B* is close—a boom city is one that becomes quickly populated, but it is not necessarily *always* populated by residents from the east coast. Choice *C* is incorrect because a boom city is not one that catches fire frequently, but one made up of people who are looking to make quick fortunes from the resources provided on the land. Choice *E* is incorrect because although it describes a characteristic of Portland, the passage does not state that in order for a city to be a "boom city," it *must* be located on a river.

29. D: Choice *D* is the best answer because of the surrounding context. We can see that the fact that Portland is a "boom city" means that the "floating class"—a group of people who only have temporary roots put down—go through. This would cause the main focus of the city to be on employment and industry, rather than society and culture; thus, Choice *E* is incorrect. Choice *A* is incorrect, as we are not told about the inhabitants being social or antisocial. Choice *B* is incorrect because the text does not talk about the culture in the East regarding European influence. Finally, Choice *C* is incorrect; this is an assumption that has no evidence in the text to back it up.

30. E: The author would say that it has as much culture as the cities in the East. The author says that Portland has "as fine churches, as complete a system of schools, as fine residences, as great a love of music and art, as can be found at any city of the East of equal size," which proves that the culture is similar in this particular city to the cities in the East.

31. B: Approximately 240,000. We know from the image that San Francisco has around 300,000 inhabitants at this time. From the text (and from the graph) we can see that Portland has 60,000 inhabitants. Subtract these two numbers to come up with 240,000

32. C: This question requires close attention to the passage. Choice *A* can be found where the passage says, "no less than six named and several unnamed varieties of the peach have thus produced several varieties of nectarine, so this choice is incorrect. Choice *B* can be found where the passage says, "it is highly improbable that all these peach-trees . . . are hybrids from the peach and nectarine." Choice *D* is incorrect because we see in the passage that "the production of peaches from nectarines, either by seeds or buds, may perhaps be considered as a case of reversion." Choice *E* can be found in the last paragraph where it says, "descended from an old French variety bearing purple fruit, produced when about ten years old bright yellow plums; these differed in no respect except colour from those on the other trees." Choice *C* is the correct answer because the word "unremarkable" should be changed to "remarkable" in order for it to be consistent with the details of the passage.

33. A: The word *multiplied* is synonymous with the word *propagated,* making Choice *A* correct. Choice *B* is incorrect because *diminished* means to decrease or recede and is the opposite of *propagated.* Choice *C* is incorrect; *watered* is close, because it pertains to the growth of trees, but it is not exactly the same thing as *propagated.* Choice *D* is incorrect; *uprooted* could also pertain to trees, but this answer is incorrect. Finally, Choice *E* is appealing because it's related to trees and somewhat closer in meaning to propagated, but propagated more nearly means *spread,* while *planted* deals with the initial start.

34. B: The author's tone in this passage can be considered objective. An objective tone means that the author is open-minded and detached about the subject. Most scientific articles are objective. Choices *A, C, D,* and *E* are incorrect. The author is not very enthusiastic on the paper; the author is not critical, but rather interested in the topic. The author is not desperate in any way here.

35. B: Choice *B* is the correct answer because the meaning holds true even if the words have been switched out or rearranged some. Choice *A* is incorrect because it has trees either bearing peaches or nectarines, and the trees in the original phrase bear both. Choice *C* is incorrect because the statement does not say these trees are "indifferent to bud-variation," but that they have "indifferently [borne] peaches or nectarines." Choices *D* and *E* are incorrect; the statement may use some of the same words, but the meaning is skewed in these sentences.

36. D: *Congealed* in this context most nearly means *thickened*, because we see liquid turning into ice. Choice *B, loosened*, is the opposite of the correct answer; Choice *E, pooled*, is also somewhat opposite in meaning. Choices *A* and *C, burst* and *shrank*, are also incorrect.

37. C: Choice *A* is incorrect. We cannot infer that the passage takes place during the night time. While we do have a statement that says that the darkness thickened, this is the only evidence we have. The darkness could be thickening because it is foggy outside. We don't have enough proof to infer this otherwise. We *can* infer that the season of this narrative is in the winter time. Some of the evidence here is that "the cold became intense," and people were decorating their shops with "holly sprigs,"—a Christmas tradition. It also mentions that it's Christmastime at the end of the passage. Choice *B* is incorrect; we *can* infer that the narrative is located in a bustling city street by the actions in the story. People are running around trying to sell things, the atmosphere is busy, there is a church tolling the hours, etc. The scene switches to the Mayor's house at the end of the passage, but the answer says "majority," so this is still incorrect. Choice *D* is incorrect; we *can* infer that the Lord Mayor is wealthy—he lives in the "Mansion House" and has fifty cooks. Choice *E* is incorrect because we *can* infer that Scrooge was not kind nor receptive since he scared the caroler away.

38. E: The passage tells us that the poulterers' and grocers' trades were "a glorious pageant, with which it was next to impossible to believe that such dull principles as bargain and sale had anything to do," which means they set up their shops to be entertaining public spectacles in order to increase sales. Choice *A* is incorrect; although the word "joke" is used, it is meant to be used as a source of amusement rather than something made in poor quality. Choice *B* is incorrect; that they put on a "pageant" is figurative for the public spectacle they made with their shops, not a literal play. Choice *C* is incorrect, as this is not mentioned anywhere in the passage. Finally, Choice *D* is incorrect; although it's an appealing option because the poulterers and grocers clearly aimed to spread Christmas cheer, it's not clear that they were working tirelessly to convert non-believers.

39. B: The author, at least in the last few paragraphs, does not attempt to evoke empathy for the character of Scrooge. We see Scrooge lashing out at an innocent, cold boy, with no sign of affection or feeling for his harsh conditions. We see Choice *A* when the author talks about Saint Dunstan. We see Choices *C* and *E*, providing a palpable experience and imaginable setting and character, especially with the "piercing, searching, biting cold," among other statements. Finally, we see Choice *D* when Scrooge chases the young boy away.

40. C: The section that is talked about in the text is blazing the trail, which is Choice *C.* The passage states that one must blaze the trail by "bending down and breaking branches of trees, underbrush, and bushes."

The girl in the image is bending a branch in order to break it so that she can use it to "blaze the trail" so she won't get lost.

41. B: Choice *B* is the best answer here; the sentence states, "In unknown regions take a responsible guide with you, unless the trail is short, easily followed, and a frequented one." Choice *A* is incorrect; the passage does not state that you should try and explore unknown regions. Choice *C* is incorrect; the passage talks about trails that contain pitfalls, traps, and boggy places, but it does not say that *all* unknown regions contain these things. Choice *D* is incorrect; the passage mentions "rail" and "boat" as means of transport at the beginning, but it does not suggest it is better to travel unknown regions by rail. Choice *E* is incorrect because the passage warns against the challenges and downsides of a potential "false trail;" it does not encourage purposely creating one.

42. D: Choice *D* is correct; it may be real advice an experienced hiker would give to an inexperienced hiker. However, the question asks about details in the passage, and this is not in the passage. Choice *A* is incorrect; we do see the author encouraging the reader to learn about the trail beforehand . . . "wet or dry; where it leads; and its length." Choice *B* is also incorrect, because we do see the author telling us the time will lengthen with boggy or rugged places opposed to smooth places. Choice *C* is incorrect; at the end of the passage, the author tells us "do not go alone through lonely places . . . unless you are quite familiar with the country and the ways of the wild." Choice *E* is incorrect because the detail is found in the passage in the first sentence of the last paragraph.

43. C: The best answer here is Choice *C:* "Follow the false trail back to its beginning so that you can rediscover the real trail." Choices *A* and *D* are represented in the text; but this is advice on how to blaze a trail, not what to do when being led astray by a false trail. Choice *B* is incorrect; this is the opposite of what the text suggests doing. Choice *E* is incorrect because the author suggests bending the branches so that the light side of the leaf points upward to help make the trail clear. This advice is also in reference to blazing the main trail, not what to do should you be led astray on a false trail.

44. A: The author is doing translation work. We see this very clearly in the way the author talks about staying truthful to the original language of the text. The text also mentions "translation" towards the end. Criticism is taking an original work and analyzing it, making Choice *B* incorrect. The work is not being tested for historical validity, but being translated into the English language, making Choice *C* incorrect. The author is not writing a biography, as there is nothing in here about Pushkin himself, only his work, making Choice *D* incorrect. Similarly, while the author mentions rhythm, which is often a characteristic ascribed to poetry, and Pushkin was a poet, the author himself is not creating poetry but trying to translate already-written work.

45. D: You would most likely find this in the preface. A preface to a text usually explains what the author has done or aims to do with the work. An appendix is usually found at the end of a text and does not talk about what the author intends to do to the work, making Choice *A* incorrect. A table of contents does not contain prose, but bullet points listing chapters and sections found in the text, making Choice *B* incorrect. Choice *C* is incorrect; the first chapter would include the translation work (here, poetry), and not the author's intentions. Choice *E* is incorrect because there would be no need for an associated graphic here and this passage would not likely be the caption for a graphic.

46. B: To retain the truth of the work. The author says that "music and rhythm and harmony are indeed fine things, but truth is finer still," which means that the author stuck to a literal translation instead of changing up any words that might make the English language translation sound better.

47. A: The author is trying to say that he is not regretful for any crudeness on the part of the text because the translation was done to the best of the author's ability. The author asks for "no forgiveness" because what was done was the best the author could do with the text following a literal translation. Choice *B* is incorrect; the author does *not* ask for forgiveness. Choice *C* is incorrect; the author does mention God, but as a rhetorical device to make the translation seem an act of service rather than a hobby. Choice *D* is incorrect; no fighting is mentioned in this paragraph. Choice *E* is incorrect because the paragraph is not really explaining or teaching how translation work is done.

48. A: To show the audience one of the effects of criminal rehabilitation by comparison. Choice *B* is incorrect because although it is obvious the author favors rehabilitation, the author never asks for donations from the audience. Choice *E* is incorrect because the passage is not intended to be entertaining, but informative in its aim to address serious subject matter. Choices *C* and *D* are also incorrect. We can infer from the passage that American prisons are probably harsher than Norwegian prisons. However, the best answer that captures the author's purpose is Choice *A*, because we see an effect by the author (recidivism rate of each country) comparing Norwegian and American prisons.

49. D: The likelihood of a convicted criminal to reoffend. The passage explains how a Norwegian prison, due to rehabilitation, has a smaller rate of recidivism. Thus, we can infer that recidivism is probably not a positive attribute. Choices *A* and *B* are both positive attributes, the lack of violence and the opportunity of inmates to receive therapy, so Norway would probably not have a lower rate of these two things. Choice *C* is possible, but it does not make sense in context, because the author does not talk about tactics in which to keep prisoners inside the compound, but ways in which to rehabilitate criminals so that they can live as citizens when they get out of prison. Choice *E* can be ruled out because the passage wouldn't be explaining why the prison system is better in Norway if the likelihood that a citizen would commit a crime was lower. Instead, the passage would explain why the structure or policies in Norway lead to fewer misdemeanors.

50. E: 74g. Choice *A* has the correct number, but the unit of measurement is in "mg" instead of "g." Choices *C* and *D* are incorrect. Choice *B* is the number of grams of carbohydrate in ½ serving.

51. C: Choice *C* correctly identifies the main point in dispute. The director and critic are arguing about the director's role. The director argues that directors should be allowed to offend people, if that would accurately reflect reality, so the audience can maintain its suspension of disbelief. The critic would argue that this violates the director's social responsibility to avoid offending people.

Choice *A* is incorrect. Both the director and critic would agree that movie audiences suspend their disbelief. This is the director's main point, and the critic acknowledges its existence by claiming that censoring hate speech and racial slurs won't break the audience's disbelief.

Choice *B* is incorrect. This is the critic's main point, and the director would likely also agree. The director isn't claiming that movies aren't offensive, but that offending people is justified to protect the suspension of disbelief.

Choice *D* is incorrect. This isn't the main point in dispute. In addition, both the director and critic imply that they believe this to be true. For the director, creative control is required to structure a universe where an audience can suspend its disbelief. For the critic, the director would need creative control to censor what the critic deems inappropriate.

Choice *E* is incorrect. The critic would agree that movies have enormous cultural relevancy—that's why the critic is calling for self-censorship—but it's unclear whether the director would agree or disagree.

52. B: Choice *B* correctly identifies the best investment opportunity. The cardinal rule has three requirements—privately held small business, sells tangible goods, and no debt. Elizabeth's store is a privately held small business (standalone and owned by her), it sells tangible goods (board games), and it has no debt. The lack of profitability is irrelevant, acting as a red herring. The cardinal rule doesn't mention it, presumably since the businessman thinks he can increase profitability as long as the business meets those three requirements.

Choice *A* is incorrect. Jose's grocery store owes the bank three months' worth of mortgage payments, so it has debt, violating the cardinal rule.

Choice *C* is incorrect. The accounting firm violates the cardinal rule, because it does not sell a tangible good.

Choice *D* is incorrect. A multinational corporation is not a small business, so it violates the cardinal rule.

Choice *E* is incorrect. The regional chain of liquor stores has debt (small business loan), so it's a worse investment than the board game store according to the businessman's cardinal rule.

53. C: Choice *C* correctly identifies a necessary assumption in the argument. The argument is that hunting licenses for endangered species should be sold to support conservation efforts. If the revenue from those licenses isn't funding conservation efforts, then the ecologist's entire argument falls apart.

Choice *A* is incorrect. Hunting licenses for non-endangered species could be profitable, and the ecologist's argument wouldn't be impacted one way or another. The ecologist could still argue that hunting licenses should be expanded to further increase funding for species that are still endangered.

Choice *B* is incorrect. The ecologist would definitely agree that all one hundred animal species should be saved, but it isn't a necessary assumption. The argument would function the same if the ultimate goal were to save ten endangered animal species.

Choice *D* is incorrect. Like Choice *B*, the ecologist would agree that conservation efforts should've begun earlier, but it isn't a necessary assumption.

Choice *E* is incorrect. The ecologist likely supports hunting licenses for endangered species due to old and lame animals' diminished capacity to reproduce. But reproduction being physically impossible isn't a necessary assumption. The argument would be the same even if those animals were reproducing on a limited basis.

54. A: Choice *A* correctly identifies the statement that most strengthens the argument. The argument is that the city must ban smoking, because every cigarette that's smoked costs the city $1,000. Choice *A* eliminates a possible counterargument for a less extreme measure—taxing tobacco. Since the tax didn't work, the city would be more likely to pursue a total ban.

Choice *B* is incorrect. If smoking cigarettes was already banned in bars and restaurants, it might strengthen the argument by laying the foundation for a total ban. However, a total ban is much more extreme, and Choice *A* is stronger since it eliminates a primary counterargument against changing the law.

Choice *C* is incorrect. Non-smoking related pollution in the waterways and airways might increase the need to avoid additional pollutants, but it's not as strong as Choice *A*.

Choice *D* is incorrect. The existence of tobacco substitutes doesn't justify banning tobacco. It also doesn't necessarily mean that they'll be better for the healthcare system and environment.

Choice *E* is incorrect. The state government's decision to ban tobacco could encourage the city government to do the same, but Choice *A* has a more direct impact on that debate as it pertains to the city.

55. B: Whatever happened in his life before he had a certain internal change is irrelevant. Choices *A, C, D,* and *E* use some of the same language as the original passage, like "revolution," "speak," and "details," but they do not capture the meaning of the statement. The statement is saying the details of his previous life are not going to be talked about—that he had some kind of epiphany, and moving forward in his life is what the narrator cares about.

56. B: First-person omniscient. This is the best guess with the information we have. In the world of the passage, the narrator is first-person because we see them use the "I," but they also know the actions and thoughts of the protagonist, a character named "Webster." First-person limited tells their own story, making Choice *A* incorrect. Choice *C* is incorrect; second person uses "you" to tell the story. Third person uses "them," "they," etc., and would not fall into use of the "I" in the narrative, making Choices *D* and *E* incorrect.

57. E: Webster is a washing machine manufacturer. This question depends on reading comprehension. We see in the second sentence that Webster "was a fairly prosperous manufacturer of washing machines," making Choice *E* the correct answer.

58. A: According to the map, Volcano Terevaka is the highest point on the island, reaching 507m. Of the peaks listed in the other answer choices, Volcano Puakatike is the next highest, reaching 307m, and then Mount Pui, which is 302 m. Vaka Kipo is the next highest reaching 216m. Finally, Maunga Ana Marama is the next highest, reaching 165m.

Writing

Text Production: Writing Arguments

Producing an Argumentative Essay to Support a Claim Using Relevant and Sufficient Evidence

An argumentative essay is written for the purpose of persuading readers to agree with the author's position with the subject matter about which he or she is writing. Rather than presenting information objectively, the author treats the subject matter subjectively so that the information presented supports his or her position. In his or her argumentation, the author presents information that refutes or weakens opposing positions.

An argumentative essay typically includes the following five main elements:

- Introduction: In the introduction, the writer should draw readers in, encourage readers to perceive him or her as a trustworthy authority on the subject, and establish the purpose or thesis. Shocking statistics, new ways of restating issues, or quotations or anecdotes focusing the text can pique readers' interest. Personal statements, parallel instances, or analogies can also begin introductions—so can bold thesis statements if the author believes readers will agree. The introduction should typically narrow down to a clear, sound thesis statement. If readers cannot locate one sentence in the introduction explicitly stating the writer's position or the point the writer supports, the writer probably has not refined the introduction sufficiently.

- Narration: In the narration portion, the writer summarizes pertinent background information, informs the readers of anything they need to know regarding the circumstances and environment surrounding and/or stimulating the argument, and establishes what is at risk or at stake in the issue or topic. Literature reviews are common examples of narrations in academic writing.

- Confirmation: The confirmation states all claims supporting the thesis and furnishes evidence for each claim, arranging this material in logical order—e.g. from most obvious to most subtle or strongest to weakest. It is where the writer explains why he or she believes the stated thesis. The writer builds a chain of reasoning by developing several individual supporting claims and explaining why that evidence supports each claim and also supports the overall thesis of the argument.

- Refutation and Concession: The refutation and concession discuss opposing views and anticipate readers' objections without weakening the thesis, yet permitting as many oppositions as possible. In the refutation, writers disarm reader opposition by anticipating and answering their possible objections, persuading them to accept the author's viewpoint. In the concession, writers can concede those opposing viewpoints with which they agree.

- Summation: The summation strengthens the argument while summarizing it, supplying a strong conclusion and showing readers the superiority of the author's solution. Writers should revisit the issues and the narration part of the argument, reminding readers of what is at stake.

Writing Clearly and Coherently

Addressing the Assigned Task Appropriately for an Audience of Educated Adults

One consideration when planning and writing an essay—whether argumentative, informative, or otherwise—is the intended audience of readers. Writers should tailor their language, reasoning, and inclusion or exclusion of relevant background information depending on the perceived expertise, education, and age of the majority of anticipated readers. For example, if writing a persuasive essay about the need to increase our country's reliance on renewable energy resources for power, the author must decide how much background information to provide about the types, availability, pros and cons, cost, etc. of renewable resources as well as those of more conventional finite resources such as coal and oil. If the writer is intending his or her work to be read by an audience of adults reasonably informed about the subject matter, the need for significant background information is unnecessary and may even detract from the strength of the argument by bogging down the text with extensive data, statistics, and textbook-like information dumping. In contrast, if the essay is intended for a less informed population with little knowledge about energy and resources, such as a class of middle school students, background information would be important so that readers could follow the logic of the argument and understand the factors involved in the issue. Moreover, the language and vocabulary used for these two populations should also differ somewhat. Even greater contrast would exist between educated adults and young children.

While it's not always possible to accurately predict the entire audience for a written piece of work (and there's likely too much variety within the audience to sufficiently tailor the writing to each subset), writers should do their best to consider the likely audience or write for a specific audience in mind to facilitate their readers' comprehension and reception of the essay. On the Praxis Core Writing test, essays should be geared toward an audience of educated adults. Language, reasoning, structure, and information should be expressed accordingly.

Organizing and Develop Ideas Logically

An essay is only successful if readers can understand its reasoning, follow its logic, determine its focus or thesis, and understand the included points that support the main idea. Readers must have confidence that the writer is presenting the full gamut of evidence and presenting the ideas without bias. If readers cannot follow the chain of reasoning or easily and decisively identify the thesis, they are likely to stop reading or walk away without being convinced of the point that the author intended to support. Likewise, a reader will not be persuaded to adopt the author's opinion (if it is different from his or her own) if the essay is disjointed, if the ideas don't flow or follow logically, if conflicting points are argued such that the thesis is not consistent throughout, and if the language and writing style is not coherent. It is the writer's responsibility to guide readers through the essay and through its reasoning. The former involves producing writing that is clear, coherent, grammatically correct, and understandable. The use of transitional words and phrases that help link ideas with the appropriate connection will remove the guesswork for readers. Words like *thus, consequently, therefore, as such, however, besides*, and *accordingly* are helpful in this regard. It is also useful to include words that insinuate or shepherd readers toward a particular interpretation of statements that the writer wants the reader to adopt after reading the statement. Words like *fortunately, unfortunately,* and *thankfully* are examples of these types of qualifiers. The takeaway of a sentence, or it's emotional impact, can vary significantly by the tacking on of one of these words. As such, such words can be useful tools for a writer when crafting an argumentative piece to persuade readers to side with the writer's opinion. Consider the following example and notice how the meaning of the same sentence varies significantly when the sole qualifying word changes:

Fortunately, her role as hall monitor has changed.

Unfortunately, her role as hall monitor has changed.

While this sentence is short and it is difficult to get a sense of who "she" is and why her role as hall monitor has changed because there's no surrounding context, it is possible to see how the two sentences carry opposite meanings. In the first, it's a good thing that her role has changed. Perhaps she was bad at her role as hall monitor, disliked it, or now has a better job. Although we don't know why it's a favorable change, we are left with the takeaway that this change is a positive thing. The opposite can be said for the second sentence. Here, we see that regardless of the reason she's no longer acting as hall monitor, it's a negative change.

Lastly, writers can include temporal words like *first, next,* and *finally* to help readers follow along in the list of evidence or points made. For example, if the writer asserts that there are four reasons why renewable energy sources are actually the most energy-efficient choices these days, he or she could use *firstly . . . , secondly . . . , thirdly . . . , lastly . . ..* Writers will increase the effectiveness of their arguments and the ease with which they can be followed by using language that helps guide the reader.

Providing and Sustaining a Clear Focus or Thesis

The **thesis statement** typically appears near the end of the first paragraph of the introduction. It should clearly state the writer's position on the subject matter in a single sentence. It should be easy for readers to quickly identify the thesis statement. The thesis itself should be stated clearly in language that avoids ambiguity. It should be concise, while still providing ample verbiage to express the crux of the writer's main idea.

The thesis should provide a road map for the entire essay in that the writer should then use the subsequent body paragraphs of the essay to provide supporting details and reasons that he or she believes whatever is stated in the thesis. The thesis statement should be used to focus the entire essay.

Writers should be mindful that whatever details, examples, and explanations they provide stay on topic with their thesis and/or the main idea of the essay. The strength of an argument is decreased if readers are taken on irrelevant tangents or provided superfluous information that veers off topic. While it may be appealing to pad an essay with some of the inevitably large amount of research obtained while working on it or demonstrate one's command and expertise on the subject by inserting lots of facts and information, doing so actually detracts from the quality of the essay and the degree to which it logically flows. When choosing to include a given example, reason, or idea, writers should ask themselves if that item is unique (in that it hasn't already been stated elsewhere in the essay), if it is relevant to the main idea or thesis, if it adds anything to the argument, and if it will enhance readers' comprehension and support of the essay as a whole. Points or sentences that fail to accomplish one of these goals should be omitted.

Using Supporting Reasons, Examples, and Details to Develop Clearly and Logically the Ideas Presented

Arguments need supporting reasons and examples to support the points the author is trying to make. Unsubstantiated claims can weaken an argument because they give reason to question the credibility and accuracy of the writer's ideas and points. Tangible details and relatable examples also help readers connect with the ideas and "buy in" to the author's ideas. They help bring the ideas to life and provide evidence of their validity. It's particularly important to provide details that facilitate the ability of readers follow the logic of an argument and connect the points made and their implications. Writers should use a variety of credible primary and secondary sources to substantiate their points. It is important to credit the source and cite it appropriately to give the original author due credit and so that readers can locate the source of their own, should they be interested in further information.

Using a Variety of Sentence Structures

All complete sentences contain the same two basic components: a subject and a predicate. The **subject** is who or what is doing the action or being described in the sentence. The **predicate** is everything else in the sentence; the predicate includes the **verb,** which describes the action the subject is doing or the condition of the subject. The predicate, therefore, describes what the subject does or is.

Although all sentences contain these same two basic elements, there are different ways that the subject and predicate can be combined. There are four general sentence structures used in the English language.

Simple sentences contain one subject and one verb, but still express a complete thought:

> The mouse ate cheese.

The subject is *the mouse.* The verb is *ate.*

A sentence can still be considered a simple sentence if it has a compound subject or compound verb. A **compound** noun or verb consists of more than one elements. The following sentence contains a compound subject:

> *The mouse and the gerbil* ate cheese.

When two or more simple sentences are joined together to form a single sentence with more than one subject-verb combinations, it is considered a **compound sentence:**

> *The mouse ate cheese,* and *the boy built him a maze.*

198

This structure contains two independent clauses: (1) *the mouse ate cheese* and (2) *the boy built him a maze*. These two clauses are independent because they can stand on their own. However, they are combined with a comma and a coordinating conjunction *(and)* to form a compound sentence. Other coordinating conjunctions, such as *but* and *so* can also be used to form compound sentences.

Jenny read for two hours, *but* she did not finish her reading assignment.

The book was dense, *so* she was unable to understand it.

Complex sentences are formed from an independent clause and at least one dependent clause. Subordinating conjunctions, such as *although, because, unless, while, as soon as, since, if,* and *when*, are used to connect the dependent clause to the sentence.

Pablo bought a new bike helmet *because* his old one was cracked.

Unless you plan to renew your library books, they must be returned in two weeks.

The necessary punctuation in a complex sentence depends on the order of the clauses. When the dependent clause begins the sentence, a comma is used after it to separate it from the independent clause. However, when an independent clause precedes a dependent clause, a comma is not necessarily required.

Lastly, a **compound-complex sentence** consists of at least two independent clauses and at least one dependent clause:

Before you go home, please recycle your scrap paper, and stack your chair on your desk.

The first independent clause in the compound sentence structure includes a subordinating clause—*before you go home*. Therefore, the sentence structure is both complex and compound.

Constructing Effective Sentences that are Generally Free of Errors in Standard Written English

For fluent composition, writers must use a variety of sentence types and structures, and also ensure that they smoothly flow together when they are read. To accomplish this, they must first be able to identify fluent writing when they read it. This includes being able to distinguish among simple, compound, complex, and compound-complex sentences in text; to observe variations among sentence types, lengths, and beginnings; and to notice figurative language and understand how it augments sentence length and imparts musicality. Once students/writers recognize superior fluency, they should revise their own writing to be more readable and fluent. They must be able to apply acquired skills to revisions before being able to apply them to new drafts.

One strategy for revising writing to increase its sentence fluency is flipping sentences. This involves rearranging the word order in a sentence without deleting, changing, or adding any words. For example, the student or other writer who has written the sentence, "We went bicycling on Saturday" can revise it to, "On Saturday, we went bicycling." Another technique is using appositives. An **appositive** is a phrase or word that renames or identifies another adjacent word or phrase. Writers can revise for sentence fluency by inserting main phrases/words from one shorter sentence into another shorter sentence, combining them into one longer sentence, e.g. from "My cat, Peanut, is a gray and brown tabby. He loves hunting rats." to "My cat, Peanut, a gray and brown tabby, loves hunting rats." Revisions can also connect shorter sentences by using conjunctions and commas and removing repeated words: "Scott likes eggs. Scott is allergic to eggs" becomes "Scott likes eggs, but he is allergic to them."

One technique for revising writing to increase sentence fluency is "padding" short, simple sentences by adding phrases that provide more details specifying why, how, when, and/or where something took place. For example, a writer might have these two simple sentences: "I went to the market. I purchased a cake." To revise these, the writer can add the following informative dependent and independent clauses and prepositional phrases, respectively: "Before my mother woke up, I sneaked out of the house and went to the supermarket. As a birthday surprise, I purchased a cake for her." When revising sentences to make them longer, writers must also punctuate them correctly to change them from simple sentences to compound, complex, or compound-complex sentences.

One way writers can increase fluency is by varying the beginnings of sentences. Writers do this by starting most of their sentences with different words and phrases rather than monotonously repeating the same ones across multiple sentences. Another way writers can increase fluency is by varying the lengths of sentences. Since run-on sentences are incorrect, writers make sentences longer by also converting them from simple to compound, complex, and compound-complex sentences. The coordination and subordination involved in these also give the text more variation and interest, hence more fluency. Here are a few more ways writers can increase fluency:

> Varying the transitional language and conjunctions used makes sentences more fluent.
> Writing sentences with a variety of rhythms by using prepositional phrases.
> Varying sentence structure adds fluency.

Text Production: Writing Informative/Explanatory Texts

Producing an Informative/Explanatory Essay to Examine and Convey Complex Ideas and Information

The purpose of an informative or explanatory essay is to communicate information to the reader. Accordingly, the tone is typically formal and the language should be objective. Informative writing does not usually appeal to pathos, logos, or ethos. Instead, it simply aims to provide facts, evidence, observations, and objective descriptions of the subject matter in an organized, understandable fashion.

When tasked with writing an essay, whether informative, persuasive, or otherwise, writers typically follow a set of stages, which include the following:

> Pre-Writing/Planning: One of the most important steps in writing is pre-writing. Before drafting an essay or other assignment, it's helpful to think about the topic for a moment or two, in order to gain a more solid understanding of what the task is. Then, spend about five minutes jotting down the immediate ideas that could work for the essay. **Brainstorming** is a way to get some words on the page and offer a reference for ideas when drafting. Scratch paper is provided for writers to use any pre-writing techniques such as webbing, freewriting, or listing. Some writers prefer using graphic organizers during this phase. The goal is to get ideas out of the mind and onto the page. Like brainstorming, **freewriting** is another prewriting activity to help the writer generate ideas. This method involves setting a timer for two or three minutes and writing down all ideas that come to mind about the topic using complete sentences. Once time is up, writers should review the sentences to see what observations have been made and how these ideas might translate into a more unified direction for the topic. Even if sentences lack sense as a whole, freewriting is an

200

excellent way to get ideas onto the page in the very beginning stages of writing. Using complete sentences can make this a bit more challenging than brainstorming; however, overall it is a worthwhile exercise, as it may force the writer to come up with more complete thoughts about the topic. Once the ideas are on the page, it's time for the writer to turn them into a solid plan for the essay. The best ideas from the brainstorming results can then be developed into a more formal outline.

Organizing: Although sometimes it is difficult to get going on the brainstorming or prewriting phase, once ideas start flowing, writers often find that they have amassed too many thoughts that will not make for a cohesive and unified essay. During the organization stage, writers should examine the generated ideas, hone in on the important ones central to their main idea, and arrange the points in a logical and effective manner. Writers may also determine that some of the ideas generated in the planning process need further elaboration, potentially necessitating the need for research to gather information to fill the gaps. Once a writer has chosen his or her thesis and main argument, selected the most applicable details and evidence, and eliminated the "clutter," it is time to strategically organize the ideas. This is often accomplished with an outline.

Outlining: An **outline** is a system used to organize writing. When composing essays, outlining is important because it helps writers organize important information in a logical pattern using Roman numerals. Usually, outlines start out with the main ideas and then branch out into subgroups or subsidiary thoughts or subjects. Not only do outlines provide a visual tool for writers to reflect on how events, ideas, evidence, or other key parts of the argument relate to one another, but they can also lead writers to a stronger conclusion. The sample below demonstrates what a general outline looks like:

      I. Introduction
          1. Background
          2. Thesis statement
      II. Body
          1. Point A
              a. Supporting evidence
              b. Supporting evidence
          2. Point B
              a. Supporting evidence
              b. Supporting evidence
          3. Point C
              a. Supporting evidence
              b. Supporting evidence
     III. Conclusion

    1. Restatement of main points.

      2. Memorable ending.

Drafting/Writing: Now it comes time to actually write the essay. In this stage, writers should follow the outline they developed in the brainstorming process and try to incorporate the useful sentences penned in the freewriting exercise. The main goal of this phase is to put all the thoughts together in cohesive sentences and paragraphs. It is helpful for writers to remember that their work here does not have to be perfect. This process is often referred to as **drafting** because writers are just creating a rough draft of their work. Because of this, writers should avoid getting bogged down on the small details.

Revising: The main goal of the revision phase is to improve the essay's flow, cohesiveness, readability, and focus. For example, an essay will make a less persuasive argument if the various pieces of evidence are scattered and presented illogically or clouded with unnecessary thought. Therefore, writers should consider their essay's structure and organization, ensuring that there are smooth transitions between sentences and paragraphs. There should be a discernable introduction and conclusion as well, as these crucial components of an essay provide readers with a blueprint to follow.

Editing: Rather than focusing on content (as is the aim in the revising stage), the editing phase is all about the mechanics of the essay: the syntax, word choice, and grammar. This can be considered the proofreading stage. Successful editing is what sets apart a messy essay from a polished document.

While the writing process may have specific steps, the good news is that the process is **recursive,** meaning the steps need not be completed in a particular order. Many writers find that they complete steps at the same time such as drafting and revising, where the writing and rearranging of ideas occur simultaneously or in very close order. Similarly, a writer may find that a particular section of a draft needs more development and will go back to the prewriting stage to generate new ideas. The steps can be repeated at any time, and the more these steps of the recursive writing process are employed, the better the final product will be.

Like any other useful skill, writing only improves with practice. While writing may come more easily to some than others, it is still a skill to be honed and improved. Regardless of a person's natural abilities, there is always room for growth in writing. Practicing the basic skills of writing can aid in preparations for the Praxis Core Writing test and future writing endeavors.

One way to build vocabulary and enhance exposure to the written word is through reading. This can be through reading books, but reading of any materials such as newspapers, magazines, and even social media count towards practice with the written word. This also helps to enhance critical reading and thinking skills, through analysis of the ideas and concepts read. Think of each new reading experience as a chance to sharpen these skills.

Drawing Evidence from Informational Texts to Support Analysis

Whether engaging in a research project, completing an assignment or exam that requires reading and answering questions using informational texts, or writing an informative essay, it's critical that students master the skills needed to draw relevant evidence from informational texts that can be used to support their analysis of a topic.

Text evidence is specific information included in the text that supports the ideas and points that a writer is trying to make in his or her own essay. When a writer is tasked with writing an informative essay, he or she needs to read informational texts to cultivate text evidence that can be used to support the points he or she wants to make in the essay. These texts may be primary or secondary sources. **Primary sources** are the author's firsthand view of some specific event, phenomenon, character, place, process, ideas, field of study or discipline, or other subject matter. Whereas primary sources are original treatments of their subjects, **secondary sources** are a step removed from the original subjects; they analyze and interpret primary sources. These include journal articles, newspaper or magazine articles, works of literary criticism, political commentaries, and academic textbooks. Text evidence can be drawn from both categories of sources, but the strengths and weaknesses of the type of source should be considered when drawing evidence from it. For example, a history textbook is a secondary source that might recount the events of a certain war. However, because presumably the writer of the text was not present at the war, there may be bias and inaccuracies in the text. It is often wise to consult several sources regarding the same topic to ensure consistency, which helps increase the likelihood that the source is accurate. Students should exercise the same prudence when using online resources. Not all webpages are equally valid sources. With the ease of publishing a webpage these days, there are many sites that include inaccuracies and falsehoods stated as fact. When using any source, whether electronic or otherwise, it's important to consider the author's experience and education and the overall trustworthiness of the site. Websites produced by educational institutions (usually ending with the domain .edu) or governmental institutions (usually ending in .gov) tend to be reliable, although they should still be vetted and approached with some degree of critical evaluation.

One strategy for finding text evidence in an informational text that will directly relate or support to one's essay topic or ideas is to use the text features in the source. Textbooks, for example, usually contain an index in the back of the book with a list of included topics and the pages dedicated to them. This, along with the chapter list included in the table of contents at the front of the book, can help focus the researcher's use of the book and pinpoint where relevant information will be found. Then, instead of needing to skim or read the whole book, the reader can jump to the pertinent pages and make more efficient use of time. **Typographical emphasis** is another helpful text feature. Key words or vocabulary terms, for example, might be printed in boldface or italics to offset them from the surrounding text. This enables readers to scan and look for these terms and hone in on the particular sections of the text they may need. It also helps clarify the meaning of potentially unfamiliar words. These vocabulary words, and their definitions, are often included in a glossary at the end of the chapter as well.

Teachers can help strengthen their students' ability to find text evidence from informational texts by asking **text-dependent questions**. These are questions that most students should only be able to answer after reading a given text. Instead of relying on prior knowledge, students should be able to point to specific passages in the text that inform them as to the answer to the question. The following list also provides some specific question stems that can help encourage text evidence skill building:

- What are the exact words the author uses to describe _____ in paragraph ___?
- What clues from the text show us that _____?
- Where is the evidence (in terms of a sentence or two) that describes _____?
- What reasons does the text give for _____ and where are these reasons located?

Synthesizing Information from Multiple Sources

Informative or explanatory papers require research. Once the student chooses or is assigned his or her topic, research sources must be selected. The student may begin by conducting an Internet or library search of the topic, may refer to a reading list provided by the instructor, or may use an annotated bibliography of works related to the topic. In nearly all cases, multiple sources must be used and the information garnered from them must be integrated and synthesized together in the final paper. This involves keeping careful notes about what information is obtained from each source and then grouping the categories of facts and evidence found in the sources. Then, the writer must find a way to organize his or her paper to logically structure and present findings and ideas.

Sources may include books, journal articles, encyclopedias and dictionaries, webpages, newspapers, documentary videos, etc.

Integrating and Attributing Information from Multiple Sources on the Subject

Any time a text is used to inform one's writing, the writer must credit the text. This is usually accomplished by either in-text citations or footnotes that then lead the reader to the bibliography or works cited list, which gives the full citation for the source. There are different styles and conventions for citations; MLA, APA, and Chicago/Turabian are among the most common. The components of the citation are similar, regardless of the style, but the order and formatting of the components differ. Additionally, the form of the source (book, website, journal article, etc.) determines which components are needed. Components that are usually required in some order include the following:

Author's or authors' full name/s
Title of the source
Title of the article and the journal it was found in
Publication date
Name of editor
Version/volume
Number/issue
Publisher
URL and date of access (for electronic sources)
Page numbers
City and state of publication

In addition to the full citation found at the end of a paper, writers must attribute the supporting evidence they includes in their papers to the source where it was found using in-text citations. The form and included information for in-text citations also varies depending on the style guide followed, but all require some form of citation directly after the sentence that uses the information obtained from the source. In-text citations are condensed versions of the full citation. They contain details that correspond to the first element of the full citation in the bibliography, which is usually the author. They also often contain the page number and publication year. Students should be introduced to all three of the common styles and learn the conventions for each. It is important to note that direct quotes taken from a source must have quotation marks around the copied text along with the appropriate attribution. Even ideas that are paraphrased require attribution, although in such cases (where the writer uses his or her own wording to restate what the original author wrote), quotation marks are not needed. Failing to properly attribute an idea, quote, or fact from another writer is plagiarism.

Text Production: Revision

Developing and Strengthening Writing as Needed by Revising and Editing

Skilled writers undergo a series of steps that comprise the writing process. The purpose of adhering to a structured approach to writing is to develop clear, meaningful, coherent work.

The stages are pre-writing or planning, organizing, drafting/writing, revising, and editing. Not every writer will necessarily follow all five stages for every project, but will judiciously employ the crucial components of the stages for most formal or important work. For example, a brief informal response to a short reading passage may not necessitate the need for significant organization after idea generation, but larger assignments and essays will likely mandate use of the full process.

Revising and editing should be stages in any writing project, even a timed essay on an exam. Together, they help strengthen a piece of writing by getting the writer to consider the essay's readability, flow, logic, and writing quality. Sections of text may be reorganized, reordered, or eliminated. Grammatical and spelling mistakes should be corrected. Transitions may be enhanced to improve the flow of the essay and help readers follow the argument. Ultimately, undergoing the revising and editing stages after the essay has been written allows the writer to get his or her ideas out without getting bogged down in making sure every sentence is perfect, but then the essay can be improved by taking a finer-toothed comb through it and tidying up the work.

Recognizing How a Passage Can Be Strengthened Through Editing and Revising

Revising

Revising offers an opportunity for writers to polish things up. Putting one's self in the reader's shoes and focusing on what the essay actually says helps writers identify problems—it's a movement from the mindset of writer to the mindset of editor. The goal is to have a clean, clear copy of the essay.

The main goal of the revision phase is to improve the essay's flow, cohesiveness, readability, and focus. For example, an essay will make a less persuasive argument if the various pieces of evidence are scattered and presented illogically or clouded with unnecessary thought. Therefore, writers should consider their essay's structure and organization, ensuring that there are smooth transitions between sentences and paragraphs. There should be a discernable introduction and conclusion as well, as these crucial components of an essay provide readers with a blueprint to follow.

Additionally, if the writer includes copious details that do little to enhance the argument, they may actually distract readers from focusing on the main ideas and detract from the strength of their work. The ultimate goal is to retain the purpose or focus of the essay and provide a reader-friendly experience. Because of this, writers often need to delete parts of their essay to improve its flow and focus. Removing sentences, entire paragraphs, or large chunks of writing can be one of the toughest parts of the writing process because it is difficult to part with work one has done. However, ultimately, these types of cuts can significantly improve one's essay.

Lastly, writers should consider their voice and word choice. The voice should be consistent throughout and maintain a balance between an authoritative and warm style, to both inform and engage readers. One way to alter voice is through word choice. Writers should consider changing weak verbs to stronger ones and selecting more precise language in areas where wording is vague. In some cases, it is useful to modify sentence beginnings or to combine or split up sentences to provide a more varied sentence structure.

Editing

Rather than focusing on content (as is the aim in the revising stage), the editing phase is all about the mechanics of the essay: the syntax, word choice, and grammar. This can be considered the proofreading stage. Successful editing is what sets apart a messy essay from a polished document.

The following areas should be considered when proofreading:

Sentence fragments
Awkward sentence structure
Run-on sentences
Incorrect word choice

Grammatical agreement errors
Spelling errors
Punctuation errors
Capitalization errors

One of the most effective ways of identifying grammatical errors, awkward phrases, or unclear sentences is to read the essay out loud. Listening to one's own work can help move the writer from simply the author to the reader.

During the editing phase, it's also important to ensure the essay follows the correct formatting and citation rules as dictated by the assignment.

How Language Functions in Different Contexts and Making Effective Choices for Meaning or Style

Language can function differently depending on its context. The same words can convey meaning in nuanced ways depending on the surrounding context and the style and tone of the composition. Just as how people can speak with a variety of tones and inflections that can alter the meaning of the same sentence, so too can writers insert tone into written words. Punctuation choice is one example of how the same sentence can be interpreted slightly differently.

Consider the following three sentences:

Camille hates dogs.

Camille hates dogs!

Camille hates dogs?

Although the wording is identical in these three simple sentences, the end punctuation affects the tone, and each option allows for a slightly different interpretation. The first sentence is simply stating that Camille hates dogs; the period at the end of the sentence elicits no significant emotional response. The exclamation point at the end of the second sentence could evoke surprise, exasperation, or urgency/alarm. Perhaps, for example, someone was about to introduce a large mastiff to Camille who had her back turned to the dog. One of Camille's friends who saw what was about to happen may have shouted that sentence in caution to prevent a terrified Camille. The last sentence is obviously a question, but that doesn't mean it's affectless. It could have been asked simply out of desire for clarification or confirmation, or it could have been asked in an incredulous or surprised tone because the speaker found it hard to believe that Camille could hate dogs.

The writer could further display tone by italicizing one of the words to indicate emphasis. Consider the difference between the following three examples:

Camille hates dogs?

Camille *hates* dogs?

Camille hates *dogs*?

The first example places the emphasis on Camille. The speaker could be surprised that Camille, not another person, supposedly hates dogs. In the second example, the speaker's focus is on the word *hate*. He or she is seeking clarity or confirmation that Camille actually hates dogs (as opposed to simply being

206

annoyed by them, allergic to them, afraid of them, etc.). The italicized *dogs* in the last sentence indicates the speaker is verifying or expressing shock that Camille hates dogs in particular (rather than cats, spiders, rats, etc.). Other punctuation marks, especially commas, can also shape the way a sentence is read and interpreted.

Choosing Words and Phrases for Effect

Skillful writers are artists. They breathe life into the words they've written by choosing language that provides details that enable their readers to visualize what they have read and that makes the writing more exciting and engaging. Adjectives, adverbs, and more descriptive noun and verb choices can all help animate a piece of writing and make it more memorable. More specific words can also be used instead of vague or general ones. For example, instead of *I walked to the steps and slowly got in the water,* the sentence could be *I gingerly walked to the steps, and slowly eased myself into the water.* This second variation paints a clearer picture that the speaker is hesitant to swim. Writers should try to vary the words they choose to use as well to reduce the monotony of repetitiveness.

Choosing Words and Phrases to Convey Ideas Precisely

Writers communicate their ideas through their word choice and the way they structure the chosen words into sentences and paragraphs. The best way for writers to ensure that readers interpret a piece of writing appropriately is to be as precise as possible with word choice. **Synonyms** are words with similar meanings, like *happy* and *glad* or *arrogant* and *pompous.* While a piece of writing that uses a variety of vocabulary words is often more interesting to read and less monotonous, it's important for writers to ensure that the specific words chosen best convey the intended meaning. Even synonyms have nuances between them and just because a certain word sounds more impressive or novel, it does not mean it's necessarily the best choice in the context of the piece of writing.

Maintaining Consistency in Style and Tone

The style and tone of a piece of writing should match the intended audience and purpose. The **style** of a piece of writing refers to the way the writer has composed it. It entails the specific words chosen, the selection and arrangement of sentence structures, and the paragraph structure. The **tone** of a piece relates to the how the writer has conveyed his or her ideas. A tone, for example, might be serious, humorous, or somber. The tone of most formal pieces is impersonal or authoritative because the purpose is to inform and demonstrate a command of a topic or idea. Argumentative essays tend to be more emotional and passionate, as they usually attempt to evoke an emotional reaction in the reader.

Writers should strive to maintain consistency in the style and tone used in a given essay. For example, if the essay uses formal writing, it should be free from informal language, slang, and grammatical rule bending that is somewhat more permissible in conversational or informal writing. If the tone of a piece is authoritative and the writer is striving to assert himself or herself as an expert, the writer should not switch to a silly or playful tone. Writers can help ensure that style and tone remain consistent by maintaining the same "voice" in a given essay and remembering to write in a way that reflects the purpose and audience of the piece.

Language Skills

Conventions of Standard English Grammar and Usage

Grammatical Relationships

Adjectives and Adverbs

Adjectives are descriptive words that modify nouns or pronouns. They may occur before or after the nouns or pronouns they modify in sentences. For example, in "This is a big house," *big* is an adjective modifying or describing the noun *house*. In "This house is big," the adjective is at the end of the sentence rather than preceding the noun it modifies.

A rule of punctuation that applies to adjectives is to separate a series of adjectives with commas. For example, "Their home was a large, rambling, old, white, two-story house." A comma should never separate the last adjective from the noun, though.

Whereas adjectives modify and describe nouns or pronouns, **adverbs** modify and describe adjectives, verbs, or other adverbs. Adverbs can be thought of as answers to questions in that they describe when, where, how, how often, how much, or to what extent.

Many (but not all) adjectives can be converted to adverbs by adding *–ly*. For example, in "She is a quick learner," *quick* is an adjective modifying *learner*. In "She learns quickly," *quickly* is an adverb modifying *learns*. One exception is *fast*. *Fast* is an adjective in "She is a fast learner." However, *–ly* is never added to the word *fast*; it retains the same form as an adverb in "She learns fast."

Noun-Noun Agreement

When multiple nouns are included in the same sentence and are related to one another in that sentence, they need to agree in number. This means that if one noun is singular, all other related nouns in the sentence must be singular as well. Similarly, if one noun is plural, the rest should follow in form and be plural as well. Consider the following sentence with an error in noun-noun agreement:

> Mary and Sharon both have jobs as a teacher.

Because the noun *jobs* is plural, the noun *teachers*, which is also plural, must be used in place of *teacher*, which is singular.

> Mary and Sharon both have jobs as teachers.

Pronoun-Antecedent Agreement

Pronouns within a sentence must refer specifically to one noun, known as the **antecedent**. Sometimes, if there are multiple nouns within a sentence, it may be difficult to ascertain which noun belongs to the pronoun. It's important that the pronouns always clearly reference the nouns in the sentence so as not to confuse the reader. Here's an example of an unclear pronoun reference:

> After Catherine cut Libby's hair, David bought her some lunch.

The pronoun in the examples above is *her*. The pronoun could either be referring to *Catherine* or *Libby*. Here are some ways to write the above sentence with a clear pronoun reference:

> After Catherine cut Libby's hair, David bought Libby some lunch.

> David bought Libby some lunch after Catherine cut Libby's hair.

But many times, the pronoun will clearly refer to its antecedent, like the following:

> After David cut Catherine's hair, he bought her some lunch.

Pronoun Case

There are three **pronoun cases**: subjective case, objective case, and possessive case. Pronouns as subjects are pronouns that replace the subject of the sentence, such as *I, you, he, she, it, we, they* and *who*. Pronouns as objects replace the object of the sentence, such as *me, you, him, her, it, us, them,* and *whom*. Pronouns that show possession are *mine, yours, hers, its, ours, theirs,* and *whose*. The following are examples of different pronoun cases:

> Subject pronoun: *She* ate the cake for her birthday. *I* saw the movie.
> Object pronoun: You gave *me* the card last weekend. She gave the picture to *him*.
> Possessive pronoun: That bracelet you found yesterday is *mine*. *His* name was Casey.

Intensive Pronoun Errors

An **intensive pronoun** ends in "self" or "selves" and adds emphasis to the sentence's subject or antecedent. Like reflexive pronouns, intensive pronouns include the singular pronouns *myself, yourself, himself, herself,* and *itself,* and the plural pronouns *ourselves, yourselves,* and *themselves*. However, intensive and reflexive pronouns differ in that removing a reflexive pronoun will cause the sentence to no longer make sense, whereas intensive pronouns can be removed because they only add emphasis; they are not mandatory. An example of a sentence with an intensive pronoun is the following:

> We want to hear the author herself read the story.

The intensive pronoun *herself* adds emphasis that the speakers want to specifically hear the author read the story, rather than anyone else.

The most common error in the use of intensive pronouns is choosing the wrong pronoun; for example, using the plural pronoun when the singular one is needed, or using a singular pronoun when a plural one is needed. Using the same example from above, an error in agreement occurs in the following sentence:

> We want to hear the author themselves read the story.

Author is singular and *themselves* is plural, so there is an error in number agreement.

Pronoun Number and Person Errors

Pronouns must agree in number and person. However, it is common, unfortunately, for writers to shift between persons or numbers when using pronouns. For example, a sentence might start with third person pronouns (*he, she, it, they,* etc.), but then switch to second person. Or, a sentence might start in second person and switch to first or third person. The following sentence contains a pronoun shift in person:

> If you drink more water, most people see improvements in their skin and body composition.

This example begins with second person (using the pronoun *you*), but switches to third person (*their*). Consistency in person is needed. Therefore, the sentence should be one of the following two options:

If you drink more water, you will likely see improvements in your skin and body composition.

If they drink more water, most people see improvements in their skin and body composition.

Inappropriate pronoun shifts also occur when writers switch from using singular pronouns to plural ones, or vice versa. Sometimes, sentences will have errors in pronoun number and person.

Everyone should keep a journal about their life because you will want to pass the stories of your life along.

These sentences are usually easier to spot because the errors are two-fold and more apparent.

Vague Pronouns

A **pronoun** replaces a noun in a sentence, which is called the **antecedent.** It should be clear which noun the pronoun is replacing. Vague pronouns are unclear, cause ambiguity and confusion, may refer to more than one antecedent, and disturb the meaning of the sentence. Consider the following example:

Tommy gave Greg a gift card, and he blushed.

In the above sentence, *he* is the pronoun, but it isn't readily apparent who *he* refers to. Did Tommy blush or did Greg blush? It's plausible that either person blushed. Instead, the name of the person, the antecedent, needs to be used instead:

Tommy gave Greg a gift card, and Greg blushed.

The pronoun *it* is often the culprit in cases of a vague pronoun. Consider the following:

Grandma dropped the glass frame on her hand and it broke.

Did the frame break or did grandma's hand break? The pronoun *it* should be replaced with the proper antecedent to clarify the intended meaning.

Other times, there is no clear antecedent, which also causes ambiguity and confusion:

Mom called the store, but they didn't answer the phone.

Why is *they?* The store cannot answer the phone. A person answers a phone. Therefore, this sentence is incorrect. Instead, it should be amended in some way, such as the following:

Mom called the store, but no employees answered the phone.

Subject-Verb Agreement

Lack of subject-verb agreement is a very common grammatical error. One of the most common instances is when people use a series of nouns as a compound subject with a singular instead of a plural verb. Here is an example:

Identifying the best books, locating the sellers with the lowest prices, and paying for them *is* difficult.

The sentence should say "*are* difficult." Additionally, when a sentence subject is compound, the verb is plural:

He and his cousins *were* at the reunion.

However, if the conjunction connecting two or more singular nouns or pronouns is "or" or "nor," the verb must be singular to agree:

That pen or another one like it is in the desk drawer.

If a compound subject includes both a singular noun and a plural one, and they are connected by "or" or "nor," the verb must agree with the subject closest to the verb: "Sally or her sisters go jogging daily"; but "Her sisters or Sally goes jogging daily."

Simply put, singular subjects require singular verbs and plural subjects require plural verbs. A common source of agreement errors is not identifying the sentence subject correctly. For example, people often write sentences incorrectly like, "The group of students *were* complaining about the test." The subject is not the plural "students" but the singular "group." Therefore, the correct sentence should read, "The group of students *was* complaining about the test." The converse also applies, for example, in this incorrect sentence: "The facts in that complicated court case *is* open to question." The subject of the sentence is not the singular "case" but the plural "facts." Hence the sentence would correctly be written: "The facts in that complicated court case *are* open to question." New writers should not be misled by the distance between the subject and verb, especially when another noun with a different number intervenes as in these examples. The verb must agree with the subject, not the noun closest to it.

Inappropriate Shifts in Verb Tense

A **verb** is a word or phrase that expresses action, feeling, or state of being. Verbs explain what their subject is *doing*. Three different types of verbs used in a sentence are action verbs, linking verbs, and helping verbs.

Action verbs show a physical or mental action. Some examples of action verbs are *play, type, jump, write, examine, study, invent, develop,* and *taste.* The following example uses an action verb:

Kat *imagines* that she is a mermaid in the ocean.

The verb *imagines* explains what Kat is doing: she is imagining being a mermaid.

Linking verbs connect the subject to the predicate without expressing an action. The following sentence shows an example of a linking verb:

The mango *tastes* sweet.

The verb *tastes* is a linking verb. The mango doesn't *do* the tasting, but the word *taste* links the mango to its predicate, sweet. Most linking verbs can also be used as action verbs, such as *smell, taste, look, seem, grow,* and *sound.* Saying something *is* something else is also an example of a linking verb. For example, if we were to say, "Peaches is a dog," the verb *is* would be a linking verb in this sentence, since it links the subject to its predicate.

Helping verbs are verbs that help the main verb in a sentence. Examples of helping verbs are *be, am, is, was, have, has, do, did, can, could, may, might, should,* and *must,* among others. The following are examples of helping verbs:

> Jessica *is* planning a trip to Hawaii.
>
> Brenda *does* not like camping.
>
> Xavier *should* go to the dance tonight.

Notice that after each of these helping verbs is the main verb of the sentence: *planning, like,* and *go.* Helping verbs usually show an aspect of time.

Verb tense helps indicate when an action or a state existed occurred or existed.

Simple present tense is used to indicate that the action or state of being is currently happening or happens regularly:

> He *plays* guitar.

Present continuous tense is used to indicate that the action or state of being is in progress. It is formed by the proper to be + verb + *-ing.*

> Unfortunately, I can't go to the park right now. I *am fixing* my bicycle.

Past tense is used to indicate that the action or state of being occurred previously. It should be noted, however, that in conversational English, speakers frequently use a mix of present and past tense, or simply present tense when describing events in the past. With that said, it is important for writers (and speakers in formal situations) to be consistent and grammatically correct in their verb tenses to avoid confusing readers. Consider the following passage:

> I scored a goal in our soccer game last Saturday. At the start of the first half, Billy kicked me the ball. I run toward it and strike it directly toward the goal. It goes in and we won the game!

The passage above inappropriately switches from past tense—*scored, kicked*—to present tense—*run, strike, goes*—and then back to past tense—*won.* Instead, past tense should be carried throughout the passage:

> I *scored* a goal in our soccer game last Saturday. At the start of the first half, Billy *kicked* me the ball. I *ran* toward it and strike it directly toward the goal. It *went* in and we *won* the game!

Structural Relationships
The Placement of Phrases and Clauses Within a Sentence

Clauses contain a subject and a predicate, while **phrases** only contain a noun with no verb or a verb with no noun, and they do not have a predicate. Clauses can be independent or dependent. **Independent clauses** can stand on their own as simple sentences. For example:

> She collects stamps.

Dependent clauses need independent clauses to form a complete sentence; they cannot stand alone. For example:

> Although she collects stamps . . .

Phrases can take on many forms including prepositional phrases, gerund phrases, noun phrases, infinitive phrases, verb phrases, etc. Regardless of the type, phrases cannot stand alone as complete sentence.

Phrases and clauses must be appropriately placed in a sentence such that it is clear to readers what they are modifying.

Consider the following misplaced prepositional phrase:

> At the bottom of the pile, Lila found her scarf.

In the above sentence, the phrase *at the bottom of the pile* is intended to modify the noun phrase *the scarf* by providing details about where the scarf was found. However, as written, the prepositional phrase is next to the subject, Lila, so it is modifying Lila. This is incorrect because presumably Lila herself wasn't at the bottom of a pile, her scarf was.

Misplaced and Dangling Modifiers

Modifiers are optional elements that can clarify or add details about a phrase or another element of a sentence. They are a dependent phrase and removing them usually does not change the grammatical correctness of the sentence; however, the meaning will be changed because, as their name implies, modifiers modify another element in the sentence. Consider the following:

> Nico loves sardines.

> Nico, who is three years old, loves sardines.

The first simple sentence is grammatically correct; however, we learn a lot more from the second sentence, which contains the modifier *who is three years old*. Sardines tend to be a food that young children don't like, so adding the modifier helps readers see why Nico loving sardines is noteworthy.

Beginning writers sometimes place modifiers incorrectly. Then, instead of enhancing comprehension and providing helpful description for the reader, the modifier causes more confusion. A **misplaced modifier** is located incorrectly in relation to the phrase or word it modifies. Consider the following sentence:

> Because it is salty, Nico loves fish.

The modifier in this sentence is "because they are salty," and the noun it is intended to modify is "fish." However, due to the erroneous placement of the modifier next to the subject, Nico, the sentence is actually saying that Nico is salty.

> Nico loves fish because it is salty.

The modifier is now adjacent to the appropriate noun, clarifying which of the two elements is salty.

Dangling modifiers are so named because they modify a phrase or word that is not clearly found in the sentence, making them rather unattached. They are not intended to modify the word or phrase they are placed next to. Consider the following:

Walking home from school, the sky opened and Bruce got drenched.

The modifier here, "walking home from school," should modify who was walking (Bruce). Instead, the noun immediately after the modifier is "the sky"—but the sky was not walking home from school. Although not always the case, dangling modifiers are often found at the beginning of a sentence.

Coordinating and Subordinating Conjunctions
Conjunctions connect or coordinate words, phrases, clauses, or sentences together, typically as a way to demonstrate a relationship.

Tony has a cat *and* a rabbit.

Tony likes animals, *but* he is afraid of snakes.

Coordinating conjunctions join words or phrases that have equal rank or emphasis. There are seven coordinating conjunctions, all short words, that can be remembered by the mnemonic FANBOYS: *for, and, nor, but, or, yet, so.* They can join two words that are of the same part of speech (two verbs, two adjectives, two adverbs, or two nouns). They can also connect two phrases or two independent clauses.

Subordinating conjunctions help transition and connect two elements in the sentence, but in a way that diminishes the importance of the one it introduces, known as the dependent, or subordinate, clause. They include words like *because, since, unless, before, after, whereas, if,* and *while.*

Fragments and Run-Ons
Every sentence must have a subject and a verb to be complete. As mentioned, **sentence fragments** are caused by absent subjects, absent verbs, or dangling/uncompleted dependent clauses. An example of a fragment is "Raining all night long," because there is no subject present. "It was raining all night long" is one correction. Another example of a sentence fragment is the second part in "Many scientists think in unusual ways. Einstein, for instance." The second phrase is a fragment because it has no verb. One correction is "Many scientists, like Einstein, think in unusual ways." Finally, look for "cliffhanger" words like *if, when, because,* or *although* that introduce dependent clauses, which cannot stand alone without an independent clause. For example, to correct the sentence fragment "If you get home early," add an independent clause: "If you get home early, we can go dancing."

A **run-on sentence** combines two or more complete sentences without punctuating them correctly or separating them. For example, a run-on sentence caused by a lack of punctuation is the following:

There are too many people here for the number of available seats however there is nobody around who has access to the room with additional chairs.

One correction is, "There is a malfunction in the computer system; however, there is nobody available right now who knows how to troubleshoot it." Another is, "There is a malfunction in the computer system. However, there is nobody available right now who knows how to troubleshoot it."

An example of a **comma splice** of two sentences is the following:

Xavier decided to buy the chicken, he had enough money.

Replacing the comma with a period or a semicolon corrects this. Commas that try and separate two independent clauses without a contraction are considered comma splices.

Correlative Conjunctions

Correlative conjunctions are pairs of conjunctions that must both be used in the sentence, though in different spots, to make the sentence grammatically sound. They help relate one aspect of the sentence to another. Examples of correlative conjunctions pairs are *neither/nor, both/and, not/but, either/or, as/as, such/that* and *rather/than*. They tend to be more like coordinating conjunctions rather than subordinating conjunctions in that they typically connect two words or phrases of equal weight in the sentence.

Parallel Structure

As mentioned, **parallel structure** in a sentence matches the forms of sentence components. Any sentence containing more than one description or phrase should keep them consistent in wording and form. Readers can easily follow writers' ideas when they are written in parallel structure, making it an important element of correct sentence construction. For example, this sentence lacks parallelism: "Our coach is a skilled manager, a clever strategist, and works hard." The first two phrases are parallel, but the third is not. Correction: "Our coach is a skilled manager, a clever strategist, and a hard worker." Now all three phrases match in form. Here is another example:

Fred intercepted the ball, escaped tacklers, and a touchdown was scored.

This is also non-parallel. Here is the sentence corrected:

Fred intercepted the ball, escaped tacklers, and scored a touchdown.

Word Choice

Idiomatic Expressions

Idiomatic expressions are phrases or groups of words that have an established meaning when used together that is unrelated to the literal meanings of the individual words. For example, consider the following sentence that includes a common idiomatic phrase:

I know Phil is coming to visit this weekend because I heard it straight from the horse's mouth.

The speaker of this sentence did not consult a horse nor hear anything uttered from a horse in relation to Phil's visit. Instead, "straight from the horse's mouth" is an idiom that means the information came directly from an original or reliable source. As in the sentence above, it often means whatever said should be taken as truth because it was spoken by the person to which it pertains (in this case, Phil). The phrase is derived from the fact that sellers of horses at auctions would sometimes try to lie about the age of the horse. However, the size and shape of a horse's teeth can provide a fairly accurate estimate of the horse's true age. Therefore, the truth regarding the horse's age essentially comes straight from their mouth. The idiomatic expression came to mean getting the truth in any situation.

Finding errors in idiomatic expressions can be difficult because it requires familiarity with the idiom. Because there are more than one thousand idioms in the English language, memorizing all of them is impractical. However, it is helpful to review the most common ones. There are many webpages dedicated to listing and explaining frequently used idioms.

Errors in the idiomatic expressions are typically one of two types. The idiomatic expression may be stated improperly, or it may be used in an incorrect context. In the first type of issue, the prepositions used are often incorrect. For example, it might say "straight in the horse's mouth" or "straight with the horse's mouth." In the second error type, the idiomatic expression is used improperly because the meaning it carries does not make sense in the context in which it appears. Consider the following:

> He was looking straight from the horse's mouth when he complained about the phone his father bought him.

Here, the writer has confused the idiom "straight from the horse's mouth" with "looking a gift horse in the mouth," which means to find fault in a gift or favor.

Either type of error can be difficult to detect and correct without prior knowledge of the idiomatic phrase. Practicing usage of idioms and studying their origins can help you remember their meanings and precise wordings, which will then help you identify and correct errors in their usage.

Frequently Confused Words

The English language can be confusing and it is common for students to make mistakes in word choice, meaning, or spelling. **Homophones** are words that sound the same in speech, but have different spellings and meanings. For example, *to, too,* and *two* all sound alike, but have three different spellings and meanings. Homophones with different spellings are also called **heterographs**. **Homographs** are words that are spelled identically, but have different meanings. If they also have different pronunciations, they are heteronyms. For instance, *tear* pronounced one way means a drop of liquid formed by the eye; pronounced another way, it means to rip. Homophones that are also homographs are **homonyms**. For example, *bark* can mean the outside of a tree or a dog's vocalization; both meanings have the same spelling. *Stalk* can mean a plant stem or to pursue and/or harass somebody; these are spelled and pronounced the same. *Rose* can mean a flower or the past tense of *rise*. Many non-linguists confuse things by using "homonym" to mean sets of words that are homophones but not homographs, and also those that are homographs but not homophones.

The word *row* can mean to use oars to propel a boat; a linear arrangement of objects or print; or an argument. It is pronounced the same with the first two meanings, but differently with the third. Because it is spelled identically regardless, all three meanings are homographs. However, the two meanings pronounced the same are homophones, whereas the one with the different pronunciation is a **heteronym**. By contrast, the word *read* means to peruse language, whereas the word *reed* refers to a marsh plant. Because these are pronounced the same way, they are homophones; because they are spelled differently, they are heterographs. Homonyms are both homophones and **homographs**— pronounced and spelled identically, but with different meanings. One distinction between homonyms is of those with separate, unrelated etymologies, called "true" homonyms, e.g. *skate* meaning a fish or *skate* meaning to glide over ice/water. Those with common origins are called **polysemes** or **polysemous homonyms**, e.g. the *mouth* of an animal/human or of a river.

There are some words that do not abide by the typical rules when turning them into their plural form, and it's common for students to struggle forming and using these irregular plurals. While many words in English can become plural by adding –s or –es to the end, there are some words that have irregular plural forms. One type includes words that are spelled the same whether they are singular or plural, such as deer, fish, salmon, trout, sheep, moose, offspring, species, aircraft, etc. The spelling rule for making these words plural is simple: they do not change. Other irregular English plurals change form based on vowel shifts, linguistic mutations, or grammatical and spelling conventions from their languages of origin, like Latin or German. Some examples include *child* and *children; die* and *dice; foot* and *feet; goose* and *geese; louse* and *lice; man* and *men; mouse* and *mice; ox* and *oxen; person* and *people; tooth* and *teeth;* and *woman* and *women.*

Wrong Word Usage

One of the most common reasons that a writer chooses the wrong word for a given application is if the word has multiple meanings and spellings. Words that have different meanings and spellings but sound the same are called **homophones**. These can be confusing for English Language Learners (ELLs) and beginning students, but even native English-speaking adults can find them problematic unless informed by context. Whereas listeners must rely entirely on context to differentiate spoken homophone meanings, readers with good spelling knowledge have a distinct advantage since homophones are spelled differently. For instance, *their* means belonging to them; *there* indicates location; and *they're* is a contraction of *they are*, despite different meanings, they all sound the same. *Lacks* can be a plural noun or a present-tense, third-person singular verb; either way it refers to absence—*deficiencies* as a plural noun, and *is deficient in* as a verb. But *lax* is an adjective that means loose, slack, relaxed, uncontrolled, or negligent. These two spellings, derivations, and meanings are completely different. With speech, listeners cannot know spelling and must use context; but with print, readers with spelling knowledge can differentiate them with or without context.

One other issue that students may is misspelling certain difficult words. Spelling errors not only negatively affect the polished feel of an essay, but they can result in confusion, particularly if the spelling mistake results in the formation of a different, unintended word. One source of spelling errors is not knowing whether to drop the final letter *e* from a word when its form is changed; some words retain the final *e* when another syllable is added while others lose it. For example, *true* becomes *truly; argue* becomes *arguing; come* becomes *coming; write* becomes *writing;* and *judge* becomes *judging*. In these examples, the final *e* is dropped before adding the ending. But *severe* becomes *severely; complete* becomes *completely; sincere* becomes *sincerely; argue* becomes *argued;* and *care* becomes *careful*. In these instances, the final *e* is retained before adding the ending. Note that some words, like argue in these examples, drops the final e when the –ing ending is added to indicate the participial form, but the regular past tense form keeps the e and adds a –d to make it argued.

Other commonly misspelled English words are those containing the vowel combinations ei and ie. Many people confuse these two. Some examples of words with the ei combination include:

> *ceiling, conceive, leisure, receive, weird, their, either, foreign, sovereign, neither, neighbors, seize, forfeit, counterfeit, height, weight, protein,* and *freight*

Words with *ie* include *piece, believe, chief, field, friend, grief, relief, mischief, siege, niece, priest, fierce, pierce, achieve, retrieve, hygiene, science,* and *diesel*. A rule that also functions as a mnemonic device is "I before E except after C, or when sounded like A as in 'neighbor' or 'weigh'." However, it is obvious from the list above that many exceptions exist.

People often misspell certain words by confusing whether they have the vowel a, e, or i. For example, in the following correctly spelled words, the vowel in boldface is the one people typically get wrong by substituting one of the others for it:

> cem**e**tery, quant**i**ties, ben**e**fit, priv**i**lege, unpleas**a**nt, sep**a**rate, independ**e**nt, excell**e**nt, categ**o**ries, indispens**a**ble, and irrelev**a**nt

Some words with final syllables that sound the same when spoken but are spelled differently include *unpleasant, independent, excellent,* and *irrelevant.* Another source of misspelling is whether or not to double consonants when adding suffixes. For example, double the last consonant before –ed and –ing endings in controlled, beginning, forgetting, admitted, occurred, referred, and hopping; but do not double before the suffix in *shining, poured, sweating, loving, hating, smiling,* and *hoping.*

One final example of common misspellings involves either the failure to include silent letters or the converse of adding extraneous letters. If a letter is not pronounced in speech, it is easy to leave it out in writing. For example, some people omit the silent *u* in *guarantee,* overlook the first *r* in *surprise,* leave out the *z* in *realize,* fail to double the *m* in *recommend,* leave out the middle *i* from *aspirin,* and exclude the *p* from *temperature.* The converse error, adding extra letters, is common in words like *until* by adding a second *l* at the end; or by inserting a superfluous syllabic *a* or *e* in the middle of *athletic,* reproducing a common mispronunciation.

Redundancy

Redundancy, in terms of word choice, refers to repeating the same words or phrases or using different words to restate the same thing. Writers should strive to be concise in stating their points and backing them up with adequate and relevant examples. Wordiness detracts from the overall takeaways from an essay and redundancy can bore readers. State the point and move forward. It only makes sense to reword it and reiterate the point if it needs explicit emphasis.

An example of wordiness can be seen in the following sentence:

In spite of the fact that I stayed home from school today, I still feel sick.

In spite of the fact is wordy. The five-word phrase can be replaced by the single word *although.*

Although I stayed home from school today, I still feel sick.

The following sentence demonstrates redundancy:

We often shop there most days .

Instead, one of the following two options is preferable:

We often shop there.

We shop there most days.

Conventions of Standard English Spelling and Punctuation

Capitalization

The first word of any document, and of each new sentence, is capitalized. Proper nouns, like names and adjectives derived from proper nouns, should also be capitalized. Here are some examples:

Grand Canyon
Pacific Palisades
Golden Gate Bridge
Freudian slip
Shakespearian, Spenserian, or Petrarchan sonnet
Irish song

Some exceptions are adjectives, originally derived from proper nouns, which through time and usage are no longer capitalized, like *quixotic, herculean,* or *draconian.* Capitals draw attention to specific instances of people, places, and things. Some categories that should be capitalized include the following:

brand names
companies
weekdays
months
governmental divisions or agencies
historical eras
major historical events
holidays
institutions
famous buildings
ships and other manmade constructions
natural and manmade landmarks
territories
nicknames
epithets
organizations
planets
nationalities
tribes
religions
names of religious deities
roads
special occasions, like the Cannes Film Festival or the Olympic Games

Exceptions

Related to American government, capitalize the noun Congress but not the related adjective congressional. Capitalize the noun U.S. Constitution, but not the related adjective constitutional. Many experts advise leaving the adjectives federal and state in lowercase, as in federal regulations or state water board, and only capitalizing these when they are parts of official titles or names, like Federal Communications Commission or State Water Resources Control Board. While the names of the other planets in the solar system are capitalized as names, Earth is more often capitalized only when being described specifically as a planet, like Earth's orbit, but lowercase otherwise since it is used not only as a proper noun but also to mean *land, ground, soil,* etc.

Names of animal species or breeds are not capitalized unless they include a proper noun. Then, only the proper noun is capitalized. Antelope, black bear, and yellow-bellied sapsucker are not capitalized. However, Bengal tiger, German shepherd, Australian shepherd, French poodle, and Russian blue cat are capitalized.

Other than planets, celestial bodies like the sun, moon, and stars are not capitalized. Medical conditions like tuberculosis or diabetes are lowercase; again, exceptions are proper nouns, like Epstein-Barr syndrome, Alzheimer's disease, and Down syndrome. Seasons and related terms like winter solstice or autumnal equinox are lowercase. Plants, including fruits and vegetables, like poinsettia, celery, or avocados, are not capitalized unless they include proper names, like Douglas fir, Jerusalem artichoke, Damson plums, or Golden Delicious apples.

Titles and Names

When official titles precede names, they should be capitalized, except when there is a comma between the title and name. But if a title follows or replaces a name, it should not be capitalized. For example, "the president" without a name is not capitalized, as in "The president addressed Congress." But with a name it is capitalized, like "President Obama addressed Congress." Or, "Chair of the Board Janet Yellen was appointed by President Obama." One exception is that some publishers and writers nevertheless capitalize President, Queen, Pope, etc., when these are not accompanied by names to show respect for these high offices. However, many writers in America object to this practice for violating democratic principles of equality. Occupations before full names are not capitalized, like owner Mark Cuban, director Martin Scorsese, or coach Roger McDowell.

Some universal rules for capitalization in composition titles include capitalizing the following:

The first and last words of the title
Forms of the verb *to be* and all other verbs
Pronouns
The word *not*

Universal rules for NOT capitalizing include the articles *the, a,* or *an;* the conjunctions *and, or,* or *nor,* and the preposition *to,* or *to* as part of the infinitive form of a verb. The exception to all of these is UNLESS any of them is the first or last word in the title, in which case they are capitalized. Other words are subject to differences of opinion and differences among various stylebooks or methods. These include *as, but, if,* and *or,* which some capitalize and others do not. Some authorities say no preposition should ever be capitalized; some say prepositions five or more letters long should be capitalized. The *Associated Press Stylebook* advises capitalizing prepositions longer than three letters (like *about, across,* or *with*).

Punctuation

Commas

Commas separate words or phrases in a series of three or more. The Oxford comma is the last comma in a series. Many people omit this last comma, but many times it causes confusion. Here is an example:

I love my sisters, the Queen of England and Madonna.

This example without the comma implies that the "Queen of England and Madonna" are the speaker's sisters. However, if the speaker was trying to say that they love their sisters, the Queen of England, as well as Madonna, there should be a comma after "Queen of England" to signify this.

Commas also separate two coordinate adjectives ("big, heavy dog") but not cumulative ones, which should be arranged in a particular order for them to make sense ("beautiful ancient ruins").

A comma ends the first of two independent clauses connected by conjunctions. Here is an example:

I ate a bowl of tomato soup, and I was hungry very shortly after.

Here are some brief rules for commas:

- Commas follow introductory words like however, furthermore, well, why, and actually, among others.

- Commas go between city and state: Houston, Texas.

- If using a comma between a surname and Jr. or Sr. or a degree like M.D., also follow the whole name with a comma: "Martin Luther King, Jr., wrote that."

- A comma follows a dependent clause beginning a sentence: "Although she was very small, . . ."

- Nonessential modifying words/phrases/clauses are enclosed by commas: "Wendy, who is Peter's sister, closed the window."

- Commas introduce or interrupt direct quotations: "She said, 'I hate him.' 'Why,' I asked, 'do you hate him?'"

Semicolons

Semicolons are used to connect two independent clauses, but should never be used in the place of a comma. They can replace periods between two closely connected sentences: "Call back tomorrow; it can wait until then." When writing items in a series and one or more of them contains internal commas, separate them with semicolons, like the following:

People came from Springfield, Illinois; Alamo, Tennessee; Moscow, Idaho; and other locations.

Apostrophes

One use of the **apostrophe** (') is followed by an *s* to indicate possession, like *Mrs. White's home* or *our neighbor's dog*. When using the *'s* after names or nouns that also end in the letter *s*, no single rule applies: some experts advise adding both the apostrophe and the *s*, like "the Jones's house," while others prefer using only the apostrophe and omitting the additional *s*, like "the Jones' house." The wisest expert advice is to pick one formula or the other and then apply it consistently. Newspapers and magazines often use *'s* after common nouns ending with *s*, but add only the apostrophe after proper nouns or names ending with *s*. One common error is to place the apostrophe before a name's final *s* instead of after it: "Ms. Hasting's book" is incorrect if the name is Ms. Hastings.

Plural nouns should not include apostrophes (e.g. "apostrophe's"). Exceptions are to clarify atypical plurals, like verbs used as nouns: "These are the do's and don'ts." Irregular plurals that do not end in *s* always take apostrophe-*s*, not *s*-apostrophe—a common error, as in "childrens' toys," which should be "children's toys." Compound nouns like mother-in-law, when they are singular and possessive, are followed by apostrophe-*s*, like "your mother-in-law's coat." When a compound noun is plural and possessive, the plural is formed before the apostrophe-*s*, like "your sisters-in-laws' coats." When two people named possess the same thing, use apostrophe-*s* after the second name only, like "Dennis and Pam's house."

Ellipses

Ellipses (. . .) signal omitted text when quoting. Some writers also use them to show a thought trailing off, but this should not be overused outside of dialogue. An example of an ellipsis would be if someone is quoting a phrase out of a professional source but wants to omit part of the phrase that isn't needed: "Dr. Skim's analysis of pollen inside the body is clearly a myth . . . that speaks to the environmental guilt of our society."

Hyphens

Here are some rules concerning **hyphens (-)**:

- Compound adjectives like state-of-the-art or off-campus are hyphenated.

- Original compound verbs and nouns are often hyphenated, like "throne-sat," "video-gamed," "no-meater."

- Adjectives ending in *–ly* are often hyphenated, like "family-owned" or "friendly-looking."

- "Five years old" is not hyphenated, but singular ages like "five-year-old" are.

- Hyphens can clarify. For example, in "stolen vehicle report," "stolen-vehicle report" clarifies that "stolen" modifies "vehicle," not "report."

- Compound numbers twenty-one through ninety-nine are spelled with hyphens.

- Prefixes before proper nouns/adjectives are hyphenated, like "mid-September" and "trans-Pacific."

Parentheses

Parentheses ( ) enclose information such as an aside or more clarifying information: "She ultimately replied (after deliberating for an hour) that she was undecided." They are also used to insert short, in-text definitions or acronyms: "His FBS (fasting blood sugar) was higher than normal." When parenthetical information ends the sentence, the period follows the parentheses: "We received new funds ($25,000)." Only put periods within parentheses if the whole sentence is inside them: "Look at this. (You'll be astonished.)" However, this can also be acceptable as a clause: "Look at this (you'll be astonished)." Although parentheses appear to be part of the sentence subject, they are not, and do not change subject-verb agreement: "Will (and his dog) was there."

Quotation Marks

Quotation marks (" ") are typically used when someone is quoting a direct word or phrase someone else writes or says. Additionally, quotation marks should be used for the titles of poems, short stories, songs, articles, chapters, and other shorter works. When quotations include punctuation, periods and commas should *always* be placed inside of the quotation marks.

When a quotation contains another quotation inside of it, the outer quotation should be enclosed in double quotation marks and the inner quotation should be enclosed in single quotation marks. For example: "Timmy was begging, 'Don't go! Don't leave!'" When using both double and single quotation marks, writers will find that many word-processing programs may automatically insert enough space between the single and double quotation marks to be visible for clearer reading. But if this is not the case, the writer should write/type them with enough space between to keep them from looking like three single quotation marks. Additionally, non-standard usages, terms used in an unusual fashion, and technical terms are often clarified by quotation marks. Here are some examples:

My "friend," Dr. Sims, has been micromanaging me again.

This way of extracting oil has been dubbed "fracking."

Contractions are formed by joining two words together, omitting one or more letters from one of the component words, and replacing the omitted letter(s) with an apostrophe. An obvious yet often forgotten rule for spelling contractions is to place the apostrophe where the letters were omitted. For example, didn't is a contraction of did not; therefore, the apostrophe replaces the "o" that is omitted from the "not." Another common error is confusing contractions with possessives because both include apostrophes, e.g. spelling the possessive *its* as "it's," which is a contraction of "it is"; spelling the possessive *their* as "they're," a contraction of "they are"; spelling the possessive *whose* as "who's," a contraction of "who is"; or spelling the possessive *your* as "you're," a contraction of "you are."

No Error

Sentences that adhere to the rules and conventions of capitalization, punctuation, spelling, and grammar are considered free from error. On the Praxis Core Writing test, test takers will encounter some sentences that are grammatically sound. In most cases, they will indicate this by selecting answer choice A, unless otherwise indicated.

Research Skills

Recognizing and Applying Appropriate Research Skills and Strategies

Assessing the Credibility and Relevance of Sources

Before a writer uses a source for a research project, he or she must determine if the source is credible. A **credible source** is reliable and trustworthy.

The following questions will help writers decide if a source is credible:

- Does the author have the appropriate credentials and experience in the subject matter?

- Has the author written anything else that's been cited and used by other established organizations or publications?

- Is the publisher well-known and established as objective and reputable in the field or subject matter?

- Is the writing free from bias and are the author and publisher, or their affiliated organizations, known to be biased?

- Are there any references and are they also credible?

- Is it a peer-reviewed resource?

- Is writing and presentation of high quality?

- Is there sufficient, trustworthy evidence to support each claim or idea?

- Is the resource current or published within the past five years?

Particularly when using digital resources, students must exercise caution and don their critical thinking caps when evaluating whether a source is credible or not. Webpages that are affiliated with educational or governmental institutions (with domains that end in .edu or .gov) are typically more reliable. Articles found in peer-reviewed journals also tend to be more credible because they have to undergo a certain level of scrutiny in order to be accepted and published.

A source is **relevant** if it relates to the topic at hand and provides helpful information, examples, statistics, or other background details.

The Different Elements of a Citation

Anytime a writer quotes or paraphrases another text, they will need to include a citation. A citation is a short description of the work that a quote or information came from. The style manual that students are told to follow will dictate exactly how to format that citation. For example, this is how one would cite a book according to the APA manual of style:

Format: Last name, First initial, Middle initial. (Year Published) *Book Title.* City, State: Publisher.
Example: Sampson, M. R. (1989). *Diaries from an Alien Invasion. Springfield, IL:* Campbell Press.

As mentioned, regardless of the style guide followed, the elements that are usually required in some order in a citation include the following:

Author's or authors' full name/s
Title of the source
Title of the article and the journal it was found in
Publication date
Name of editor
Version/volume
Number/issue
Publisher
City of publication
URL and date of access (for electronic sources)
Page numbers
City and state of publication

Effective Research Strategies

Engaging in research and writing research papers can be daunting. However, by employing some basic strategies, the process can be relatively seamless, and perhaps even enjoyable. Because the purpose of research is to provide an answer to question, writers should begin the process of writing their research papers by posing their assigned or chosen topic in the form of a question. They will use this question as a guide to help them formulate a clear answer or argument, which is to be backed with supporting evidence and rationale.

After the topic is selected, the **research question** needs to be formed. It should pertain to a unique and very specific aspect of the topic. Generally, it helps if some amount of background research is done before writers select their exact research question because it might be that there is already copious amounts of research addressing that question (so that it is not unique), or on the contrary, that there is very little available information. A **literature review** is essentially a survey of the prior peer-reviewed research conducted pertaining to the topic or research question. The literature review step is important in selecting an original topic that can still be investigated through available sources.

An effective research question should be narrow in its focus. A research question that is too broad will result in a paper that is scattered and unable to fully cover the scope of the question. On the other hand, a research question that can be answered in a sentence or two, or relies solely on opinions, is also not a wise choice.

What is autism?

How many people in the United States are autistic?

How does autism present differently in males and females?

The first question above is too broad. It can be answered in a very general paragraph, but in order to make any sort of novel conclusions or add to the bevy of research on the condition, a researcher would need to do extensive research to adequately answer such a vague question. The second question is too specific. It can be answered with one sentence, after estimations from various sources are obtained and compared. The final question is a better starting point. A question of this general scope could provide enough focus, while permitting ample research to be conducted, to write a research paper of a reasonable length that adequately addresses the question.

Recognizing Information Relevant to a Particular Research Task

Any resource is only valuable to a student for a given research project if it contains information that is relevant to his or her research question. To be relevant, the resource must contain information that pertains to the research topic.

To evaluate the worth of the book for the research paper, the student should first consider the book title to get an idea of its content. Then the student can scan the book's table of contents for chapter titles and topics to get further ideas of their applicability to the topic. The student may also turn to the end of the book to look for an alphabetized index. Most academic textbooks and scholarly works have these; students can look up key topic terms to see how many are included and how many pages are devoted to them. A relevant book should have a couple of pages or more dedicated to the topic.

To assess whether a journal article will be a useful source for a particular paper topic, a student can first get some idea about the content of the article by reading its title and subtitle, if any exists. Many journal articles, particularly scientific ones, include abstracts. These are brief summaries of the content. The student should read the abstract to get a more specific idea of whether the experiment, literature review, or other work documented is applicable to the paper topic.

Online sources can be overwhelming because of the sheer volume of published webpages. Students can use Boolean searches when using search engines, which are searches that involve words like *AND, OR,* and *NOT,* which work to help filter results to only the most relevant pages. While not perfect in their ability to weed out non-pertinent pages, Boolean searches tend to increase the efficiency of finding relevant webpages.

Practice Questions

Usage

Please select the portion of the sentence below that contains a usage error. These errors can be incorrect grammar, word use, punctuation, or capitalization.

1. Why must I always (A) <u>be last?</u> (B) <u>I'm the last one in line</u> at the cafeteria, (C) <u>I'm the last</u> (D) <u>one to my locker</u>, and I'm always (E) <u>last</u> one to class.

2. Having also been the last of (A) <u>all the siblings</u>, my older sisters always (B) <u>teasing me</u>. I was the last to be potty-trained, (C) <u>the last to get</u> a big (D) <u>girl's bed</u>, and (E) <u>the last to start school</u>.

3. My older sisters (A) <u>did spoil me</u>, though. When (B) <u>they gotten</u> their driver's licenses, (C) <u>they would take</u> me out for ice cream or to the movies, and I even got (D) <u>to tag along</u> from time to time when they (E) <u>went out on dates</u>.

4. (A) <u>I guess they thought I was cute</u> or something. (B) <u>Each time I would complain</u> about (C) <u>being last</u>, (D) <u>my mother would say</u>, (E) <u>'Don't ever worry about being last. That means you're the best!'</u>

5. (A) <u>Of course</u>, I'm not being (B) <u>completely honest</u> with you (C) <u>and</u> I've never been the last in my class. (D) <u>In fact</u>, I always seem to score (E) <u>in the top tenth percentile which isn't too bad at all</u>.

6. (A) <u>Café Adriatico being</u> the best place in town to go for authentic Italian cuisine. (B) <u>The entire restaurant consisted</u> of the kitchen in the far back of the restaurant, (C) <u>one small bathroom</u>, and a (D) <u>quaint</u> dining area (E) <u>that comfortably held ten tables</u>.

7. There was always (A) <u>Italian classical music</u> playing in the background, (B) <u>and the atmosphere</u> always (C) <u>put me in mind</u> of being in my own (D) <u>grandparents</u> (E) <u>home</u>.

8. (A) <u>Angela the sole owner</u> and head chef, (B) <u>was a unique character</u>. (C) <u>She loved</u> her guests and (D) <u>treated them like</u> (E) <u>her extended family</u>.

9. (A) <u>One famous story she used to tell</u> was of her younger years in Italy, and how once she won a (B) <u>National Beauty Contest</u>. (C) <u>She wouldn't tell the story</u> in an arrogant way. (D) <u>She would just</u> matter-of-factly tell us (E) <u>what it was like when she was honored with this award</u>.

10. (A) <u>The school bell was about to ring</u> at Juniper High, (B) <u>but Matt wasn't ready.</u> He wasn't ready because (C) <u>he hadn't studied</u> for (D) <u>today's science</u> test in (E) <u>Mr. Jones class</u>.

11. (A) <u>When he was a teenager</u>, he started collecting CDs, and (B) <u>within no time at all he had</u> an impressive collection of artists. (C) <u>Therefore</u> what he really wanted was (D) <u>his very own</u> synthesizer (E) <u>so he could create</u> his own music.

12. (A) <u>He played for hours</u> and tested every button on his (B) <u>synthesizer before</u> he knew it, (C) <u>the clock struck midnight</u>, and (D) <u>he fell into</u> a deep sleep (E) <u>with music playing</u> in his head.

13. (A) <u>The bell rang.</u> Matt slowly walked into (B) <u>school, wondering</u> how he was going to pass this test. It was the last test of the (C) <u>semester and</u> it was the one (D) <u>that was</u> supposed to (E) <u>bring up his average</u>.

Sentence Correction

Choose the answer choice that best corrects the sentence. If you think the sentence is correct as is, choose Choice A.

14. Everybody has their own version of the perfect <u>peanutbutter</u> and banana sandwich.
   a. peanutbutter
   b. peanut-butter
   c. peanut butter
   d. peanutbutter,
   e. Peanut Butter

15. My grandmother started <u>making me and my brothers peanut butter and banana</u> sandwiches before we could speak.
   a. making me and my brothers peanut butter and banana
   b. making peanut butter and banana sandwiches my brothers and me
   c. making me peanut butter and my brothers banana
   d. making I and my brothers peanut butter and banana
   e. making my brothers and I peanut butter and banana

16. She would start by setting out the slices of bread along the counter, <u>and then carefully add</u> one thin layer of butter to each slice.
   a. and then carefully add
   b. carefully add
   c. then carefully adding
   d. then carefully added
   e. then she would carefully add

17. <u>For what its worth,</u> the train arrived two hours late.
   a. For what its worth,
   b. For what it's worth,
   c. For what its worth
   d. For what it's worth
   e. For what its' worth

18. After lunch <u>I went swimming, played with my dog, and cleaning up my room</u>.
   a. I went swimming, played with my dog, and cleaning up my room.
   b. I went swimming, playing with my dog, and cleaning up my room.
   c. I was going swimming, played with my dog, and cleaned up my room.
   d. I went swimming, playing with my dog, and cleaned up my room.
   e. I went swimming, played with my dog, and cleaned up my room.

19. When writing an academic paper, <u>spelling, punctuation, and content development are key.</u>
   a. spelling, punctuation, and content development are key.
   b. students should consider spelling, punctuation, and content development.
   c. spelling, punctuation, and content development, are key.
   d. the paper needs to contain proper spelling, punctuation, and convent development.
   e. being key are spelling, punctuation, and content development.

20. <u>Transitions are an extremely important part of writing. Without proper transitions, a paper might seem choppy and disconnected.</u>

    a. Transitions are an extremely important part of writing. Without proper transitions, a paper might seem choppy and disconnected.

    b. Transitions are an extremely important part of writing without which, a paper might seem choppy and disconnected.

    c. Transitions are an extremely important part of writing. Additionally, without them, a paper might seem choppy and disconnected.

    d. Transitions are an extremely important part of writing without them, a paper might seem choppy and disconnected.

    e. Transitions are an extremely important part of writing. Might seem choppy and disconnected.

21. There are transitional words and phrases that emphasize a point, <u>demonstrating</u> an opposing point of view, present a condition, introduce examples in support of an argument, and so much more.

    a. demonstrating

    b. to demonstrate

    c. demonstrate

    d. for demonstrating

    e. demonstrated

22. Transitional words act as a <u>bridge connecting</u> ideas and strengthening a paper's coherency.

    a. bridge connecting

    b. bridge of connection

    c. bridge connecting,

    d. bridge to connections

    e. bridge connection

23. <u>"Please sit down" the teacher said.</u>

    a. "Please sit down" the teacher said.

    b. 'Please sit down,' the teacher said.

    c. 'Please sit down' the teacher said.

    d. "Please sit down", the teacher said.

    e. "Please sit down," the teacher said.

Revision in Context

Questions 24–28 are based on the following passage.

Nobody knew where she went. She wasn't in the living room, the dining room, or the kitchen. She wasn't underneath the staircase, and she certainly wasn't in her bedroom. The bathroom was thoroughly checked, and the closets were emptied. Where could she have possibly gone? Outside was dark, cold, and damp. Each person took a turn calling for her. <u>"Eva! Eva!"</u> (24) they'd each cry out, but not a sound was heard in return. The littlest sister in the house began to cry. "Where could my cat have gone?" Everyone just looked at <u>each other</u> (25) in utter silence. <u>Lulu was only five years old and brought this kitten home only six weeks ago and she was so fond of her.</u> (26) Every morning, Lulu would comb her fur, feed her, and play a cat-and-mouse game with her before she left for school. At night, Eva would curl up on the pillow next to Lulu and stay with her <u>across the night</u> (27). They were already becoming best friends. But this evening, right after dinner, Eva snuck outside when Lulu's brother came in from the yard. It was already dark out and Eva ran so quickly that nobody could see where she went.

It was really starting to feel hopeless when all of a sudden Lulu had an idea. She remembered how much Eva loved the cat-and-mouse game, so she decided to go outside and pretend that she was playing with Eva. Out she went. She curled up on the grass and began to play cat and mouse. Within seconds, Lulu could see shining eyes in the distance. The eyes got closer, and closer, and closer. Lulu continued to play <u>in order that</u> (28) she wouldn't scare the kitten away. In less than five minutes, her beautiful kitten had crawled right up to her lap as if asking to join in the game. Eva was back, and Lulu couldn't have been more thrilled! Gently, she scooped up her kitten, grabbed the cat-and-mouse game, and headed back inside, grinning from ear to ear. That night, Eva and Lulu snuggled right back down again, side by side, and had a very restful sleep.

24. Choose the best replacement punctuation.
    a. NO CHANGE
    b. 'Eva! Eva!'
    c. 'Eva, Eva'!
    d. "Eva, Eva"!
    e. "Eva!" "Eva!"

25. Choose the best replacement word or phrase.
    a. NO CHANGE
    b. one another
    c. themselves
    d. each one
    e. eachother

26. Choose the best replacement sentence.
    a. NO CHANGE
    b. Lulu brought this kitten home only six weeks ago and she was so fond of her
    c. Lulu brought this kitten home only six weeks ago, and she was so fond of her
    d. Lulu was only five years old, and brought this kitten home only six weeks ago, and she was so fond of her
    e. Lulu bringing this kitten home six weeks ago and so fond of her.

27. Choose the best replacement word or phrase.
    a. NO CHANGE
    b. below the night
    c. among the night
    d. amidst the night
    e. through the night

28. Choose the best replacement word or phrase.
    a. NO CHANGE
    b. so,
    c. so that
    d. so that,
    e. because that

Questions 29–33 are based on the following passage.

In our busy family, there are chores that each member must do every day. There are chores for our daughter, for me, and for my husband. There is always so much going on in our family and so many scheduled events every week that without a set list of <u>chores and</u> (29) without ensuring the chores are completed, our household would be utterly chaotic.

I work days, from home. My husband works evenings about a half-hour away, and our <u>13-year-old</u> (30) daughter, Niamh, attends a homeschooling program. She is an avid hockey player and the third-highest scorer on the team. She simply lives for hockey. Three times a week, she has hockey practice, and <u>once, approximately, a week</u> (31), she has a hockey game. Niamh is responsible for washing her jerseys and her hockey pants and making sure all her gear is properly stored after every practice and game in the garage. Occasionally she forgets and leaves it all in the middle of the dining room floor. Niamh must also clean the kitchen every evening after dinner, empty the dishwasher, and feed her two guinea pigs and her cat. Every Saturday, we also give Niamh an allowance for doing extra chores. She sweeps and washes our floors, cleans windows, vacuums, and tidies up the bathrooms.

As for me, I am responsible for walking and feeding the dogs, preparing the lunches and dinners, and keeping up with the laundry. My husband takes out the trash and recycling, keeps up with the yard work, and pays all the bills. Both my husband and <u>myself</u> (32) drive our daughter to friends' houses, school, the arena, the grocery store, medical appointments, and more.

We very rarely seem to get a break, but we are always happy and healthy, and that's what really matters. So, now that you know the breakdown of chores between our daughter, my husband, and me, who do you think has <u>more</u> (33) chores?

29. Choose the best replacement.
   a. NO CHANGE
   b. chores, and,
   c. chores and,
   d. chores, and
   e. chores; and

30. Choose the best replacement.
   a. NO CHANGE
   b. 13 year old
   c. 13-year old
   d. 13 year-old
   e. 13-yr-old

31. Choose the best replacement.
   a. NO CHANGE
   b. approximately once a week
   c. approximately bi-weekly
   d. once a week
   e. once approximately a week

32. Choose the best replacement.
    a. NO CHANGE
    b. I
    c. me
    d. myself,
    e. ourselves

33. Choose the best replacement.
    a. NO CHANGE
    b. the most
    c. lesser
    d. less
    e. lessest

Questions 34–36 are based on the following passage.

Imagine yourself in a secluded room. There is no one to talk to. The room has a bed, a desk, and a computer, and its one window faces the yard. Every day, you must work in this isolated room, away from everyone. There isn't a sound heard <u>accept</u> (34) for the <u>birds outside</u> (35) and your own hands tapping on the computer keyboard. Imagine having to work in that somber environment every day. The only breaks you receive are to go to the bathroom or grab a quick bite to eat. It feels like solitary confinement, and you start to feel yourself slipping <u>ever-so</u> (36) slowly into a depressed state. What should you do? If you don't get the work done, you won't get paid.

Suddenly, you have an idea. You decide that at least two days a week, you can pack up and work at the library. Although it is quiet at the library, there are people coming and going. You will be able to hear the librarians helping students and visitors, and you can people-watch. Feeling optimistic, you smile for the rest of the day. When the morning arrives, you pack up your computer, notebooks, calendar, phone, and you head out the door. You arrive at the library just as the doors are opening. You find a quiet place to set up, and you settle down into your work day. At first, you are thrilled with the new scenery and you love the extra space you have to work with. But before long, you realize your work isn't getting done. You spent so much time watching the different people coming and going and daydreaming about what it would be like to casually read a book that you stopped working altogether! Perhaps the library wasn't the ideal spot for your after all.

You pack up your computer, your notebooks, your calendar, and your phone, and you head back out the door, back to the solitary room with the bed, the desk, the computer, and the window, and you settle down once again, into your work day.

34. Choose the best replacement.
    a. NO CHANGE
    b. exceptionally
    c. except
    d. expect
    e. accepting

35. Choose the best replacement.
    a. NO CHANGE
    b. birds chirping outside
    c. birds, outside
    d. birds, chirping outside
    e. outside birds

36. Choose the best replacement.
    a. NO CHANGE
    b. ever-so,
    c. ever so
    d. everso
    e. even so

Research Skills

37. A reader comes across a word they do not know in the book they are reading, and they need to find out what the word means in order to understand the context of the sentence. Where should the reader look?
    a. Table of contents
    b. Introduction
    c. Index
    d. Glossary
    e. Appendix

38. Which of the following best describes the type of document that explains how to use an LCD flat screen TV?
    a. Technical
    b. Persuasive
    c. Narrative
    d. Cause and effect
    e. Compare and contrast

39. A student encounters the word *aficionado* and wants to learn more about it. It doesn't sound like other English words he knows, so the student is curious to identify the word's origin. What resource should he consult?
    a. A thesaurus
    b. A dictionary
    c. A style guide
    d. A grammar book
    e. A map

40. Which domain is likely to be used by a website run by a nonprofit group?
    a. .com
    b. .edu
    c. .org
    d. .gov
    e. .au

Answer Explanations

Usage

1. E: Choice *E* is the correct answer because it is missing the word *the* before the word *last*. The other answers do not contain errors.

2. B: Choice *B* is the correct answer because it is missing a helping verb "were." Or, the word "teasing" should be "teased." The answer is incorrect as it is now.

3. B: *Gotten* is the past participle version of the word *get*, and here it must have the helping verb "had" in front of it. "They gotten" is not correct verb usage.

4. E: Choice *E* is the correct answer because any dialogue represented within a sentence must have double quotes around it. Choice *E* has single quotes around the dialogue.

5. C: The way ideas are connected is important. In this case, the second independent clause gives an example of the first. The author says she has been dishonest; the next clause shows the instance of her dishonesty. The word "and" is not grammatically wrong, but it suggests the two facts are on the same level. The *and* should be replaced with the word *because* or with a semicolon.

6. A: Choice *A* is the correct answer because the verb *being* should be *was*. "Café Adiatico was the best place in town to go for authentic Italian cuisine."

7. D: Choice *D* is the correct answer because it's missing an apostrophe. Anything that shows possession, like "grandparent's house," must have an apostrophe either before or after the *s*, depending on if the word is singular or plural.

8. A: The phrase "the sole owner and head chef" modifies the noun "Angela" and should be separated by commas. Therefore, there should be a comma after the word "Angela" for this sentence to be grammatically sound.

9. B: There is no need to use any uppercase letters in the name "national beauty contest" because the specific name of a contest is not being used. The first letter of the words in a proper noun would be capitalized, but this is not a proper noun.

10. E: Since Mr. Jones is in possession of "class," it should have an apostrophe after the "s." All of the other answer choices do not have errors.

11. C: Choice *C* is the best answer because it should have a comma after the word "Therefore." Any transitional words that begin a sentence, like "therefore," "however," or "additionally," should have a comma after the word.

12. B: Choice *B* is the correct answer because it is missing a period or a semicolon after the word "synthesizer." Without a proper stop here, this sentence is considered a run-on.

13. C: Choice *C* is the best answer; there should be a comma after the word "semester" because we have two independent clauses in one sentence. Two independent clauses are always separated by a comma.

Sentence Correction

14. C: The best answer is Choice *C.* "Peanut butter" is spelled as two separate words without a hyphen.

15. A: The best answer is Choice *A.* The original sentence is correct. There is a joke in which a boy says to a genie, "Make me a peanut butter sandwich." The genie interprets the sentence incorrectly, and the boy is turned into a sandwich. However, there is nothing grammatically wrong with the way the boy expresses his wish, and there is nothing wrong with the original sentence. The word "sandwiches" is the direct object of the verb "make"; sandwiches are what the grandmother makes. The words "me and my brothers" are indirect objects of the verb "make"; the grandmother makes sandwiches for them. Choices *D* and *E* are incorrect, because the pronoun "I" is a subject, and the sentence requires the indirect object "me."

16. E: The best answer is Choice *E.* To refer to repeated past actions as in this case, the word "would" is used, and in an independent clause like this one, the pronoun "she" needs to be repeated.

17. B: Choice *B* is the best answer choice here. It contains the contraction "it's" for "it is," and also has a comma after the introductory phrase before the independent clause.

18. E: The best answer is Choice *E,* which says: "After lunch I went swimming, played with my dog, and cleaned up my room." This answer is correct because it is in parallel structure, which means the verbs "went, played, and cleaned" are all the same verb tense.

19. B: Choice *B* is the best answer: "students should consider spelling, punctuation, and content development." This is an example of a dangling modifier. The writing of the paper is not done by the spelling, punctuation, or content development. The writing is done by the students, so the clause has to use "students" as the subject.

20. A: The best answer is Choice *A.* Choice *B* is incorrect because there is a comma after "without which," and this comma interrupts the sentence. Choice *C* is incorrect because of the superfluous word "additionally." "Additionally" is not needed here because the second sentence acts as an explanation to the first. Choice *D* is incorrect because it is a run-on sentence; there should be a semicolon or period after "writing" and before "without them." Choice *E* is incorrect because the second sentence is a fragment; it contains no subject.

21. C: The best answer is Choice *C.* Each verb in the relative clause should show parallelism with the use of the third-person singular present tense. The clause is about words that demonstrate, words that emphasize, words that present, and so on. Therefore "demonstrate" should be parallel with the verbs "emphasize," "present," and "introduce." Choices *A, C, D,* and *E* are not parallel.

22. A: The best answer is Choice *A.* The gerund form of the verb "to connect" is "connecting." Using this form of the verb creates a parallel structure, because the sentence also uses the gerund form of "to strengthen," which is "strengthening."

23. E: Choice *E* is the best answer choice because it has double quotes which is appropriate around dialogue. Additionally, the comma is inside the quotes, which is appropriate punctuation placement when it comes to dialogue.

Revision in Context

24. A: Choice *A* is the best answer. To write a direct quotation, double quotation marks are placed at the beginning and ending of the quoted words. All punctuation specifically related to the quoted phrase or sentence is kept inside the quotation marks. Single quotation marks, as used in Choices *B* and *C*, are not used for dialogue in American English.

25. B: The best answer is Choice *B*. The reciprocal pronoun "one another" generally refers to more than two people.

26. C: The best answer is Choice *C*, which says: "Lulu brought this kitten home only six weeks ago, and she was so fond of her." There are two independent clauses in one sentence, so separating the two clauses with a comma is the best option. The other sentences have incorrect comma placement. Additionally, the information that Lulu was only five years old is not necessary in this particular sentence—it is out of context.

27. E: Choice *E* is the best answer. We would use the preposition "through," when talking about staying with someone "through the night."

28. C: Choice *C* is the best answer here: "Lulu continued to play so that she wouldn't scare the kitten away." Usually the words "in order" are used with the word "to." Choice *A* is incorrect because the words "in order" are usually followed by the word "to" not "that." For Choice *D*, there is no need for a comma after "so that", and for Choice *B*, there is no need for a comma after "so." Choice *E* is incorrect; "because that" is awkwardly placed in this sentence.

29. D: The best answer is Choice *D*, which says: "without a set list of chores, and without ensuring the chores are completed, our household would be utterly chaotic." In this sentence, there is an interrupting phrase that must be set apart by two commas on either side of it.

30. A: Choice *A* is the best answer because "13-year-old" is correct. When an age is describing a noun and precedes the noun, a hyphen is required.

31. B. Choice *B* is the best answer: "approximately once a week." Choice *A* is not the best answer, because the adverb "approximately" interrupts the phrase "once a week," producing the awkward if grammatically correct phrase "once, approximately, a week." Choice *C* is not correct, because "bi-weekly" means twice a week or every two weeks. Choice *D* is not the best answer, because it changes the meaning to a firm "once a week." Choice *E* is incorrect because the phrase "once a week" is interrupted by the adverb "approximately" which is not correct usage. The adverb should come before the phrase.

32. B: The best answer is Choice *B*, which says: "Both my husband and I drive our daughter." "I" is a subject pronoun, and in this sentence "I" is part of a compound subject, "my husband and I." A helpful way to answer this question is to take out the phrase "my husband" and read the sentence with each choice. Choice *A*, "myself drive our daughter" is incorrect, and so is Choice *D*, "myself, drive our daughter." Choice *C*, "me drive our daughter" is also incorrect. "I drive our daughter" is the best answer. Choice *E* is incorrect because the speaker already mentioned her husband, so ourselves would be referring to just her, which is incorrect.

33. B: Choice *B*, "who do you think has the most chores?", is the best answer. Since the sentence is comparing three people's chores, it is necessary to use a superlative adjective. If there were only two people, it would be correct to use the comparative adjective "more."

34. C: Choice *C* is the best answer. The words "accept" and "except" are often confused. There is no need to use the adverb "exceptionally" here, so Choice *B* is incorrect. Choice *C* is incorrect, because "expect" is a verb with a different meaning than "except."

35. B: The best answer is Choice *B*. The word "birds" doesn't necessarily evoke a sound, but any number of actions birds make will create sound. It is best to use a qualifier here, to indicate which bird sound the person hears.

36. C: The best answer is Choice *C*. "Ever so" is a common phrase in English. The other options are incorrectly spelled.

Research Skills

37. D: Glossary. A glossary is a section in a book that provides brief definitions/explanations for words that the reader may not know. Choice *A* is incorrect because a table of contents shows where each section of the book is located. Choice *B* is incorrect because the introduction is usually a chapter that introduces the book about to be read. Choice *C* is incorrect because an index is usually a list of alphabetical references at the end of a book that a reader can look up to get more information. Choice *E* is incorrect; an appendix is a section of additional matter toward the end of a book.

38. A: Technical document. Technical documents are documents that describe the functionality of a technical product, so Choice *A* is the best answer. Persuasive texts, Choice *B*, try to persuade an audience to follow the author's line of thinking or to act on something. Choice *C*, narrative texts, seek to tell a story. Choice *D*, cause and effect, try to show why something happened, or the causes or effects of a particular thing. Choice *E*, compare and contrast, is usually used in persuasive papers to show how two things are different or similar to one another.

39. B: A word's origin is also known as its *etymology*. In addition to offering a detailed list of a word's various meanings, a dictionary also provides information about a word's history, such as when it first came into use, what language it originated from, and how its meaning may have changed over time. A thesaurus is for identifying synonyms and antonyms, so Choice *A* is incorrect. A style guide provides formatting, punctuation, and syntactical advice for a specific field, and a grammar book is related to the appropriate placement of words and punctuation, which does not provide any insight into a word's meaning. Therefore, Choices *A, C, D,* and *E* are incorrect.

40. C: The .org domain on websites is generally used by nonprofit groups or community organizations. A government website uses .gov, and .edu is used for educational institutions. Private companies and businesses use .com, and .au is used for the Australia domain, so Choices *A, B, D,* and *E* are incorrect.

Essay Prompt

Essay 1

Read the passage below then answer in an essay format.

> According to the plan of the convention, all judges who may be appointed by the United States are to hold their offices *during good behavior*, which is conformable to the most approved of the State constitutions and among the rest, to that of this State. Its propriety having been drawn into question by the adversaries of that plan, is no light symptom of the rage for objection, which disorders their imaginations and judgments. The standard of good behavior for the continuance in office of the judicial magistracy is certainly one of the most valuable of the modern improvements in the practice of government. In a monarchy, it is an excellent barrier to the despotism of the prince; in a republic, it is a no less excellent barrier to the encroachments and oppressions of the representative body. And it is the best expedient which can be devised in any government, to secure a steady, upright, and impartial administration of the laws.

Write an essay and explain what the author means by the passage above. Then, choose a side on the issue and argue why you agree or disagree. Give specific examples to support the argument.

Essay 2

Read the two articles below, then write a 500-word essay where you synthesize the two essays and give your opinion on the subject. Choose a specific side on the issue and use specific examples and evidence from each passage to support your own opinion. Be sure to use the authors' last names or the title of the passage when referring to each specific text.

(from "Free Speech in War Time" by James Parker Hall, written in 1921, published in Columbia Law Review, Vol. 21 No. 6)

> In approaching this problem of interpretation, we may first put out of consideration certain obvious limitations upon the generality of all guaranties of free speech. An occasional unthinking malcontent may urge that the only meaning not fraught with danger to liberty is the literal one that no utterance may be forbidden, no matter what its intent or result; but in fact it is nowhere seriously argued by anyone whose opinion is entitled to respect that direct and intentional incitations to crime may not be forbidden by the state. If a state may properly forbid murder or robbery or treason, it may also punish those who induce or counsel the commission of such crimes. Any other view makes a mockery of the state's power to declare and punish offences. And what the state may do to prevent the incitement of serious crimes which are universally condemned, it may also do to prevent the incitement of lesser crimes, or of those in regard to the bad tendency of which public opinion is divided. That is, if the state may punish John for burning straw in an alley, it may also constitutionally punish Frank for inciting John to do it, though Frank did so by speech or writing. And if, in 1857, the United States could punish John for helping a fugitive slave to escape, it could also punish Frank for inducing John to do this, even though a large section of public opinion might applaud John and condemn the Fugitive Slave Law.

(from "Freedom of Speech in War Time" by Zechariah Chafee, Jr. written in 1919, published in Harvard Law Review Vol. 32 No. 8)

The true boundary line of the First Amendment can be fixed only when Congress and the courts realize that the principle on which speech is classified as lawful or unlawful involves the balancing against each other of two very important social interests, in public safety and in the search for truth. Every reasonable attempt should be made to maintain both interests unimpaired, and the great interest in free speech should be sacrificed only when the interest in public safety is really imperiled, and not, as most men believe, when it is barely conceivable that it may be slightly affected. In war time, therefore, speech should be unrestricted by the censorship or by punishment, unless it is clearly liable to cause direct and dangerous interference with the conduct of the war.

Thus our problem of locating the boundary line of free speech is solved. It is fixed close to the point where words will give rise to unlawful acts. We cannot define the right of free speech with the precision of the Rule against Perpetuities or the Rule in Shelley's Case, because it involves national policies which are much more flexible than private property, but we can establish a workable principle of classification in this method of balancing and this broad test of certain danger. There is a similar balancing in the determination of what is "due process of law." And we can with certitude declare that the First Amendment forbids the punishment of words merely for their injurious tendencies. The history of the Amendment and the political function of free speech corroborate each other and make this conclusion plain.

Greetings!

First, we would like to give a huge "thank you" for choosing us and this study guide for your Praxis Core exam. We hope that it will lead you to success on this exam and for your years to come.

Our team has tried to make your preparations as thorough as possible by covering all of the topics you should be expected to know. In addition, our writers attempted to create practice questions identical to what you will see on the day of your actual test. We have also included many test-taking strategies to help you learn the material, maintain the knowledge, and take the test with confidence.

We strive for excellence in our products, and if you have any comments or concerns over the quality of something in this study guide, please send us an email so that we may improve.

As you continue forward in life, we would like to remain alongside you with other books and study guides in our library. We are continually producing and updating study guides in several different subjects. If you are looking for something in particular, all of our products are available on Amazon. You may also send us an email!

Sincerely,
APEX Test Prep
info@apexprep.com

Free Study Tips DVD

In addition to the tips and content in this guide, we have created a FREE DVD with helpful study tips to further assist your exam preparation. **This FREE Study Tips DVD provides you with top-notch tips to conquer your exam and reach your goals.**

Our simple request in exchange for the strategy-packed DVD is that you email us your feedback about our study guide. We would love to hear what you thought about the guide, and we welcome any and all feedback—positive, negative, or neutral. It is our #1 goal to provide you with top quality products and customer service.

To receive your **FREE Study Tips DVD**, email freedvd@apexprep.com. Please put "FREE DVD" in the subject line and put the following in the email:

      a. The name of the study guide you purchased.

      b. Your rating of the study guide on a scale of 1-5, with 5 being the highest score.

      c. Any thoughts or feedback about your study guide.

      d. Your first and last name and your mailing address, so we know where to send your free DVD!

Thank you!

Made in the USA
Monee, IL
18 July 2021